Watchmen as Literature

Watchmen as Literature

A Critical Study
of the Graphic Novel

SARA J. VAN NESS

McFarland & Company, Inc., Publishers
Jefferson, North Carolina, and London

Library of Congress Cataloguing-in-Publication Data

Van Ness, Sara J.
    Watchmen as literature : a critical study of the graphic novel /
Sara J. Van Ness.
        p.   cm.
    Includes bibliographical references and index.

    ISBN 978-0-7864-4475-5
    softcover : 50# alkaline paper ∞

    1. Moore, Alan, 1953– Watchmen. 2. Graphic novels.
3. Watchmen (Motion picture) 4. Film adaptations. I. Title.
PN6728.W386V36 2010
741.5'942 — dc22   2009050584

British Library cataloguing data are available

Cover design by Mark Durr

Manufactured in the United States of America

McFarland & Company, Inc., Publishers
  Box 611, Jefferson, North Carolina 28640
  www.mcfarlandpub.com

Acknowledgments

I would first like to thank Dr. Stanley Blair, my professor and mentor at Monmouth University, who first introduced me to *Watchmen*, and without whose tireless support and guidance this book would not have been possible. I would also like to thank the collective support of the English department and the School of Education at Monmouth for encouraging me to pursue this project. Special thanks also go to Michelle Giles for her helpful comments on the work, Glenn Romanelli for his insight on Zack Snyder's *Watchmen*, and John Kowalcyk for always being there to provide unending encouragement. Most important, I want to thank my dad and mom, Garrett and Terry Van Ness, for always reminding me of what is most important.

Table of Contents

Preface

It is 1985, and an ever-present threat of global thermonuclear war seems out of mankind's control. The *Bulletin of the Atomic Scientists* pushes the minute hand of the Doomsday Clock closer to midnight, while powerless Americans look on with a sense of impending doom. In response to the threatening haze of Cold War confusion, Alan Moore and Dave Gibbons' *Watchmen* reveals a world of retired masked adventurers, vigilantes, and semi-deities, who are virtually powerless after the 1977 Keene Act forcibly retired them. Eight years later, a strange string of murders catches the attention of Rorschach, a slovenly transient vigilante who has refused to comply with the government mandate. Where others see the murders as a random result of the chaotic times, Rorschach sees a pattern, a conspiracy that subsequent events seem to prove.

In the process of Rorschach's seemingly irrational hunch turning out to be the truth, *Watchmen* explores a variety of complex themes that question the heroic ideal, the validity of utopias, the fundamental qualities of good and evil, and the dangers of possible world destruction and even world peace. For more than twenty years, *Watchmen* has sustained attention among scholarly and popular audiences. In fact, its popularity would seem to suggest that scholarly attention is appropriate. *Watchmen* is the only graphic novel to date to earn a Hugo Award from the World Science Fiction Society ("Nominations"). In 2005, *Time* magazine's Lev Grossman and Richard Lacayo ranked *Watchmen* among their selections for the top 100 English-language novels since 1923, the only graphic novel to be included on the list. Over twenty years after its first publication, *Watchmen* topped best-seller lists, gaining so much attention in the summer of 2008 that DC Comics printed an unprecedented one million copies to keep up with demand (Romanelli, "Effect"). Within its pages, *Watchmen* has the potential to teach us not only about the nature of reading in the 21st century, but also, perhaps more importantly, about ourselves as readers.

The first chapter of this critical examination, "Invading the Ivory Tower," begins with a study of the history and reception of the novel by popular and scholarly audiences. The work (intentionally or not) changed the face of the industry, ushering in the age of the "graphic novel," along with Frank Miller's *The Dark Knight Returns* and Art Spiegelman's *Maus*. Many were unsure of what to make of the so-called graphic novel or even how to define it. Some were defiantly dismissive of this new form, others recognized a lucrative new market for popular fiction, and still others saw beyond the flurry of news coverage to find that several of these works were worthy of academic study. Structurally and thematically, *Watchmen* was a work unlike any before it. Within a self-contained narrative first presented as twelve comic-book installments, it offered readers a broken cast of half-hearted heroes who appeared as anything but heroic in a world that proved just as fragile as the characters themselves. Racking up awards and recognition both within and outside of the comic-book industry, *Watchmen*'s popularity steadily increased as the cadre of *Watchmen* readers and admirers expanded.

Chapter 2, "I^^@ge$ and Wo(r)d$," and chapter 3, "A Language All Its Own," examine how the visual and written aspects of *Watchmen* individually and collectively affect reading and interpretation. The relationship between images and words are analyzed and synthesized, starting with their similar origins and moving to an understanding of their distinct contributions. Applying the comics theory of Will Eisner and Scott McCloud, chapter 2 considers the function of such graphic narrative elements as the word balloon, handwriting and typographic style, panel composition, color, and much more. Chapter 3 addresses the different ways in which images and words combine in what McCloud metaphorically defines as both a "dance" and a "language" in his groundbreaking *Understanding Comics*. Also discussed are how images and words function as both text and context within each panel, and how both text and context function continuously and discontinuously within *Watchmen*'s intricately complex narrative structure.

Chapter 4, "The Watchmen," takes a closer look at this intricate and multilayered narrative structure, using French critic and rhetorician Gérard Genette's schematic on narrative levels. The work's structure is reflexive and self-referential. The final panel's composition mirrors that of the first, and the novel begins and ends with a focus on a character's writings or story within the larger story structure: Rorschach's journal. This chapter addresses the question posed in *Watchmen*'s famous epigraph — who watches the watchmen? — in relation to the work's unidentified narrative voice. The novel alludes to some potential answers to the more fundamental question of who the watchmen *are*; however, whether or not the reader arrives at these possibilities depends on his or her interpretive decisions after reading the final page.

Chapter 5, "Parallel Histories," analyzes how the unidentified yet all-seeing narrator presents *Watchmen*'s story, one that spans a timeline of more than 50 years, two generations of characters, and two planets. Moore has referred to *Watchmen*'s narrative structure as a "massively complex, simultaneous event with connections made of coincidence and synchronicity" (*Mindscape*). This chapter begins by applying linguist Ferdinand de Saussure's conceptions of diachronic and synchronic time to the way in which different times and places are associated with one another throughout the narrative, and drawing on philosopher Paul Ricoeur's concept of narrative time, then elaborates on some of the strategies used to manipulate its presentation. Dr. Manhattan, the only character who has a perspective on time and space analogous to that of the narrator, helps Laurie Juspeczyk, the second Silk Spectre, to re-imagine her past, thereby affecting her present understanding of herself and her future as a daughter, adult, lover, and masked adventurer.

Similar to the way Dr. Manhattan aids Juspeczyk in finding a new perspective on herself, the novel's treatment of heroism provides readers the opportunity to do the same. Chapters 6 through 8 examine heroism throughout the work. *Watchmen* questions the hero's role in a world where deity-like figures, the average man, and vigilantes alike may or may not be heroes. Through an evaluation of the criteria, history, and characterization of each, these chapters show how the novel destabilizes the concept of heroism, thereby provoking the reader to *re*construct a meaning for him or herself. Chapter 6, "Hooded Honor," shows how Dan Dreiberg (aka the second Nite Owl), Adrian Veidt (aka Ozymandias), Rorschach (aka Walter Joseph Kovacs), and Dr. Manhattan (aka Jon Osterman) are heroic by using Greimas' semiotic rectangle to suggest the semiological complexity of the terms "heroism" and "masked adventurer." After the imposition of the Keene Act, each character's course of action determines whether or not he believes the conventional laws of the society to be valid for guiding his work. Those characters who choose to disavow the conventional law subscribe to natural law, leaving them open to harsh criticism and serious legal repercussions.

Throughout the novel there are many different labels for these heroes, not all of which are positive. The definitions and connotations of each label, as well as how they fit into the social structure of the world in *Watchmen*, cause some characters to appear more heroic than others. Chapter 7, "Not So Black and White," addresses just this: why many readers are seemingly incongruously drawn to see Rorschach, the crazed and unkempt vigilante, as the hero of the work, and Adrian Veidt, the successful and driven celebrity entrepreneur, as the villain. This chapter contrasts how, in the novel's rhetorical presentation of the masked adventurers, public personas ironically disguise their true motives. How each character publicly presents himself and how he interacts with others literally and metaphorically mask details that are likely to detract from Veidt's credibility and lend Rorschach sympathy.

Whereas chapter 6 examines how the four main characters could each be considered a type of hero, chapter 8, "Faceless Heroes," examines how *none* of the characters lives up to a standard heroic ideal. This chapter examines the tension between characters finding their identities and fulfilling previously defined roles as they discover (willingly or not) their heroic potentials. Through an examination of Joseph Campbell's monomyth theory from his classic, though often disputed, *The Hero with a Thousand Faces*, each character is shown to partially conform to the hero's journey; however, none of the characters complete Campbell's designated stages. *Watchmen* builds the characters sufficiently enough so that they are recognizable as heroic but not as heroes.

Chapter 9, "Measuring Up: Zack Snyder's *Watchmen*" considers the initial reception of the film that was thought to be "unfilmable." The chapter focuses on Zack Snyder's theatrical release version of the film, which debuted in theaters in March of 2009. The reviews were varied and reflected the strong feelings that so many *Watchmen* fans (and detractors) brought with them to the film. Many of the reviewers used similar rhetorical strategies, ones that reflected their inability to separate the film from its various contexts: the original graphic novel, Alan Moore's writing in general, graphic-novel and comic-book fandom, and even other superhero films. When Snyder set out to create a film from source material to which he was clearly devoted, it appeared as though he was fighting a losing battle, as so many viewers were similarly invested in and passionate about the work.

My personal experience with *Watchmen* began in college, when I first picked up the work upon the recommendation of my professor and mentor, Dr. Stanley Blair, at Monmouth University. That same evening I bought my copy at the local bookstore. Once I began, it was impossible for me to stop, and, like many readers, I read into the early hours of the morning. I was drawn into the text by the reality of the characters and setting, the action and suspense of the text, and the beautifully detailed images. What began as recommended reading material became the focus of both my undergraduate and graduate work. Over the years I continued to research graphic novels, now not only as a scholar in an academic setting, but also as a fan. I devoured other titles, found myself visiting fan websites and blogs, and learning about the long, fluctuating history of comics and graphic novels. I even attended comic conventions, and had the pleasure of meeting some of the authors and illustrators whose work I had come to so greatly admire. For me, writing *Watchmen as Literature* has bridged a gap between the scholarly and popular, and my purpose has been to provide readers from a variety of backgrounds, experiences, and perspectives the opportunity to do the same. For fans of *Watchmen*, I hope that this book will provide insight into the complexity and profundity of what is, on the surface, a really great story. For scholars and teachers of literature, I hope that this book will give you the opportunity to understand and appreciate the graphic-narrative form, and to see how literary theory can be applied to a text that is truly on the fringe of literary studies. Finally, it is my hope that this work will inspire all readers to return to *Watchmen* to enjoy and study once more a work that has truly become an iconic part of 20th century Anglo-American fiction and culture.

CHAPTER 1

Invading the Ivory Tower

What is a graphic novel? In the late 1980s it appeared as if everyone in the television and print news media was asking the question; however, few seemed able to provide any clear answers.[1] The buzzword splashed across headlines with the seemingly concurrent release of Frank Miller's *The Dark Knight Returns* (1986), Alan Moore and Dave Gibbons' *Watchmen* (1987), and Art Spiegelman's *Maus* (1987), three works that brought nationwide attention to the form. In the most basic terms, these works were simply lengthy comic books. They were repackaged and printed on a higher quality of paper, with pages that were squarebound and glued into a binding, rather than held together with staples in the traditional comic-book style. However, these works were so much more. All dealt with some weighty issues (Holocaust, Cold War, vigilantism, justice), employed complex narrative structures, and were targeted for an adult readership. Even though the massive media coverage suggested otherwise, the graphic novel was not a new concept. In fact, Will Eisner's 1978 *A Contract with God* was considered by many to be the first graphic novel, even donning the label on its cover.[2] When he first proposed the book to a New York publisher, Eisner recalls, "A little voice inside me said, 'Hey stupid, don't tell him it's a comic or he'll hang up on you.' So I said, 'It's a graphic novel'" (qtd. in Arnold). Eisner's intuitive hesitation in labeling his work as a comic book suggests that he was conscious of some negative implications that the comic book label carried. What began as (and perhaps still is) a marketing strategy aimed at distancing the comic book from its lengthier counterpart flourished into a media-hyped movement led by Miller's, Moore and Gibbons,' and Spiegelman's work.

In an April 1989 article for the *Los Angeles Times*, Charles Solomon aptly summarized the graphic novel's definition dilemma: "Acclaimed as a new art form, damned as 'comic books for adults,' graphic novels are easier to recognize than they are to define." George Beahm of *Publishers Weekly* titled his November 6, 1987, article "Graphic Novels: Comics, Magazines, or Books?" and tried to clarify the confusion over the newly popularized form. First, Beahm explained the graphic novel's physical features: "A graphic novel is typically a trade paperback, 7" × 10" or 8½" × 11", usually in full color, priced from $6.95 to $12.95 ... a graphic novel is usually a minimum of 64 pages but can extend to over 100 pages." By providing these parameters, it was as if Beahm was attempting to suggest a way for consumers to quickly and easily identify a graphic novel visually. Yet, the description also applied to traditional novels, illustrated books, and even expensive magazines or other print media. The definition was general, offering readers little clarification on the form. To refine this broad definition, Beahm also provided a more narrow lexical one: "As implied, a graphic novel is an adaptation of a novel in comic-art form." However, this was also not necessarily true. To say that a graphic novel was an "adaptation" suggested that the images (or the "comic-art") was there to support, enhance, or modify some original story that did not include images. In this case, the implication was that the original or primary narrative was solely derived from the words on the page. The definition could be applied correctly only to those works that were truly adaptations, like works from *Classics Illustrated*, a popular comic-book series in publication between 1941 and 1971 that adapted literary works such as Shelley's *Frankenstein*, Melville's *Moby Dick*, and Cooper's *The Last of the Mohicans* into a comic-book format.

Although Beahm's definition could apply to some graphic novels, it did not apply to all, and with no clear definition for what the graphic novel was, he attempted to define the form based on "things that graphic novels are not":

- They are not slick comic books for kids or adults whose lips move when they read.
- Graphic novels are not comics or magazines.
- Graphic novels are not necessarily about comic-book superheroes.
- Graphic novels are not simple stories simply told.

The list suggested that there were many misconceptions about the form; not only were some having trouble defining the graphic novel, but many were prejudging it based on its association with comic books and other media that combined images and words. The first bullet countered the misconception that graphic novels would only appeal to children or uneducated adults. In his June 23, 1989, article for the *Star Tribune* entitled "Comics Are Good for More Than a Laugh," Joseph Diliberto frankly explained how comics readers were often unfairly stereotyped: "The classic image of the illiterate is a grown person reading a comic book and shoving a finger up his nose." His explanation of the stereotype echoed Beahm's description of the comic-book reader "whose lips move" while reading, but Diliberto challenged the misconception. He rightly added, "The perpetrators of this stereotype don't stop to consider that an illiterate doesn't read anything, let alone something as complicated as some of today's new adult comic books." Complex and certainly not for the illiterate, these works, Beahm and Diliberto agreed, required some education or reading skills to comprehend. Beahm's second bullet point separated graphic novels from "comics" and "magazines." The two latter media were often considered disposable, reading materials that were read once or twice before being thrown away. The graphic novel, however, was constructed out of higher-quality materials and was a work that one would place on a bookshelf rather than in the trash after a first read. The third bullet, where Beahm asserts that graphic novels include subject matter on other topics besides the "comic-book superhero," suggested that there were different genres of graphic novels, just as there were different genres of novels. Of course, there were also different genres of comic books; however, the bullet point implied that many people closely associated the superhero genre with the comic-book form, one that was often perceived as unsophisticated or only for children. Beahm's final bullet stressed the complexity of graphic novels, one that was perhaps *too* complex for young or inexperienced readers.

What all of the features in Beahm's list had in common were attempts to legitimate the graphic novel by distancing it from the comic book. There is a long history[3] behind many of these stereotypes, which helped to foster the perception that comics was a medium unable to convey intricate plots, complex themes, or intriguing characters for an educated, "well-adjusted" adult readership (Versaci 2). Perhaps the most notable event that helped to closely associate comics with children's reading materials was Fredrick Wertham's 1954 book entitled *Seduction of the Innocent*, which lead to strict regulations for comic-book content. His book sparked

> a Senate subcommittee['s] investigat[ion of] their link to juvenile delinquency. [Comic books] were destroyed in community bonfires. They were blamed for everything from asthma to poor eyesight. Even the writers who created them sometimes denied they worked in the field" [Voger].

As a direct result of Wertham's work and these investigations, the Comics Magazine Association of America established the Comics Code, which outlined "standards for such aspects as depiction of crime, authority figures, religion, weapons, violence, sex, and marriage" (Ellis and Highsmith 23). Believed to be a form strictly for children, the content of comics was diluted for young readers. Eventually, some writers and artists chose to publish their works without the Comics Code's seal of approval, and portions of the code were eventually changed to suit changing times; however, in the eyes of many, the comic book remained an unsophisticated and simplistic storytelling form. The graphic novel label was an attempt to redeem the comic book's denigrated status.

With a new name and a new look, many were hopeful that the form would get the attention and respect that it rightly deserved outside of the comic-book industry; however, some were skeptical of what appeared to be a simple marketing ploy. In the January 7, 1987, issue of the *St. Petersburg Times*, Peter Smith sarcastically remarked that graphic novels were named as such "because 'expensive comic books' d[id]n't have the same ring to it" (3D). Some of the writers and artists from inside the industry were likely to agree with Smith. Any attempt to distance the graphic novel from the comic book appeared to be a blatant denial of the form's ancestry. Some comics creators saw no need to rename the form, knowing that there already were plenty of sophisticated works published as comic books; the general public was just unaware of it. Even though the graphic novel was not as new as everyone seemed to be claiming, and its predecessor, the comic book, was the victim of a seriously bad rap for quite some time, Miller's *Dark Knight*, Moore and Gibbons' *Watchmen*, and Spiegelman's *Maus* caught the attention of more that just the comics community:

> Suddenly, there was grittier superhero fare! Suddenly, there was a comic book taking on a "serious subject!" In actuality, the "suddenly" part was more a product of perception than reality: superhero comics had been dealing with more mature subject matter as early as the 1970s, and independent comics in the 1980s had many more practitioners than Art Spiegelman" [Versaci 10].

So what accounted for the sudden interest surrounding these three works? What made them so appealing or, at the very least, newsworthy? This chapter will attempt to answer this question, with particular attention paid to the reception, both scholarly and popular, of Moore and Gibbons' *Watchmen*.

Movin' on Up

In the documentary *The Mindscape of Alan Moore*, Moore recalled that *Watchmen* "was one of the books that was responsible for the ridiculous blizzard of publicity that comic books, or 'graphic novels,' as somebody in a marketing department decided by them that they should be called, became popular." Gibbons later expressed similar sentiments in his book *Watching the Watchmen*: "The term 'graphic novel' was shiny new, and, frankly, considered a little pretentious by industry insiders" (237). *Watchmen* was originally released as twelve issues of a comic-book series between September 1986 and October 1987 that featured a self-contained narrative, original characters,[4] and a setting separate from the rest of the DC Comics Universe. The work surely appeared as though it fit the graphic novel label more so than some other works that were considered as such. With no clear definition for what graphic novels were, the label was widely applied to works that ranged in theme, narrative style, and format. Gary Groth of Fantagraphic Books explained that the graphic novel label was used for "cartoon collections, long comic books and collected short comic stories that are sold in book form. I'd be surprised if more than a half-dozen books out there could legitimately be called graphic novels" (qtd. in Solomon). *Watchmen*, however, seemed more suited for the label than most, as Gibbons explained: "Lofty though the term might have seemed, *Watchmen*'s narrative certainly had the weight and complexity of a prose novel, and it was, after all, indisputably graphic in its presentation. In addition, it was a complete story, needing no prior knowledge and requiring no further reading to be a satisfying fictional experience" (Gibbons 237). Even before it was packaged as a graphic novel, *Watchmen* won three prestigious Jack Kirby Awards in 1987 for

Best New Series, Best Writer, and Best Writer/Artist. The individual comics from the series also racked up three additional nominations for Best Single Issue (*Watchmen* #1 and #2), and Best Artist. Once published in graphic-novel form, *Watchmen* won every Will Eisner Comic Industry Award for which it was nominated in 1988, sweeping the categories of Best Finite Series, Best Graphic Album, Best Writer, and Best Writer/Artist (Hahn).

Outside of the comic book industry, a landmark moment in *Watchmen*'s history came when it was recognized in, what Gibbons referred to as, "the next ghetto up": science fiction (263). In 1988, *Watchmen* won a Hugo Award in the category of Other Forms. The Hugo Awards, presented by the World Science Fiction Society (WSFS), are the science fiction industry's most prominent awards, and to date, *Watchmen* is the only graphic novel to ever win ("Nominations").[5] For the science fiction community to acknowledge *Watchmen* was quite an achievement, as Gibbons explained: "Science fiction fans have always seemed to consider themselves superior to comics fans (and possibly to the entire remainder of the human race), so to be awarded a Hugo, the most coveted trophy in their field, was a signal honor" (263). Gibbons acknowledged an element evident in many early reviews of both *Watchmen* and the graphic-novel form in general: there was an implied stratification of value for different genres and forms of literature. That is, science fiction was perceived as being "superior" or one "up" in rank above graphic novels. This hierarchical structure was what many of the critics relied on, knowingly or unknowingly, to make judgments of the texts (i.e., comic books are bad, graphic novels are good, but science fiction is even better). Perhaps the phenomenon is best exemplified by a passage from *Watchmen*: in chapter 3, Benny Anger's attempt at comedy leads him to begin his interview with Dr. Manhattan by asking, "What's up, doc?" Dr. Manhattan poignantly responds that "'up' is a relative concept. It has no intrinsic value" (Moore and Gibbons 3.12).[6] And neither does any attempt at creating a hierarchical structure based on genre or medium. Unfortunately, however, categories of judgment do not follow critical judgment, but rather precede it, instantaneously containing or confining *Watchmen* to a category or strata. The acceptance of *Watchmen* into the science fiction genre is notable, but science fiction as a hierarchical level was still inarguably considered a "ghetto" by some, especially in relation to other genres of literature.

Early reviews of *Watchmen* (both positive and negative) made value judgments based on its narrative structure, its inclusion of superhero themes and science fiction elements, its violent content, and even the perceived maturity level of its readership. Some reviewers were quick to express their admiration for the series, and, not surprisingly, many science-fiction reviewers were especially approving of the work. For the December 6, 1987, edition of the *San Francisco Chronicle*, Michael Berry wrote in his review that although "Alan Moore has yet to fulfill his contract for a full-length prose novel ... he has already proved with his science fiction 'graphic novel,' *Watchmen*, that he is a storyteller of the first order.... *Watchmen* expertly combines pictures and text into an emotionally compelling piece of literature." In other words, Berry understood *Watchmen* to be just as satisfying as, or even more satisfying than, a "full-length prose novel." That is, its graphic-novel format did not detract from the narrative, but, in fact, enhanced it, making it worthy of the label "literature." Similarly, Darren Harris-Fain's review in a 1989 edition of *Extrapolation*, a scholarly journal of science fiction and fantasy works that was published by Kent State University Press at the time, acknowledged *Watchmen* for its use of complex narrative techniques. Harris-Fain admired how the work seemed to take full advantage of the graphic-novel form's potential, with its inclusion of expository materials after each chapter, the ironic juxtaposition of images and words in panels, and the manipulation of time and space throughout the narrative. Here too, Harris-Fain saw no need to defend a positive and sophisticated review of the work. He acknowledged that "other comic book writers have done much to raise expectations for the medium through their work, but their comics have often failed to transcend the level of sophisticated adventure and realistic storytelling. In my opinion *Watchmen* possesses a depth which makes it unique" (Review 411). For Harris-Fain, *Watchmen* stood apart from other graphic novels and comics that came before it, even going so far as to say that "despite the sophistication of *Watchmen*, the book has enjoyed popular success as well as critical acclaim" (Review 411–12). Harris-Fain was suggesting that *Watchmen*'s popularity came "despite" the complexity of the narrative. That is, *readers* may not have been "sophisticated" enough to comprehend the work, a distinction which was certainly different than the common stereotype that comic books or graphic novels were easy reads. *Watchmen* transcended literary strata and opened the path for others to follow: *Watchmen* was "not simply a comic book phenomenon, but a fascinating experiment in broadening a limited genre which deserves wider attention than it has received" (Harris-Fain, Review 412).

For some reviewers, *Watchmen* far exceeded other works in the graphic-novel form. Larry Kart's December 2, 1987, review of *Watchmen* for the *Chicago Tribune* boasted the title "A Comic Book as Gripping as Dickens." The review's title immediately suggested that the work was on the same level as those by Dickens, ones that were already widely respected and considered by many to be in a much higher literary strata. Kart continued by also comparing the work to other comic books, noting that *Watchmen* was of more value than those that "would-be intellectuals have tried to claim the comics in the name of art ... which usually means that one is about to encounter a comic that is willfully brutal or self-consciously hip." Moore and Gibbons were not these "would-be intellectuals," but instead, their graphic novel was different and truly intellectual. He referred to the work as a "comic-book novel," and the use of both "book" and "novel" emphasized the work as more literary than "comic." Kart ended his review with the affirmation that "*Watchmen* really works," but ironically warned readers to "think twice" before showing it to children, believing that perhaps some readers would unknowingly suspect the work to be for children because of its format.

Beth Levine's May 22, 1987, article for *Publishers Weekly* preceded and in fact anticipated[7] the release of *Watchmen* in graphic-novel form. In her analysis of other graphic novels, she explained that the form's level of sophistication was contingent upon its content. She compared Spiegelman's *Maus*, a Holocaust memoir, with Miller's *Dark Knight*, a work of the superhero genre:

> Are the books little more than comics in paperback bindings? (Many graphic novels in fact derive from comics, including *Dark Knight*.) Or are they like *Maus*, a medium of serious expression? Are graphic novels for adults or children? "You are mixing apples and oranges when you compare *Dark Knight* to *Maus*," says Esther Mitgang, editorial director, Harmony books. But 80,000 copies of *Maus* and 70,000 copies of *Dark Knight* in print clearly indicate that the graphic novel can appeal to wide audiences and that the format is sufficiently flexible to accommodate both the serious and the light-hearted [45].

For Levine, the fact that *Dark Knight* derived from a storyline originating in comic books proved that it was not a "medium of serious expression" like *Maus*. The quote from Mitgang used here is unclear: why did she perceive the two titles so differently ("apples and oranges")? Was it because of the inclusion of superheroes? Both works used a graphic-narrative format, and both dealt with mature themes; however, the inclusion of superheroes, a staple of the comic-book medium, implied that the title was somehow less "sophisticated" or for "children."

In the December 26, 1987, issue of *The Nation*, Maria Margaronis and Elizabeth Pochoda placed *Watchmen* at the top of their lists of holiday book picks among other titles in all-word formats. Margaronis wrote, "I can recommend no better disorientation manual than *Watchmen*, a comic book by Alan Moore and Dave Gibbons" (Navasky et al.). Pochoda agreed, going even further in her praise of the work: "If I were to give any of this year's books for Christmas ... I'd begin with DC Comics' *Watchmen*." However, Pochoda quickly qualified her recommendation by adding, "I'm not slumming. This stuff is smart. Many of my serious-minded colleagues were transfixed by these narratives of superheroes, costume heroes, plain-wrap heroes and plain psychopaths at play in the fevered history of the past four decades" (Navasky et al.). Her use of the word "slumming" here was based as much on her perception of literary stratification as on how she believed her readers would perceive her selection. That is, she suspected readers would be surprised that a graphic novel surpassed other works (in more respected literary formats) as one of her favorite items for the gift-giving season. The term was used similarly to the way Gibbons later referred to science fiction as the next "ghetto up" above graphic novels. Pointing to her "serious-minded colleagues" for support, Pochoda acknowledged the negative stereotypes that some readers held about graphic-novel narratives. Her comment also suggested, however, that by referring to herself and her supporters as "colleagues," this in some way acknowledged their collective identity as professionals— professionals who are well-read and trusted enough to write book reviews.

But all of Pochoda's colleagues at *The Nation* may not have agreed with her appreciation for *Watchmen*. In fact, in the October 10, 1987, edition of *The Nation*, less than three months before Pochoda and Margaronis proclaim *Watchmen* a worthy read, Fredric Paul Smoler wrote a review of the graphic novel that differed quite drastically in its approach. Rather than attempting to justify his appreciation of the narrative in relation to other professionals, Smoler distanced himself from *Watchmen* and what he believed to be its readers. He began his review with this assertion: "*Watchmen* comics were brought to my attention by a man in Los Angeles who got the tip from a friend who was on serious speaking terms with some teen-agers" (386). The first line of the review implied that the source of the recommendation was in some way juvenile. Even if he were to find value in the work, the immaturity of the readers would discredit it. He continued, describing how his friend was uncomfortable recommending the work to Smoler: "My friend was ... cagy, almost furtive: Check these out.... No, its not that they're exactly *good*, Just check 'em out. So I did" (386). After reading, Smoler explained that he understood his friend's hesitation in recommending the work. Although *Watchmen* was "weirdly interesting," it had a "melodramatic and hyperbolic" tone, suited to match a target audience of teenagers and young adults (387). His assessment of *Watchmen* concluded that it contained "an authentic response to a cultural dilemma ... the problem of an adolescence occurring in a period of right-wing dominance, in which the available cultural resources are insipid or toxic" (387). In other words, he found *Watchmen* merely a reactionary work in the context of the times aimed at appealing to an adolescent audience. One might question if Smoler's "friend" was uncomfortable in explaining the title's worth to him because he personally felt it to be suited for teens, or if he was simply uncomfortable at being judged for enjoying it.

Joe Queenan's April 30, 1989, article "Drawing on the Dark Side" for *The New York Times* was more direct in its attack on *Watchmen* and its readers. He acknowledged the recent surge in news coverage of graphic novels over the past few years, noting the "countless newspaper and magazine articles [that] have cited the topicality of today's comic-book plot lines as a sign of the art form's maturity," but he argued that, in reality, comics had simply gone from being filled with "campy repartee" to "remorseless violence," and had "pretensions to be more than just popular art." His article opened with descriptions of some of the major characters present in the Gotham City of contemporary comics: Catwoman was a "prostitute [who] squats in the shadows," Batman was "unhinged," Lex Luthor was "murderous," and the Joker was "depraved," all of which Queenan believed reflected how the comic book industry was "determined to dispel any lingering notion that its products are for children." In other words, the violence, insanity, and raunchiness were simply there to serve as a signal of the form's maturity. Although acknowledging that *Watchmen* was "well-written and elegantly drawn," he claimed that "the vindictive, sadistic tone of comics of the 1980's [sic] is best exemplified by the work of Alan Moore, author of *Watchmen*, which appeared in 1986." His basis for such an analysis was as follows:

> *Watchmen* features a boy who laughs when he finds out his mother committed suicide by drinking Drano, a heroine forced into early retirement because of lesbianism, and a child hacked to pieces and fed to German shepherds. This is all in the service of a sophisticated literary technique called "foreshadowing" that prepares the reader for the riveting climax, in which half of New York City's population gets annihilated. (In the comic-book universe, anything Armageddon-like that takes place in New York is generally viewed as an improvement.)

After spending the better part of his article detailing brutal murder scenes, women in bondage, and "titillating sex," Queenan selected *Watchmen* as the "best exemplifie[r]" of graphic novels that were striving to be taken seriously. The use of "sophisticated literary technique[s]" was, for Queenan, *Watchmen*'s feeble attempt to be considered among other works in a higher literary strata.

Queenan's use of the phrase "comic-book universe" is revealing, especially for its ambiguity. Was he referring to the universe created within the novel (that is, the alternative 1985 New York City where the action of the narrative takes place), or was he referring to a "universe," separate from his own, that included graphic-narrative works and their readers? The biting tone surrounding his descriptions of *Watchmen* and graphic novels in general suggested that the latter interpretation is plausible. That is, Queenan obviously saw himself as somehow removed from these works and their readers. Who, exactly, was Queenan referring to when he wrote, "Anything Armageddon-like that takes place in New York is generally viewed as an improvement"? Certainly there are characters in *Watchmen* (such as Rorschach) who do not view Adrian Veidt's "Armageddon-like" plan as an "improvement." Outside the context of the graphic novel, it seemed as though Queenan was suggesting that those inside the "comic-book universe" (i.e., readers of comic books) collectively viewed the destruction of New York City as positive, which thereby accounted for the massive success of the work, not the fact that it was "well-written and elegantly drawn."

Watchmen certainly left an indelible mark on other comic-book and graphic-novel narratives that followed it, and perhaps this was what Queenan was reacting to when examining the "dark side" of comics. David Hughes explained that "although intended to be the last word on comic book superheroes, ironically *Watchmen* breathed new life into the genre, establishing the cynical comic book hero as a staple of the superhero fiction, and leading to a succession of mostly inferior imitations which continue to this day" (148).

Hughes' suggestion that *Watchmen* "intended" to pulverize the superhero genre is debatable; however, the work undeniably spawned a proliferation of copy-cat works with similar themes. Gibbons explained that "in *Watchmen*'s wake there were some, frankly, tediously grim'n'gritty comics done, but these completely missed the point. It was affection and truth that the fans bought into, not disdain and distortion" (263).

Watchmen's massive success both inside and out of the comic-book community continued to attract attention throughout the 1990s, and many, like Queenan, focused on the increasingly popular adult-themed superhero narratives. Pagan Kennedy's March 19, 1990, article in *The Nation* warned not to let the "gussied-up looks" of graphic novels "fool you." Kennedy explained that Miller's *Dark Knight* "has been hailed for reviving the vampirish 1930s Batman, but one would hope it is only fanboys weaned on costumed-hero books who are insisting that *The Dark Knight* qualifies as literature." As for *Watchmen*, Kennedy claimed, "While you wouldn't want to call this book literature either, it's a lot more sophisticated than *The Dark Knight*.... *Watchmen* may be a bit simple-minded, but it deserves recognition for the innovations it brings to the graphic novel form." These "innovations" include the reoccurrence of various motifs throughout the novel (i.e., the smiley face button), as well as the use of expository materials, such as excerpts from Hollis Mason's book, an unfinished issue of the *New Frontiersman*, or pages from Sally Jupiter's scrapbook at the ends of chapters. However, Kennedy believed *Watchmen* and *Dark Knight* could not possibly live up to Speigalman's *Maus*, which "trailblazed comics' migration from the ghetto of special interest markets to the (relatively) big bucks of book publishing." Similarly, Neil Kendricks' August 19, 1993, article for *The San Diego Union-Tribune* quoted Jim Valentino, who explained that superheroes "are an adolescent power fantasy. To ask that they be mature is like asking a tree to walk." Kendricks acknowledged that Miller's *Dark Knight* and Moore and Gibbons' *Watchmen* were part of the "landmark year" of 1986, "But comics reached a new creative peak with the release of Spiegelman's subtle masterpiece, *Maus*, published by Pantheon Books," most notably because it did not offer "tales of feuding superheroes." Like Queenan's view of comics' inclusion of violence or sexuality as a discrediting factor, Kendricks and Kennedy understood the inclusion of superheroes—regardless of the complexity of the narrative—as a factor that automatically denigrated the work to a status below those that did not. Gibbons noted the media phenomenon surrounding both *Watchmen* and Miller's *Dark Knight*: "Dealing in many of the same concerns, it [*Dark Knight*] seemed to form, along with *Watchmen*, a two-pronged assault upon the iconic values and conventions of the super-hero comic. In particular, it attracted huge interest from the public media, for whom the camp 1960s *Batman* TV show was still the perceived high point of super-hero cultural attainment" (240). Simply put, few had confidence in the superhero narrative's potential to reach a "high point" beyond a popular television series.

However, some saw a great deal of potential for the superhero genre in both the popular and scholarly arenas. Janet McConnaughey's March 28, 1993, article in the *Chicago Sun-Times* briefly addressed the issue by noting, "Superhero books aren't necessarily mindless chase sequences," while Richard Reynolds' book *Super Heroes: A Modern Mythology* took the value of the superhero genre to a new level. First published by B. T. Batsford in the United Kingdom in 1992, and then published by the University of Mississippi Press in the United States in 1994, Reynolds' book examined *Watchmen*, among other works (including Miller's *Dark Knight*), in the context of the superhero genre. Drawing on ancient mythology and scholars such as Joseph Campbell, Reynolds detailed key aspects found in many superhero narratives and exemplified this through close readings of multiple texts. Also significant about this work is the fact that a university press had published it. The University of Mississippi, known for its long support of popular culture studies, was endorsing scholarly work on *Watchmen* and other graphic narratives within the superhero genre. Even if some members of the mainstream media denounced the superhero narratives, a university endorsed it, and this work provided an early glimmer of what was to come.[8]

Scaling the Walls of the Ivory Tower

There is evidence that *Watchmen* was used as reading material in college English classrooms as early as 1988. Just a year after its release in graphic-novel form, Roger Dean Du Mars interviewed Daryl Coats, an assistant professor of English at Northwest Community College in Powell, Wyoming, in his article for *The Christian Science Monitor*. Du Mars explained that Coats "teaches the post-modern *Watchmen*, by Alan Moore ... in his 'Science Fiction Literature' course." In the interview, Coats provided justification for his use of the work: "*Watchmen* is a novel told with the aid of pictures. Is it literature? Yes, I would go that far" (qtd. in Du Mars). As an English professor, it was likely that Coats viewed the "literature" label through the context of his profession. To say that he would "go that far" in labeling *Watchmen* as literature meant that the work was worthy of a label that often (when used in an academic context) was most readily understood as referring to the classics or canonical works. Ten years later, in the "Letters" section of the Spring 1998 edition of *Extrapolation*, Harris-Fain, an associate professor of English at Shawnee State University, explained that he also used *Watchmen* as a text in one of his science fiction classes. Responding to a previously printed book review, he writes, "I also had my students read H. G. Wells' *The War of the Worlds*, Dick's *Do Androids Dream of Electric Sheep*, and Alan Moore's *Watchmen* over a ten week term..." (Letter 87).

Both Coats and Harris-Fain included *Watchmen* in classes that focused on works of science fiction, but if an English professor were to suggest that a graphic novel be included in an English course that included multiple genres, one that was thought of as above the science-fiction ghetto, he or she was likely to elicit some strong negative reactions from colleagues. In the February 28, 1992, edition of *Commonweal*, Frank McConnell explained his experience as precisely that when he decided to assign Miller's *Dark Knight* for a course entitled "The Art of Narrative":

> The consensus of my colleagues (I heard it through the grapevine) was "God —
> what's he trying to do *now*?" Well, maybe just be honest. The fact is — though
> you're not going to hear it from many of the tenured priesthood of what Ezra
> Pound contemptuously called "Kulchur" — that some of the best and most human
> fiction in America, not to mention the rest of the world, is appearing not as "nov-
> els" but as that more-than-faintly-contemptible form, the comic book [21].

It was more acceptable for *Watchmen* to be taught, among other titles, in the "next ghetto up" than if it were to be catapulted among other literary works, known for their "art of narrative." Here, too, hierarchical stratification of different genres and narratives compelled McConnell's colleagues to suspect him (covertly) of some serious misjudgment. He was quick to defend his decision, continually referring to the graphic narratives mentioned throughout his article in relation to canonical works such as *Beowulf, The Great Gatsby*, and *Sister Carrie*, to name just a few. Of *Watchmen*, McConnell wrote, "I can't begin to describe the brilliance of, say, *Watchmen*. But read it and then tell *me* that it's less admirable than Coover or Pynchon or Mailer or DeLillo" (22).

Interestingly, even though McConnell, Coats, and Harris-Fain acknowledged the value of *Watchmen*, and the latter two included it in their syllabi, none mentioned Dave Gibbons as part of the creative team, whose drawings contributed an essential part of the narrative.[9] Coats' explanation of *Watchmen* as a "novel told with the aid of pictures" suggested that the majority of the story came from the words rather than the pictures, which merely served as an "aid" or support for what was narrated through the words. If even Coats, someone who clearly found value in the graphic-novel form, explained the images as such, then it was easy to see where some would disagree with Coats and view *Watchmen* and other graphic narratives as less than "real" literature. Perhaps he placed the emphasis on the writing rather than the interaction between the words and images in order to sway readers towards believing in the work's value; however, this strategy could also have had the opposite effect, confirming the hesitations of those who believed that the images simply made the narrative easier to read by filling in the parts of the story that the reader would otherwise have to imagine for him or herself.

Some wanted to explain the graphic novel's significance as something beyond bounded literary strata, seeing it as a work that transcended the comic-book industry, while others steadfastly defended the turf of separate strata for literary value. George Dardess, in a review of four books for *College English*, explained that the combination of two media into one was nothing new. The graphic novel's battle for respect was one that other media had to fight in the past: "Like opera, the theater, the cinema, or video, it [the graphic novel] uses at least two mediums simultaneously, in this case words and pictures, to give aesthetic shape to human experience. The only important general characteristic the sequential art narrative form lacks that opera and the others share is respectability" (214). In his 1990 book *Science Fiction in the Real World*, Norman Spinrad wrote that *Watchmen* was an exemplar of the graphic-novel form: "a full-sized novel, a complex one, a sophisticated one, and Moore and Gibbons bring it all together in a manner which makes *Watchmen* to the graphic novel what *Don Quixote* was to the prose novel — the first full-scale demonstration of the mature potentials of a new art form in its adolescence" (76). *Watchmen* was no ordinary graphic novel. Spinrad, like so many other reviewers, writers, and professors, wanted to place it among other great works of art by defining it through analogy. *Watchmen* was like a canonical Dickens work, the works of Pynchon or DeLillo, or even like Cervantes's *Don Quixote*. Over the years, some began to recognize a distinction between *Watchmen* and other graphic-narrative works, and it undeniably had immense staying power.

Topping the Charts

By 1997, *Watchmen*'s tenth anniversary, the graphic novel was still garnering praise, as John Layman of *The San Diego Union-Tribune* noted: "A decade later, the miniseries remains among the most complex, thought-provoking and perfectly realized explorations of the comic-book medium, and the superhero genre in particular." He continued, explaining that the work was one that "no comic reader should be without." With the dawning of the millennium quickly approaching, *Watchmen* was reaching a sort of canonical status in the world of comic books, one representation of which was seen in DC Comics' inclusion of *Watchmen* #1 in their release of "Millennium Editions." As Bill Radford of *The Gazette* explained in his November 1999 article titled "Millennium Editions Feature Classics," these publications were "reprints of classic titles span[ning] six decades of DC history, from Golden Age to Silver Age to the modern era." *Watchmen* was included alongside such notable works as *Action Comics* #1 (the first appearance of Superman) and *Brave and the Bold* #28 (the first appearance of the Justice League of America). In 1999, *Watchmen* was also voted "Favorite Limited Comic-Book Series of the Century" in *Comic Buyer's Guide* (Radford, "Millennium"), in addition to being included in *The Comics Journal*'s 1999 list of their selections for "The Top 100 Comics of the Century."

The Comics Journal top 100 list attempted to include "the *best* work of the past 100 years — that is to say, *the most valuable for their artistic merits*, not simply the 100 most *enjoyable* comics of the 20th century" (Hick). There were numerous objections to the list, some of which were that selections were limited to English-language comics, that the list was too subjective, and that the category of "comics" was too broadly defined (Radford, "Magazine" and "The Top"). Of the three major titles popularized in the late 1980s, *Watchmen* ranks number 91; *Maus* held a top spot at number four, and *Dark Knight* did not make the list at all. To compile the list, eight members of the staff at *The Comics Journal* came up with their own top 100 lists, and "ideally, by comparing the lists in compiling the final list, elements of taste were weeded out. Works without a strong consensus simply did not make the cut" (Hick). So why did the list exclude *Dark Knight*? After all, it had been extensively praised and awarded for its artistic merit and writing.[10] Radford explained that "*The Comics Journal* champions alternative comics, so it's not surprising to see few mainstream, superhero titles on the list" ("Magazine"), but *Watchmen* had been argued as "mainstream" many times over. Not only was it published by powerhouse DC Comics, but it also dealt with superheroes. However, others saw something exceptional about *Watchmen* beyond its mainstream publisher and superhero themes. Kim Thompson, vice president for Fantagraphic Books, the publisher of *The Comics Journal*, explained on a message board: "Superman and Batman aren't on the list because, as important as they were, 99.8% of the actual comics are crap, and the .2% that aren't do not include any individual issue, story or run that can legitimately be considered one of the best 100 comics of the century" (qtd. in Radford, "Magazine"). This seems to be a direct dig at *Dark Knight*, a title that was, for some, valued as much if not more than *Watchmen*. Thompson's judgment here seemed to be somewhat subjective, which exemplified the reasons for the massive backlash when the list was first published. It was noteworthy, however, that *Watchmen* made the list, suggesting that it was in some way "alternative" and not "mainstream." Additional evidence for this emerged on Ray Mescallodo's list of "The Twenty Best Mainstream Comics," appearing along with *The Comics Journal*'s top 100. *Dark Knight* was included on this list, but *Watchmen* was not, suggesting that *Watchmen* has some artistic merit beyond its mainstream appeal.

Interest in graphic novels continued to increase throughout the first decade of the 21st century. Peter Rowe's 2007 article for *The San Diego Union-Tribune* ironically noted, "In the 20th century, comic books endured congressional hearings and parental condemnation. The industry, like Plastic Man, always bounced back. The 21st century, though, has ushered in a relentless new foe: Respectability." In a complete turn, graphic novels and comics had found the center of the media spotlight, and, along the way, steadily gained scholarly acceptance and mainstream attention. Yet, some were not thrilled with the new widespread respect for the graphic-narrative form. Rowe quoted Tom Spurgeon, editor of *The Comics Reporter*, who believed that the medium needed "some of that air of disrepute" in order to "retain ... a cool factor." Although some would disagree with Spurgeon, his comment reflected the fact that graphic novels and comics had became reputable, losing some of "that air of disrepute." Increasingly, "guides" to graphic novels were published in newspapers, magazines, and online, offering new readers lists of what were now considered "classics" of the medium. In 2005, Geoff Boucher of the *Los Angeles Times* wrote, "Graphic novels seem to be everywhere," and *Watchmen* appeared to be included on almost every one of these short lists of graphic-novel must-reads.

When *Watchmen* was included on one list in particular, however, it was highlighted for its perceived elevated status above other graphic novels. In October 2005, *Time* magazine's Lev Grossman and Richard Lacayo picked what they believed to be the best 100 English-language novels since 1923, the year *Time* magazine began. *Watchmen* made the list, and stood among literary greats such as F. Scott Fitzgerald's *The Great Gatsby*, Joseph Heller's *Catch-22*, George Orwell's *1984*, and J. R. R. Tolkien's *The Lord of the Rings*. The work also made Andrew D. Arnold's list for *Time* magazine's top ten graphic novels in English since 1923, making it the only work to be included in both novel and graphic-novel categories. Two years later, in Peter Rowe's article, Arnold is quoted as saying, "Anyone described as 'well read' would have to be at least familiar with a core sample of all the varieties of literature including poetry, essays, novels, short stories, and nonfiction.... So there should be no reason to exclude graphical literature as well." The prospective seemed quite daunting for some, as Arthur Salm indicated in his overview of Grossman and Lacayo's list, particularly with their choice to include *Watchmen*: "Someday I'm going to *have to* deal with graphic novels — but today's not that day. Words are quite enough for the time being" [my emphasis]. Bruce Eric Kaplan's cartoon for the December 13, 2004, issue of *The New Yorker* seemed to be anticipating the graphic novel's prestigious rise. His cartoon pictured a couple walking by the windows of a bookstore with a caption that read, "Now I have to start pretending I like graphic novels too?"

A month after *Time* magazine included *Watchmen* on their list, DC Comics released *Absolute Watchmen*. This edition included beautifully recolored images, essays by both Moore and Gibbons, and original notes from the work's initial planning stages. Printed on heavy paper stock in a larger hardcover format, it carried a serious price tag of 75 dollars. Reviews of the newly repackaged work were positive. David Itzkoff, for the *New York Times Book Review*, noted that *Watchmen*'s "acuteness has not dulled with age." For some, the time-tested and lasting quality of *Watchmen*'s narrative was enough to merit it a glowing review, while others believed the way in which the graphic novel had been repackaged was telling of the work's monumental status: "At Golden Apple [a large Los Angeles comic book store] you can order the new $75 hardcover edition of *The Watchmen* [sic] with a slipcase and lots of extra material, and that alone should signal the rarified stature that it enjoys ... forget the Super Friends, this is a Greek tragedy with an especially flamboyant wardrobe" (Boucher). In 2006, the comics industry also recognized the publication of the *Absolute Watchmen* with a Will

Eisner Comic Industry Award for the category Best Archival Collection/Project — Comic Books (Hahn).

Watchmen's Long Shadow

Not only was *Watchmen* renowned for its staying power and influence in the comic-book industry over twenty years after it was first published, but as Jeff Jensen pointed out in his 2005 article "*Watchmen*: An Oral History" for *Entertainment Weekly*, *Watchmen* "created seismic waves, not just in comics but rippling across all of pop culture." Jensen explained that in 1988, Bomb the Bass used an inverted version of *Watchmen*'s blood-spattered smiley face for the cover of their single "Beat Dis," which from then on linked rave scenes with the smiley face logo. Comics writers and film directors who point to *Watchmen* as having a profound influence on their careers include legendary comics writer Neil Gaiman (*The Sandman*), writer/director/producer Joss Whedon (*Buffy the Vampire Slayer* and *Serenity*), hit television series *Lost* co-creator Damon Lindelof, and directors Darren Aronofsky (*pi*) and Richard Kelley (*Donnie Darko*) (Jensen). Walt Disney and Pixar's 2004 film *The Incredibles* paid homage to *Watchmen* with a story that included a super-powered family forced into retirement and a suburbia lifestyle, an overweight and middle-aged super dad yearning to return to masked adventuring, and even a reference to the "hazards of wearing a cape" (Jensen). *Watchmen* was referenced in the November 18, 2007, *The Simpsons* episode titled "Husbands and Knives," in which Moore portrayed himself at a comic-book signing. Milhouse brings his DVD copy of "Watchmen Babies in V for Vendetta," sending Moore into a rant on the irresponsibility of Hollywood adaptations of his work. The April 23, 2007, episode of the television series *Heroes* includes a plot curiously close to the Ozymandias world-uniting plan from the graphic novel. *Heroes*' character Linderman "reveals that he knows the bomb [that will kill a portion of the population in New York City] is going to go off and wants it to — because the destruction of New York will unite the world in peace behind a new president he is grooming" (Lynch 49). *Watchmen*'s influence was far-reaching, but a new surge in *Watchmen*'s long history of popularity began in the summer of 2008.

When *The Dark Knight*, directed by Christopher Nolan, hit theaters in the summer of 2008, a teaser trailer for *Watchmen* preceded the feature film. A montage of clips from the film, some of which were scenes directly drawn from the images in the graphic novel, was accompanied by a haunting rendition of the Smashing Pumpkins' "The Beginning Is the End Is the Beginning." The only dialogue in the two-minute trailer was a single line from Rorschach's journal: "The world will look up and shout, 'save us,' and I'll whisper, 'no.'" Four short clips of explanatory text — "In 2009," "Everything we know will change," "From the visionary director of '300,'" and "The most celebrated graphic novel of all time"—left the details of the film ambiguous, and the trailer ended with the film's website, *Watchmenmovie.com*, splashed across the screen, leaving some *Watchmen* fans anxious, others excited, and those unfamiliar with the graphic novel curious to learn more.

Less than a week later, the graphic novel shot to number five on BarnesandNoble.com's sales rank, and by August the book "listed atop Amazon as one of the most requested items" (Dyer). DC Comics printed an unprecedented one million more copies to keep pace with increased demand (Romanelli, "Effect"). Jeff Dyer, for the *Telegraph-Herald*, aptly summed up the phenomenon: "Unlike other books that come and go as fads, *Watchmen* has had staying power unseen in the comic book business. It seems that year after year, new fans discover the work, and old fans rediscover it." However, the summer of 2008 created more than the usual interest in the work, as the graphic novel once again headed for the media spotlight and came to the attention of a whole new audience. In the November 9, 2008, issue of *The Independent on Sunday*, Dominic Wells wrote, "Two decades later, the hype juggernaut is picking up pace once more. Tantalizing trailers herald the release, next spring, of Hollywood's version of the book which many—including Moore—deemed unfilmable." By January 2009, *USA Today* published the 100 top-selling books for 2008, among which *Watchmen* ranked 60 (Cadden et. al.).

As anticipation built surrounding the film, publications on and about the graphic novel and film adaptation also increased. In October 2008, Gibbons' *Watching the Watchmen* was published. This companion work to *Watchmen* provided readers with Gibbons' perspective on the genesis of the work and his commentary on numerous sketches, layout roughs, page prints, and schematics from *Watchmen*'s creation. Also included were narratives detailing how Gibbons and Moore came to work together on the project, the unusual amount of creative flexibility that they were allowed, the overwhelming and somewhat unexpected acclaim for the piece, and the flurry of memorabilia and marketing strategies that ensued after the series' release. John Higgins, colorist on the original series, also provided a brief commentary about his involvement. Three books directly related to the film also hit book stores nationwide in February 2009—Peter Aperlo's *Watchmen: The Official Film Companion* and *Watchmen: The Art of the Film*, and Clay Enos' *Watchmen: The Film Portraits*.

On the scholarly front, publications on *Watchmen* sporadically appeared throughout the first decade of the 21st century. Matthew Wolf-Meyer's 2003 article for the *Journal of Popular Culture* analyzed the characters of Rorschach and Veidt in relation to their political perspectives. Mark Bernard and James Bucky Carter discussed time and space in Moore's works, including *Watchmen*, in their 2004 article for *ImageTexT: Interdisciplinary Comics Studies*. Similarly, Sean Carney's 2006 article for *ImageTexT* explored time and history's progress in *Watchmen* and other works. Iain Thomson's 2005 article for the University of Mississippi's *Comics as Philosophy* book discussed the work's deconstruction of the hero in relation to Heidegger, Nietzsche, and Kierkegaard. Jamie A. Hughes' 2006 article for the *Journal of Popular Culture* analyzed the motivations and ideologies of *Watchmen*'s characters. Geoff Klock's 2006 book *How to Read Superhero Comics and Why* included one chapter on *Watchmen*, which discussed how it and *Dark Knight* changed the face of the superhero genre. Roger Whitson's 2007 article for *ImageTexT* examined the work in relation to those of William Blake.

In reviewing the scholarship on comics studies for *Modern North American Criticism and Theory*, Christopher Eklund pointed out in 2006:

> This "holy trinity" of comic books [*Maus, Watchmen,* and *Dark Knight*] would result in the first of many furors over the "new" comics, and all have subsequently become staples of academic teaching and research. *Maus* is taught in many Holocaust literature classes, while both it and *Watchmen* have become *de rigeur* for classes on comics as literature. All three have been the subject of many journal articles book chapters [sic], but as yet none have received dedicated monographs [210].

In February 2009, *Watchmen and Philosophy: A Rorschach Test*, edited by Mark D. White, included a collection of fifteen essays all dedicated to the study of the graphic novel. Each essay (as expected from the title) attempted to analyze a different aspect of the work through a philosophical lens, with sections focusing on power, ethics, metaphysics, and the comic-book medium.

Once thought of as mere sources of adolescent entertainment, the perception of graphic novels has changed by following the path that *Watchmen* had plowed through both scholarly and popular communities. Like *Watchmen and Philosophy*, this book is a dedicated study of the work, but in the context of contemporary literary criticism, and draws from social, cultural, and political perspectives. In the coming chapters, this book will examine what constitutes "text," thereby showing the conceptual relationship between images and words, consider heroism as a stereotype and social construction, analyze the hero's journey, discuss the role of the narrator, and the way in which the narrative's construction manipulates the reader's perception of time and space.

Chapter 2

I^^@ge$ & Wo(r)d$

> *"The evolution of literature and art are kind of uncertain. The future seems to me to be much clearer for comics because the future there seems to be building the links between words and pictures, the visual verbal combinations that comics offer in all its variations is still wide open, ready to be explored...."*
> — Paul Gravett, *The Mindscape of Alan Moore*

The graphic narrative is a mode of communication through which the storyteller conveys his or her idea through a combination of images and words.[1] Outside of the graphic-narrative medium, they are often perceived as separate entities. Scholars study them separately; they are even housed in their own departments at most post-secondary schools and universities. Great literary works are comprised of all words, and great pieces of art are valued for the quality of their images. While each is a distinct vehicle of communication with separate ways of conveying information, when examined at their fundamental level, images and words are not as different as they appear. In his groundbreaking *Comics and Sequential Art*, Will Eisner explains:

> Comics deal with two fundamental communicating devices: words and images. Admittedly this is an arbitrary separation. But, since in the modern world of communication they are treated as independent disciplines, it seems valid. Actually, they are derivatives of a single origin and in the skillful employment of words and images lies the expressive potential of the medium [7].

Both words and images convey meaning through the precise combination or placement of marks on a two to three dimensional surface (i.e., ink on paper, paint on canvas, engravings on wood, pixels on a computer screen, etc). Scott McCloud, author of *Understanding Comics* and *Making Comics*, two valuable resources on the graphic-narrative form, notes, "It's easy to forget that the same few dots and lines that can draw a person—can easily write what that person says. Words and pictures for all their differences— are just two sides of the same coin. Both share a common purpose and a common heritage" (*Making* 152). The "common heritage" between images and words is perhaps most recognizable in pictographic languages, those that use simplified images to represent particular objects or things. In these languages, words *are* images and vice versa. Today, however, many languages that were once pictographic (such as Chinese) have evolved to include characters that represent single syllables, and many characters that began as pictographic no longer directly resemble the objects that they originally represented.[2] One reason for such change is that some ideas or concepts are not simply or quickly relatable through images. Images may be more direct than words in their representations of some tangible objects, but other concepts may be too challenging to represent with a simple icon. Both words and images are signifiers, representations of something else; however, words are more abstract in their representation and easily discernable as separate from the actual objects or ideas that they represent. Belgian artist René Magritte's 1929 painting "La Trahison des Images" (The Treason of Images) portrays a large pipe in the middle of the canvas, under which reads "Ceci n'est pas une pipe" (or "This is not a pipe"), and indeed it is not; it is merely a *painting* of a pipe. If the word "pipe" simply appeared on the canvas, one would perhaps be less inclined to confuse the object with its representation because the combinations of letters that form the word do not resemble an actual pipe like the visual representation.

The perceived distinction between words and images is fundamentally derived from how we read each signifier. The former has a stable set of conventions or guidelines for reading, but the latter does not. In English, we begin reading a page of text in the top left-hand corner, following each line of words from left to right until reaching the bottom right-hand portion of the page. The author therefore controls the order in which readers encounter new information; without following the conventions, decoding the narrative becomes a much more difficult task. Similar to a page of printed words, an image is presented to the reader in its entirety, but *unlike* with words, the reader's eyes are free to wander through the image with no standard for where he or she should begin or end. There are many ways an artist can manipulate the reader's gaze to focus on a particular aspect of the piece: "with experience, [artists] can reliably predict what [readers will] pay attention to—and be distracted by—and use that knowledge to [their] advantage" (McCloud, *Making* 35). However, there is never a guarantee that a reader will perceive the information in exactly the way the artist intends, as McCloud explains: "In comics the conversion follows a path from mind to hand to paper to eye to mind. Ideally the artist's 'message' will run this gauntlet without being affected by it, but in practice this is rarely the case" (*Understanding* 195).

Eisner's understanding of the distinction between reading words and reading images is one of imagination: "In writing with words alone, the author directs the reader's imagination. In comics the imagining is done for the reader. An image once drawn becomes a precise statement that brooks little or no further interpretation. When the two are mixed, the words become welded to the image and no longer serve to describe but rather to provide sound, dialogue and connective passages" (*Comics* 127). What Eisner is referring to here are some established graphic-narrative conventions that direct the reader's interpretation. Conventions such as word balloons and typographic style allude to how particular characters "sound," or provide subtle nuance of tone or vocal inflection; however, what Eisner does *not* address in his quotation are the interpretive possibilities of images. Color, panel composition, perspective, and characters' body language and facial expressions contribute to how the reader interprets the contents of each panel. Images provide just as much room for interpretation as do the written words, even though the experience of reading an image is more visceral and immediate. In graphic narratives, the "imagining" is not "done for the reader" any more than in other texts; the path leading readers to interpretation is simply paved in a different way. Using Moore and Gibbons' *Watchmen* as a guide, this chapter will explore the function of both word and image conventions commonly found in the graphic-narrative form, and will explain how style and design decisions affect how the reader perceives particular characters, their actions, and the overall tone of the narrative.

Reading Words: Word Balloons and Narrative Boxes

The most obvious way that words contribute to the meaning of a text is through their denotative and connotative meanings, but the written elements in a graphic narrative also convey meaning through their stylization. Elements such as font, size, and framing all contribute to how the reader interprets the words and their relationship to the images on the page. Throughout much of *Watchmen*'s narrative, words are hand-lettered rather than typeset. Eisner describes hand lettering as giving the words in the text a "recognizable 'human' quality" that "reflects the nature and emotion of speech" (*Comics* 26, 24). Similarly, Saraceni, author of *The Language of Comics*, writes, "We tend to associate handwriting with human agency. The irregular shapes of letters resemble the irregular patterns in the way people speak, with varying tones and loudness of voice" (21). With hand lettering, every letter is slightly different from the last, making the letters as unique as the drawings that they accompany. Standardized, rigidly consistent letters would unnecessarily distract the reader, clearly demarcating between words and images based on the uniformity of the former and the fluidity of the latter. Rather, hand lettering matches the line quality of the images with which they are housed, especially when done by the same artist, as is the case with *Watchmen*.

Word balloons are perhaps one of the most recognizable and enigmatic elements of word integration in the graphic-narrative medium. Balloons allow for the elimination of attributives (such as "he said" or "she said") by representing them visually; the words "float" over or near the characters who are speaking. McCloud describes word balloons as having an "uneasy" relationship with the panels that contain them: "Balloons don't exist in the same plane of reality as these pictures, yet here they are, floating about like physical objects!" (*Making* 142). Word balloons often include a "tail," a line or other graphical element that points to the character or object to which the words belong. Similarly to McCloud, Paul Gravett, author of *Graphic Novels: Everything You Need to Know*, understands that word balloons "can appear unnatural and unnerving, hovering like Zeppelins over people's heads" (10), but they are what Eisner calls a "desperation device ... [that] attempts to capture and make visible an ethereal element: sound" (*Comics* 24).

For most of the characters in *Watchmen*, the word balloons are a uniform oval shape with a white background, each containing hand-lettered words. Rorschach's word balloons, however, are distinct from the rest. They are defined by a tattered and uneven shape, and are rough and slightly disheveled, much like his attire. His word balloons are as unique as he is; Rorschach is the only one of his fellow masked brethren to have continued crime-fighting illegally after the 1977 institution of the Keene Act. The irregularly shaped balloons are a reflection of Rorschach's voice, which is muffled while wearing his tight-fitting mask. When he is not wearing his mask, his word balloons match those of the other characters,[3] a distinction presumably based on a variation in the sound of his voice. The shape and style merge with Rorschach's character and the image that represents him throughout the text. Word balloons function in such a dichotomous way that they are simultaneously natural and unnatural; they are extensions of the characters themselves, yet represent that which cannot be seen, the sounds of voices and the surrounding environment.

If Rorschach's word balloons remained constant throughout the narrative or always resembled the rest of the other characters' balloons, it would seem asynchronous to Rorschach's character, as every other aspect of him suggests that he is slightly removed from those around him. The only one that shares this similarly removed position is Dr. Manhattan, whose word balloons are also distinct from the conventional white oval format. As the only superhuman character in the group, Dr. Manhattan's word balloons reflect "his very different voice and worldview" (Gravett 83). After transforming into a being more powerful than any other on Earth, Dr. Manhattan is slowly losing touch with humanity. His word balloons are filled with a pale blue color and insulated by thick, white borders. His balloons are cold and detached, like his relationships with others, and they reflect his isolation as a result of his otherworldly perspective and abilities.

In many graphic narratives, voices modified through some type of electronic device are represented in a different word-balloon format than those representing characters' voices. In *Comics and Sequential Art*, Eisner visually depicts the word-balloon conventions for this and other sounds. For "sound or speech that emanates from a radio, telephone, television or any machine," Eisner shows the standard word balloon style, one that is surrounded by a hard, jagged outline with a tail that resembles a lightning bolt (25). There are a few different examples of electronically modified dialogue in *Watchmen*, each of which has a different word-balloon style to reflect the quality of the sound. When Dreiberg speaks through the PA system in the Owl Ship, the word balloons resemble Eisner's convention for electronic sound with a jagged balloon and tail (2.16–17, 7.23–26). The same balloon format is used for the police megaphone in chapter 5, with which Detective Steve Fine warns Rorschach that the building is surrounded (5.24–25). After rescuing victims from the tenement fire with Juspeczyk, Dreiberg turns on music in the cabin of the Owl Ship (7.25). Compared to the cacophonic blare of the PA system and the megaphone, the melodious lyrics of Billie Holiday's "You're My Thrill" drift from the Owl Ship in word balloons that take on a fluid-like form. The word balloons to represent the sounds that come from televisions throughout the narrative are similar to those that represent most characters' dialogue (4.13, 7.11–15, 12.28). They are characterized by the conventional white oval shape but include a jagged tail. The shape represents a sound that is less abrasive than that of the PA system, but not as melodic as the music from the Owl Ship.

A word balloon's shape also represents the sound quality of dialogue, and if it is distinct in any way from regular conversation. Placement of the balloons within the panel also affects how the reader "hears" dialogue. Eisner explains that panels "*capture* or encapsulate ... events in the flow of the narrative" (*Comics* 39). They are "sequenced segments" of the story that together form the overall narrative (Eisner, *Comics* 39). Panels frame the images and word balloons on the page in much the same way the word balloons frame or contain the words. A character's words are not necessarily contained within one word balloon per panel. Figure 2.1 shows four different constructions of the standard oval word balloon. Balloons are sometimes "pinched," giving them a figure-eight–like shape. Others are attached by a small connecting tail, and still others are completely separate, where one character's words may be represented in two disconnected balloons. This is as much an aesthetic consideration as it is a rhetorical one. In *Watchmen*, word balloons all contain solid backgrounds, which cover parts of the images in the panels. The balloons must allow room for the images. If they are too large, they take the reader's attention away and overpower the images in the panel. When accommodating a large amount of

Fig. 2.1. A pause in dialogue may be represented graphically through the separation of a character's words into more than one word balloon.

words, pinched or separated balloons allow for more of the image to show. These balloons visually create a pause in a character's dialogue. The more space between the balloons, the more time that elapses between the words. The physical act of moving one's eyes to the next balloon forces a pause.

Of course, the length of the sentences and words within the balloons also contributes to syntactical pacing. Longer sentences with longer words generally slow down the pacing of the narrative; they physically require the reader to read more words before reaching the end of a sentence. Shorter, more abrupt sentences can be read more quickly. However, a short sentence does not necessarily mean that the pacing of the dialogue accelerates, nor does a long sentence mean that the dialogue's pace slows. Word balloon placement and syntactical structure work together to counterbalance each other. When Rorschach meets with psychoanalyst Dr. Malcolm Long for the third time, their conversation shows how syntactical pacing affects meaning. Long presents Rorschach with the same inkblot tests used during his first visit. Rorschach says, "Seen this one before," and Dr. Long responds, "Yes. I know. I ... uh ... I thought you might have been holding back before and I wanted to try it again. Go on. Tell me what you really see" (6.17).[4] Long expects Rorschach to give him a different answer than his previous answer of "pretty butterfly" (6.1). He is nervous about what Rorschach might say as he hesitantly insists Rorschach to tell him what he "really see[s]." Long's word balloon is pinched before the words "go on," reflecting not only a slight pause in his speech, but also a shift away from himself and a more passive approach to working with Rorschach ("I wanted to try again") to a more active one ("Tell me what you see"). The next two panels contain no word balloons; the first focuses closely on Rorschach, who stares intently at the inkblot, and the second shows what he sees. The silent panels in the middle of the conversation extend the time lapse between question and response. McCloud notes, "Silence has the effect of removing a panel from any particular span of time. Word balloons have a perceived duration so the panels they're in do too. Without that implicit time stamp which words provide, a silent panel doesn't 'end' quite as crisply — and the effect of it can linger throughout the page" (*Making* 164). Silent panels positioned between those with dialogue can lend the conversation weight by suspending it in time.

After two silent panels amid the conversation, Rorschach finally answers, "Dog." "Dog with head split in half" (6.17). Each phrase is represented in its own word balloon, giving each of the short statements greater intensity and extending the narrative time. In the following panel, Long responds in three separate word balloons: "I ... I see." "And, Uh, what do you think split the, uh, split the dog's head." "In half." The background of the panel is blank, and all emphasis is placed on a profile of Long's face and the three balloons, which begin at the top of the panel and cascade down the right side. Long does not reply with many words, but the separate balloons, the ellipses, and the disfluencies ("uh," repetition of "split the") in his language all contribute to slowing the pace of the conversation. The next panel focuses on Rorschach's profile, and the background is again blank. Rorschach simply responds, "I did," which is represented in one small word balloon near the bottom of the panel. Both the panels and small, separated word balloons are visually quiet, signifying the unexpected turn in Dr. Long and Rorschach's conversation.

Word balloons can also simulate confusion and accelerate the narrative pacing. After Rorschach's first meeting with Dr. Long earlier in chapter 6, the prisoners call out to Rorschach, taunting and threatening him as he is led back to his cell (5–6). Word balloons reach from both sides of the cell-lined aisle. As Rorschach walks further down the hall, the balloons begin to overlap one another. Only parts of each balloon can be read, merging into a bombardment of faceless voices all at once. The balloons visually represent the seemingly overwhelming cacophonic din of the prisoners' voices. In chapter 12, Veidt's wall of televisions evokes a similar experience. Each television, set to a different channel, flashes news broadcasts of the destruction in New York City (12.18–19). Word balloons overlap with descriptions of the devastation and the ways in which it will affect the world in the years to come. Each balloon has multiple tails, and one cannot be sure of the origin of each report, emanating from any one of the screens. The barrage of sounds is overwhelming for both characters and reader, as the balloons fill much of the panels. This again visually establishes an auditory tone for the scene.

In addition to contributing quality and pacing for particular sounds, word balloons also help to reflect the volume at which characters speak. For most of the narrative, the words remain a constant size, so any change in the size of the words is an indication that a character's voice has either increased or decreased in volume. Large, bold words signify shouting, as when Juspeczyk becomes startled when she finds that Dr. Manhattan has divided himself into three separate beings, or when Rorschach attempts to escape the police by leaping from Moloch's apartment (3.4, 5.27–28). To signify the uneven waver in each character's voice while screaming, the letters alternate in a wave-like pattern. Large bold words also represent Dr. Manhattan's loud, booming voice when he morphs himself into an enormous size and crashes through the wall of Veidt's Antarctic retreat (12.18). Significantly smaller words than the standard format function in the opposite way of the large, bold words. Rather than representing the character's strength or the amplified sound of his or her voice, these words suggest that the speaker feels defeated or weak, and, as a result, is speaking more softly. When Rorschach makes a surprise visit to Happy Harry's Bar and Grill in chapter 1, Harry pleads with Rorschach: "Oh God. Please don't kill anybody" (15). His words are tiny in a large, white word balloon as he cowers behind the bar. In chapter 10, Rorschach comments on Juspeczyk's sudden departure to Mars with Dr. Manhattan: "Pity Miss Juspeczyk couldn't stay with us" (4). Dreiberg responds, "Yes. Yes, it's a pity." His words appear much smaller than Rorschach's, an indication that he feels it more than a "pity" that Juspeczyk left with Dr. Manhattan; he's hurt and defeated with the knowledge that she has perhaps returned to her significant other. Representation of a quiet voice is different from a defeated one, as seen in chapter 4. When Janey Slater is angered by Dr. Manhattan's incessant staring at Juspeczyk during the Crimebusters meeting, their word balloons' outlines are dashed rather than solid, a representation that they are whispering to each other so that the others cannot hear. Word balloons are more than the vessels that contain characters' dialogue. By adding sound to an otherwise silent medium, variations in style, color, and typography transform dialogue to express a range of human emotion beyond what the individual words signify.

Narrative boxes are like word balloons without the tails and tend to be rectangular or square rather than oval or circular. As stated earlier, the function of a word balloon's tails is attributive in nature; it signifies that the words contained within the balloon are spoken and designate which character is speaking. The absence of a tail, therefore, signifies no attribution. In *Watchmen*, the narrative box functions in two ways: to represent a character's dialogue, who is not pictured in the corresponding panel, or to represent written rather than spoken words.[5] Excerpts from Rorschach's journal and the comic book *Tales of the Black Freighter* are both written texts that are represented in narrative boxes throughout *Watchmen*. Rorschach's journal entries serve to portray the surrounding events of the main plot from his perspective. The journal entries' narrative boxes resemble the well-worn paper on which they are written. The edges are torn and tattered, and stray ink speckles the pale yellow backgrounds. Rorschach's journal entries include a mixture of upper and lower-case letters, giving the boxes a more casual and hand-written quality, as opposed to the uniform, capitalized letters of the word balloons. The issues of *Tales of the Black Freighter* are first introduced in chapter 3. Bernie reads two issues of the comic while sitting beside Bernard's newsstand. The comic book's narrative boxes evoke a sense of antiquity, resembling scrolls of weatherworn paper. When the first letter of a narrative box begins a new sentence, the initial letter or initial cap[6] is set off from the rest as slightly larger in size and in a decorative script font, contributing to this aged or old-fashioned effect. Each stylistic element contributes to the meaning of the words contained within both word balloons and narrative boxes.

Expository Materials

Watchmen includes a variety of stand-alone written documents for the readers to view in their entirety. Expository materials are documents (included after chapters 1 through 11) that provide readers with materials from within

Watchmen's world. References to most of these materials are made directly in the chapters that precede them. At times, these materials give the reader a voyeuristic look into particular characters' lives, like the materials that Rorschach and Dreiberg take from Veidt's desk in chapter 10 (21), Rorschach's classified police profile that Dr. Long is seen holding and reading through much of chapter 6, or Sally Jupiter's scrapbook that Juspeczyk brings to Mars in chapter 9 (23). These corresponding documents are made available to the reader following each respective chapter. Other documents are published materials with which the characters are familiar, such as Hollis Mason's autobiography *Under the Hood*. Two copies of the book stand on a shelf in Mason's apartment early in chapter 1, and Juspeczyk's familiarity with the text is made clear later in the same chapter (9, 21). After chapters 1 through 3, the expository materials include the first five chapters of Mason's book, which depict Mason's childhood and the rise and fall of the Minutemen, the first generation of costumed crime-fighters (1.27–32, 2.29–32, 3.29–32).

In *Comics and Sequential Art*, Eisner explains that when used in a graphic narrative, set-type can seem asynchronous: "Attempts to 'provide dignity' to the comic strip are often tried by utilizing set-type or computer-generated type instead of the less rigid hand lettering. Typesetting does have a kind of inherent authority but it also has a 'mechanical' effect that intrudes on the personality of freehand art" (25–26). Eisner is referring to the use of set-type in word balloons here, but his explanation of typesetting having "a kind of inherent authority" is noteworthy. All of the expository materials are very much a part of the overall narrative, but are separated by their presentation and form, one clearly distinct element of which is lettering style. Rather than hand-lettering, the words for materials such as the chapters from Mason's *Under the Hood* are uniform in a standard font. Documents, such as the excerpts from Mason's book, are supposed to appear "real," as if torn from the pages of the actual book and inserted at the end of the chapter. Readers should feel as if they are holding the artifact in their hands, reading from Mason's book just as Juspeczyk and other characters do in the narrative. In this sense, the "inherent authority" proves to be beneficial by allowing the reader to enter *Watchmen's* world.

Of course, not all of the expository materials include words that are in one set-type. The lettering styles are as varied as their sources. For example, there are numerous lettering styles included throughout the documents in Rorschach's police file (6.29–32). The first document, New York Police Department's "Form 2–18," includes multiple fonts. The police department's heading uses one font, indicators for placement of specific information (i.e., "Name" and "Address") uses another, and the directions on how to fill out the form ("Please type or print clearly") is distinct from the other two. The actual contents of the document are represented in a fourth style, a Courier font, which is frequently associated with words produced on typewriters.

Some of the letters are even slightly askew or improperly inked, which gives the document a realistic quality, imperfections and all.[7] It carries an "inherent authority" in the sense that it appears to be authentic. Readers are observing not only a representation of the document, but a document that has been filled out and filed with Rorschach's records. Other documents from his file include an "Early History" from the New York State Psychiatric Hospital, an essay entitled "My Parents" that young Kovacs wrote while a resident of the Lillian Charlton Home for Problem Children, his account of a dream at age thirteen, and one of Dr. Long's handwritten notes about his predictions for the case.

The last two documents are representations of different handwriting styles. Alongside Kovacs' depiction of his dream, he writes "My Dream by W. J. Kovacs Age 13" (6.32). A mixture of upper and lowercase letters are scratched into the paper with wildly uneven curves and sharp angles. Similar to the way in which the words in the word balloons throughout the narrative "match" Gibbons' drawings, Kovacs' words and the images match in style. Both show the same erratic expressiveness, which suggest that Kovacs is either extremely careless, perhaps uneducated, or that writing, talking, and drawing about this incident makes him very uncomfortable. Based on other documents contained in the file, the third reason appears to be the most likely. His "Early History" explains that while at the Charlton Home, he "did very well at school work," and although he was "quiet and shy, especially with women, Kovacs was capable of long and well-reasoned conversations with his classmates and instructors..." (6.30). Located directly above Kovacs' illustrated version, the document in which a representative from the Charlton Home transcribes Kovacs' oral account of the dream reveals the emotional impact that it has had on young Kovacs: "The dream it sort of upset me, physically. I couldn't help it. I feel bad just talking about it." The handwriting style of the dream, in conjunction with other contextual clues from the collective documents, contributes to the reader's understanding of Kovacs' troubled past.

Alternatively, Dr. Long's handwritten note, labeled "From the desk of: Dr. Malcolm Long," expresses his optimism in anticipation of working with Kovacs. This note is pictured next to Kovacs' drawing of his dream, which slightly overlaps Dr. Long's note, casting a shadow over some of the letters. Through their juxtaposition, the distinction between the two handwriting styles becomes dramatically apparent. The note is written in small, fairly consistent letters that tilt slightly to the right, alluding to Long's interest in meeting with Kovacs; he's looking forward to meeting him in the same way that the letters of his writing anxiously lean to the right on the page. He even writes that he is "looking forward to" working with Rorschach because he believes it may be a case "for possible future publication." Distinct typographic and handwriting styles lend each document of the expository materials credibility, allowing the reader to feel as if he or she is a part of *Watchmen*'s world.

The Montage

The "montage," first coined by McCloud in *Understanding Comics*, is "where words are treated as integral parts of the picture" (154). Throughout *Watchmen*, words are integrated into the images of panels in such forms as newspaper headlines, magazine cover stories, signs, billboards, advertisements, graffiti, and product packaging. As McCloud later notes in *Making Comics*, montages allow images and words to blend more easily: "Words and letters take on pictorial qualities and are combined more freely with the pictures that surround them.... The idea that words might 'cross the fence' into pictorial territory once in a while seems reasonable — considering how often they rub shoulders" (139). Montage words add texture to the narrative's world, and some help the reader to identify locations for particular scenes. When readers first meet Bernard and Bernie at the newsstand on page 1 of chapter 3, montage words are imbedded throughout the fourth panel (see figure 2.2). A white truck with a logo that includes "NY" and a large, red apple is parked in the background of the image, and the pairing of these two letters with the apple logo reinforces that New York City is the location of the scene. The window of the building in the background reads "Promethian Cab Co.," which places the company and the newsstand in relation to one another. Advertisements and product packaging from the Gunga Diner are scattered on the ground, suggesting that the diner is also nearby. Both of these locations will become more significant in the coming chapters. Later in the same chapter, Juspeczyk uses the cab company to drive her away from the Rockefeller Military Research Center into the city, and her driver, Joey, becomes a minor character later in the narrative (3.7, 5.21). Similarly, the Gunga Diner is the setting for Dreiberg and Juspeczyk's conversation, which leads to the decision that Juspeczyk will stay with him until she finds a new place to live, and the diner also serves as Rorschach's surveillance spot for his "maildrop" (5.10–11). This street intersection is even more significant in chapter 12 when it becomes the epicenter of Veidt's plans for world unity, directly affecting all of the characters and places in the immediate area.

In addition to providing context for location, the montage words in this first panel with Bernie and Bernard also suggest current events and popular culture trends. On the side of the newsstand hangs the latest copy of the *New Frontiersman*, whose cover reads "Missing Writer: Castro to Blame?" Readers later learn of the missing writer's identity, his location, and his unknowing involvement in Veidt's plans to transform the world (5.32 ,8.11, 32, 10.17–18). The "NY" truck holds stacks of signs that read "Fallout Shelter," one of which the man (wearing the same "NY" logo on his jacket) fastens to the side of the Promethean Cab Company building. The need for multiple fallout shelters indicates that fears of a nuclear attack are rising. Two copies of *Nova Express* hang inside the newsstand with a headline —"How Sick is Dick? After Third Presidential Heart-

Fig. 2.2. Bernard and Bernie at the newsstand (Moore and Gibbons 3.1).

Op?"—which indicates Richard Nixon is still president in 1985, but he is now in poor health. The copy of *Knot Top Magazine* that hangs from the front of the newsstand caters to the many (sometimes violent)[8] characters that affiliate themselves with the group through their style of dress and their namesake hair style.

Veidt products and advertisements are pervasive throughout *Watchmen*'s world, and Bernard's newsstand is no exception. An advertisement for "The Veidt Method" graces the back cover of Bernie's issue of *Tales*. At times, Veidt products are clearly labeled with the word "Veidt" somewhere on the item or advertisement; however, the Veidt logo is one word that blends the montage of words and images so well that it becomes difficult to clearly label it as word or image. Readers cannot always decipher each of the letters of the distinctive "Veidt" logo, but the recognizable outline of the logo is clearly visible. Bernie's shoes include outlined contours of the Veidt logo, as does the magazine that hangs next to the issue of *Knot Top*. Posters and billboards throughout the city include the logo, advertising everything from a benefit for Southern India Famine Relief to Nostalgia and Millennium Colognes (3.15, 8.25, 12.31). It marks such wide-ranging products as Mason's television set, Dr. Long's "Go Pain" pill bottle, Dreiberg's coffee pot, a Happy Harry's Bar patron's sweat-shirt, and even Moloch's "Veidt for Men Hair Spray" that Rorschach uses as a weapon in chapter 5 (3.17, 6.13–14, 7.3, 1.15, 5.25). With every imbedded Veidt logo, the repeated images continually remind the reader of his presence, sig-naling his prominence (and foreshadowing his power) in *Watchmen*'s world.

Reading Images: Composition

There may not be conventions or fixed "rules" on how to read images, but there are certainly elements that affect the way the reader interprets them. The smallest details are significant; just think of the previously discussed montage words in the panel featuring Bernie and Bernard at the newsstand in the begin-ning of chapter 3. When considering that these words are only a fraction of the whole, one can see just how much meaning something so little can contribute to the text. The majority of *Watchmen*'s panels contain settings that are as descriptive and expressive as the characters that inhabit them, and elements such as panel composition, the reader's point-of-view or perspective, color, and the characters' facial expressions and body language all contribute to their meaning.

The way the elements of an image are arranged within the picture plane is referred to as a panel's composition. The bounded sides of a panel's border function as a window through which the reader gains access to the narrative's world. The artist's choice on how to capture or frame a moment in space and time affects the reader's perception of the characters and objects that are rep-resented within. For the artist, this decision includes where characters or objects are positioned in the image, how near or far away the reader will view them, and whether the reader will be above, below, or at eye-level with the scene. McCloud suggests that "readers will assign importance to characters and objects placed in the center [of a panel] ... and some comics artists oblige by putting their most important subjects there" (*Making* 25). While positioning a char-acter in the center of the picture plane can make him or her the focus of the scene, this position in an image's composition can also affect the way the reader perceives the character. While on Benny Anger's television program, Doug Roth, of *Nova Express*, asks Dr. Manhattan a series of loaded questions regard-ing his causal relationship with those who have developed cancer. When Roth stands among the other audience members, he is positioned in the center of the picture plane, squarely facing the reader (3.13). He challenges the reader in a similar way that he confronts Dr. Manhattan with his intended line of questioning. The character's position as centered in the picture plane can also give the reader the sense of having another character's perspective, as is the case during Dr. Long's meetings with Rorschach throughout chapter 6. The two characters sit across the table from one another, and panels alternate between centered views of Long and Rorschach, each representing the perspective of the other.

Subjects placed off-center in a panel's composition give readers' eyes a "license to 'wander' ... such compositions create a sense of entering a setting with a person in it, rather than meeting a person with a setting behind them" (McCloud, *Making* 165). They invite the reader to explore the setting as freely as the characters. An example of this is the previously mentioned panel featuring Bernie and Bernard at the newsstand. The reader becomes an observer of the characters rather than being confronted by or in direct contact with them. Off-center placement can also suggest distance between characters, place emphasis on the characters' actions rather than on the characters themselves, portray distance that characters or objects have traveled or will travel, or note characters' absences (McCloud, *Making* 25). When Rorschach first investigates Edward Blake's murder, he shoots his grappling gun into the broken window of Blake's apartment from the street below and then proceeds to scale the side of the building (1.5). The last three panels on this page portray the hook's path up to the window, its descent into the apartment, and the way Rorschach uses it to climb up the side of the building. None of these panels depicts Rorschach in the center of the picture plane; however, each implies the space through which the hook and Rorschach move in order to gain entrance through the high-rise window.

Depth and Dimension

Panel composition considerations extend beyond the two-dimensional level (i.e., where the subject of an image is located on the flat picture plane). The basic levels of depth for an image, which include foreground, midground, and background, give panels the illusion of three-dimensional space. The foreground of a panel is what is closest to the reader. The midground represents the middle area between the objects closest to the reader and that of the background, that which is farthest away from the reader's "window" on the world. One depth does not necessarily take precedence over the other. The artist can situate the focal point or subject of a panel at any depth, and panels do not always include all three grounds. For example, many of the panels featuring close-up centered images of Dr. Long and Rorschach during their interviews in chapter 6 are virtually devoid of any background detail, simply featuring flat solid colors behind the characters. Alternatively, the previously discussed panel featuring Bernard and Bernie at the newsstand (see figure 2.2) includes intri-

cate detail in the foreground (Bernard, Bernie, the sidewalk, and the newsstand), midground (the street, the "NY" truck and the Promethean Cab Company building), and background (the city beyond this intersection seen in the
upper left corner of the panel).

The majority of *Watchmen*'s panels are like the latter rather than the former, and at times the background and foreground of a single panel are host to
two separate scenes involving the characters.[9] Some simply contribute to the
detail or texture of the narrative, while others play a more significant role in
the meaning of the text. For example, in chapter 1, Rorschach and Juspeczyk's
conversation about the late Comedian's death turns to the more sensitive subject of how the Comedian attempted to rape Juspeczyk's mother (21). While
their conversation continues in the foreground of the panel, Dr. Manhattan walks
away to resume his work, and in the background he exhibits his superhuman abilities by lifting a giant reactor above his head. The detail adds to the reader's understanding of Dr. Manhattan's character as extraordinarily powerful. On the first
page of chapter 2, the police block Rorschach, who is disguised as Kovacs, from
moving any closer to the guests as they arrive at Blake's funeral. Rorschach is in
the background of the fifth panel as Dr. Manhattan, in the foreground, glances
his way. On the following page, Kovacs assumes the foreground of the panel,
while the guests surrounding Blake's casket are pictured in the background. At
this point in the narrative, readers are unaware that Kovacs and Rorschach are
the same character, but this scene and others like it allude to the importance of
the placard-carrying Doomsday prophet. Similarly, in chapter 3, Juspeczyk walks
with Dreiberg on his way to Mason's home in the foreground of the second panel
on page 11. In the background, the *Nova Express* truck makes a delivery at
Bernard's newsstand. Seven pages later, the same moment is represented, but
from the opposite perspective; Bernard receives the late delivery of the *Nova
Express* in the foreground, and Dreiberg and Juspeczyk are pictured walking
away in the background. Detailed foregrounds, midgrounds, and backgrounds
encourage the reader to look beyond what is presented directly; all of the characters, even if by mere proximity, are in some way connected to one another.

One of the most ironic uses of the background and foreground to relate
parallel stories is found in chapter 5. On page 12, Bernard stands facing the street
behind his newsstand. Across the street and to Bernard's left, Rorschach (again
disguised as Kovacs) leaves the Gunga Diner and begins walking toward the
intersection directly across the street from Bernard. In the final panel on the
page, Kovacs is pictured rummaging through the trashcan as his characteristic
placard reading "The End is Nigh" leans against its side. Five pages later,
Bernard now sits next to the newsstand reading the paper and faces *away* from
the street. In the background, Kovacs enters from the right side of the panel
and walks toward the same trashcan. The images are disorienting, seeming to
repeat the same events from just five pages earlier. Yet, it cannot be the same
moment. Bernard faces the opposite direction; he sits rather than stands; and

Kovacs's path to the trashcan is reversed.[10] Both foreground and background events seemingly mirror those pictured just pages earlier.[11] As Rorschach once again leans over the trashcan, Bernard ironically offers a reminder of just how important it is to acknowledge more than what appears on the surface: "I bet there's all kinda stuff we never notice" (5.17).

Point-of-View

Basic composition and depth affect the way the reader interprets an image, but "the viewer's response to a given scene is [also] influenced by his position as a spectator" (Eisner, *Comics* 92). The reader views a scene from one of three basic points of view: the basic eye-level view, the bird's-eye view, and the worm's-eye view. Viewing a scene from eye-level gives the reader the feeling that he or she is witnessing the scene by standing alongside or among the characters in their environment. An eye-level point-of-view can also allow the reader to actually assume a character's perspective and see through his or her eyes. As previously discussed, many of the panels throughout chapter 6 in Dr. Long and Rorschach's interviews allow the reader to take on the perspective of each. Similarly, readers assume Moloch's perspective in chapter 2 as he recounts a recent surprise visit from the Comedian (21–23). The Comedian sits on the edge of Moloch's bed, frantically explaining how he has discovered a terrible truth that is becoming too much for him to bear. Moloch's hands and his blanket-covered feet become the reader's hands and feet as they extend from the bottom of the panel.

A bird's-eye view is one where the reader takes on a position above the action of the scene. The reader's "window" looks down over the subjects in the panel as a bird would if flying overhead. Eisner explains that "looking at a scene from above it, the viewer has a sense of detachment — he is an observer rather than a participant" (*Comics* 92). This view can be emotionally estranging by emphasizing the distance between the reader and the characters, or it can be quite empowering. McCloud writes, "Getting above a scene can give readers access to a wealth of info about a setting — and a sense of 'rising above it all' emotionally as well" (*Making* 21). All of the panels on *Watchmen*'s very first page are bird's-eye views. The first panel closely focuses on the bloodstained smiley face button that lies in the gutter, and each subsequent panel's point-of-view moves up and further away. The reader's perspective defies gravity as he or she travels in reverse along the same path that the Comedian previously took to his death. The hard diagonal lines created by the skyscrapers and street also affect the point-of-view. Located over the spot where the victim landed, the reader's perspective offers a dizzying sense of vertigo and imbalance, which ironically leaves the reader in a detached and helpless position rather than an empowering one while "rising above it all."

Rather than viewing a scene from above the action, a worm's-eye view places the reader's "window" at or near ground level. McCloud notes that this perspective can show the strength or prestige of the subject of a panel by "giv[ing] weight and grandeur to objects—and characters" (*Making* 21). Eisner explains the worm's-eye view from the reader's perspective: "When the reader views a scene from below it, then his position evokes a sense of smallness, which stimulates a sensation of fear" (*Comics* 92). When Rorschach tells of Kitty Genovese and how her tragic murder influenced his decision to fight crime, readers are placed in a position to experience this strong sense of fear or vulnerability (6.10). While working in the garment industry as an unskilled manual laborer, young Kovacs takes home a dress made of special black and white, shape-shifting material that a customer never picked up. He later learns that the customer, Kitty Genovese, was brutally murdered in the street while many of her neighbors heard her screams or even watched as the events took place, yet no one called the police for help (6.10). Rorschach recounts this story to Dr. Long in two panels, using worm's-eye view perspectives. This perspective represents Kitty Genovese's helpless position in the street as so many of her neighbors look down at her below. Another use of the worm's-eye view perspective is found in chapter 4. After Jon Osterman's intrinsic field is subtracted in the accident at Gila Flats Test Base, everyone believes him to be dead, so his reemergence is not only shocking, but also incredibly frightening for those who witness it. He appears hovering over the heads of his frightened colleagues in the Gila Flats cafeteria (4.10). Although not located on the ground (by the gravity-bound coworkers' feet), this perspective is a worm's-eye view in that the reader's perspective is on the same level as the terrified coworkers as they look up at Dr. Manhattan's glowing blue presence. The perspective lends, in McCloud's words, "weight and grandeur" to his superhuman powers, which far exceed any other being on Earth.

Color

In comics, the colorist, the person responsible for adding color to black and white line-drawn artwork, is often thought of as the "low man on the totem pole" (Gibbons 164). After the writing is complete, the images are drawn, and the word balloons are lettered, the colorist is the last person to work on the nearly completed piece, and yet, Gibbons continues, "It's an interesting paradox, too, that although theirs is the final contribution, it has the first impact on the reader. Bad coloring can kill artwork and obscure story, so Alan and I were blessed to have someone of John's reliability and talent to make the most of our efforts." Artist John Higgins served as the colorist for *Watchmen*, and he knew early on in the creative process that this work would be far from traditional. Higgins writes, "All along, Alan and Dave wanted *Watchmen* to be, visually, completely different from any other comic book that was around at the time and, of course, that we achieved" (Gibbons 164). The typical color palette for the traditional superhero-themed comics included bold and garish primary color combinations—red, yellow, and blue—whereas *Watchmen*'s color palette consists mostly of secondary colors. These colors—orange, green, and violet—are achieved by mixing the primaries with one another, and contribute an entirely different tone to the narrative than do their primary-color companions.

McCloud states that the primary color palette became popular with superhero comics as a way "[t]o counteract dulling effects of newsprint and to stand out from the competition.... The colors were picked for strength and contrasted strongly with one another." (*Understanding* 188). Unfortunately, he continues, "on most pages no one color dominated. Without the emotional impact of single-color saturation, the expressive potential of American color comics was often canceled out to an emotional grey." Color, like any aspect of the panel, is most effective when the reader can determine a change or distinction between various panels. Think, for example, the change in Rorschach's word balloon shapes or between differing points-of-view and how these affect the reader's perception of particular subjects. If all of the colors are consistently bright and bold and never placed in contrast to more muted or subtle colors, any impact that they may have on the tone of the narrative is lost. Scenes set in Moloch's apartment clearly exemplify the emotional power and visual detail that single-color saturation lends to a scene. Moloch's apartment is located next to the Rumrunner's blinking neon sign, which intermittently illuminates the interior of the apartment with a warm, orange glow. In chapter 2, when Moloch recounts the Comedian's recent visit, the panels' color schemes alternate between orange hues when the sign is lit and violet ones when the sign's lights dim (21–23).[12]

Color can also contribute to the tone of the narrative, as seen in chapter 8 when Mason calls his former fellow member of the Minutemen, Sally Jupiter (1–2). The contrasting color palettes between the two locations reflect the two characters' respective lives. Dark violet and orange hues shade the interior of Mason's apartment, while lighter tints of the primary-color palette color Jupiter's California home with rosy reds, pinks, and sunny yellows. The distinction in color is perhaps the result of the time difference between New York and California, but the colors also contribute to the reader's understanding of each character's lifestyle and values. The panels focus on various objects within the living spaces rather than on the characters themselves. Mason's television screen displays an ominous image of the Soviet Union's recent invasion of Afghanistan, while Jupiter watches a brightly colored soap opera. A can of Miller Lite, an open pack of cigarettes, and a lighter rest on Mason's table, shaded in muted violet and pale orange hues, whereas Jupiter's table holds various vitamins and supplements, colored in cheery pinks and pastel greens. These color schemes align with the characters and contribute to the tone of the settings. Similarly, Higgins' color selections in chapter 6 dramatically affect the tone of the chapter. He explains:

> I used my choice of color to complement and accentuate the art first and foremost, but also to enhance the mood and drama of the story. One prime example would be the Rorschach episode, specifically the opening scenes of Rorschach/Walter Kovacs in prison, talking to his psychiatrist. The issue starts with sunny, early morning light streaming into the prison room as the psychiatrist, in a bright and breezy manner, tries to get through to Rorschach, to cure him. As the story unfolds and the horror of Rorschach's life starts to permeate the story, the colors begin to darken and reflect the corruption and despair that created Rorschach [Gibbons 171].

The chapter begins and ends with images focusing on the pivotal inkblot tests that Rorschach first describes as a "pretty butterfly" and later as a "dog with head split in half" (1, 17). On the first page of the chapter, the inkblot rests on the table in a sunny yellow glow, but on the last page of the chapter, Dr. Long holds the card in his dimly lit bedroom, shadowing the white portion of the card in a cold, violet hue. Some of the panels that represent centered eye-level images of Dr. Long and Rorschach throughout the chapter contain solid-colored backgrounds, and as each meeting reveals more of Rorschach's murky past, the backgrounds gradually become darker in value and hue.

However effective Higgins' color selections were, they were still limited by the technology available at the time of *Watchmen*'s first publication:

> In 1986 everything was done by hand. I colored the black-and-white copies of Dave's pages with watercolor, and then marked the equivalent printing ink combinations for each color.... Then that page would be sent to hand separators who would do up the twelve separate acetate overlays for each page to create a four-color effect. Each overlay represented a 25 percent, 50 percent, 75 percent or solid tone of each of the printing colors: cyan, magenta and yellow. In addition, every color and every percentage tone within that color had hard edges; so no matter how subtle I tried to be with the color, what I was trying to get from my mind to the printed page was compromised before it had even been printed [Gibbons 171].

Higgins was eventually able to digitally recolor *Watchmen* for the 2005 *Absolute Watchmen* to a standard that suited his original vision.[13] One significant distinction between the original and the remastered publication is the coloring for panels of the comic within the comic, *Tales of the Black Freighter*. Originally, these panels were colored in much the same way as their "real world" counterparts. For example, Bernie and Bernard were colored in the same solid-color format as the characters from the issues of *Tales*. With better coloring technology nearly 20 years later, the panels featuring scenes from *Tales* now include a classic comic-book texture; each of the colors in these panels consists of a visible dot-like pattern of yellow, cyan, and magenta that combine to make the colors for each figure and object. The style mimics less-advanced printing technology, and creates an interesting juxtaposition between *Watch-*

men's world and a character's reading material within that world. New copies of *Watchmen* now include softer color transitions throughout the work, and the "hard edges" between colors have been eliminated. Some panels have been changed only slightly, while others have substantially changed from their original palette, such as the large panel on page 20 of chapter 4, which shows Dr. Manhattan's enormous presence in Vietnam.[14] This scene originally featured a flat, pale yellow background, but now includes a violet and blue gradient-filled skyline. Although these changes may seem small in relation to other aspects of the images, it is important to remember that color greatly impacts nuances in mood and tone for an image, and "when used well, color in comics can — like comics itself — amount to far more than the sum of its parts" (McCloud, *Understanding* 192).

Facial Expressions and Body Language Cues

Facial expressions and body language are two interrelated visual languages that we all use in our daily lives to convey (or suppress) information about our emotions to others and, conversely, to understand what others around us are feeling. The same holds true for representations of the human form in images; however, as McCloud explains in *Making Comics*, it can be quite challenging to represent the wide spectrum of human emotions graphically: "Expressions aren't something we can opt out of easily, as with words. They're a compulsive form of visual communication all of us use. We know how to 'read' and 'write' them with our faces— but few of us can consciously reproduce them in art with as much style and grace as we do in life" (81).[15] Facial expressions and body language cues contribute to the reader's understanding of a particular character's demeanor, mood, level or lack of confidence, desires, and much more. When Rorschach and Dreiberg arrive at Veidt's Antarctic retreat in chapter 12, they find him sitting in a large, expansive hall (16–17). His back is turned, and he is busy eating. They decide to approach him in silence to hopefully take him by surprise; however, Veidt anticipates their approach and beats each into submission, all while maintaining a chillingly calm demeanor. In the final panel on page 17, Veidt, composed and unemotional, pours himself a drink as he faces away from Rorschach and Dreiberg, who crouch on the floor in pain. Veidt's strong, square stance suggests that he is confident enough to turn away from his would-be attackers. Rorschach and Dreiberg's body language suggest that both are in pain, but their positions also ironically resemble bowing, as if they are bending their heads in respect to submit to Veidt's more powerful status. Veidt disturbingly maintains his composure in this panel and those that directly precede it during the fight sequence. He even calmly smiles as he flings a piece of dinnerware toward Dreiberg's face (12.17). Throughout the encounter, Veidt's facial expressions and body language suggest how he sees himself as above his opponents, in both physical prowess and status.

Facial expressions and body language can also contribute to the reader's understanding of characters' relationships with one another in a conversation. At the beginning of chapter 3, Bernard and Bernie's relationship is distant. They are mere acquaintances who happen to be sitting in the same location. Bernard tends his newsstand while Bernie reads a copy of *Tales*. Each character's body language expresses his informal relationship with the other. Again referring to the fourth panel on the first page of chapter 3 (figure 2.2), Bernard sits on a stool next to the newsstand, facing slightly away from Bernie even though he has been talking to him for the duration of the first four panels. Bernie's posture is equally distant from Bernard. He too sits turned slightly away, and leans over the comic book, focusing his gaze on the open pages. His face is expressionless, suggesting to the reader that he is attending to what he is reading rather than to the conversation that Bernard has begun. Bernard slouches slightly forward and rests one hand on his leg while he raises the other casually up and away from his body. His attempts at starting a conversation with Bernie are clear, yet his posture suggests that he is less than enthusiastic about its one-sidedness. His posture could even suggest a lack of confidence at not eliciting any reaction from Bernie. McCloud notes that a character's posture indicates much about his or her temperament and personality: "A ramrod straight posture ... will communicate strength and confidence by being symbolically taller. Likewise, a bent, lowered posture will be identified with the weak and dispossessed" (*Making* 106). However, posture or any element of body language is mediated by facial expression and vice versa; Bernard's facial expression does not suggest weakness, but rather a somewhat emotionally tough exterior. With his upper lip slightly snarled, he stares straight ahead and away from Bernie as he initiates a conversation.

Whereas Bernard and Bernie's facial expressions and body language suggest an indirect or passive association with one another, Jupiter's memory of when Blake attempted to rape her in chapter 2 portrays the frightening reality of each character's very different desires in an intimate setting. After she believes that everyone has left the room, Jupiter begins to undress, only to discover that Blake has returned uninvited. McCloud explains that we "indicate our desired closeness to each other through our stances," and "there are hundreds of ways to show a character resisting intimacy with another, through the ways they turn away, step back, avert their eyes or erect 'barriers' to create symbolic or even literal distances" (*Making* 107–8). In the first panel on page 6 of chapter 2, she turns away from Blake and clutches her blouse close to her body to cover herself. Her eyebrows lower and move closer together. Her body language clearly sends a message indicating her discomfort with Blake's return. In the next panel, Blake is closer and now holds her blouse in his hands. He wraps his arms around her waist and pulls her closer to him as he says, "C'mon, baby. I know what you need. You gotta have some reason for wearin' an outfit like this, huh?" Jupiter is pictured with her arms up, physically barring his advances. Her eyes widen and her brow wrinkles slightly as her facial expression turns from one of annoyance to one of fear and anger as she replies, "E-Eddie, no..." McCloud notes that one's posture is "such a powerful indicator of attitude and personality, it can even affect how we hear characters' voices" (*Making* 106). Through Jupiter's body language and fearful facial expression, readers know that she is sincere when she tells Blake "No," that she wants no part of his sexual advances. However, if these words were paired with an image of Jupiter smiling or playfully pushing Blake away, the reader may "hear" her words (and her intentions) much differently. The attempted rape scene is just one example of how the images and words in a panel, when combined, create a whole greater than the sum of the parts.

Both and Neither

Utilizing the strengths of each communicative tool, the graphic narrative tells a story through the combination of the two media, but the nature of this combination is debatable. In the introduction to *The Language of Comics: Word and Image*, coeditors Robin Varnum and Christina T. Gibbons praise McCloud's theoretical work in the field — namely, his investigation into comics theory and the way in which he attempts to define the image/word relationship in *Understanding Comics*. However, they are critical of McCloud's "contradict[ory]" treatment of comics as both "a partnership of separate elements and as a unique language" (xiv). McCloud metaphorically explains the relationship between words and images as a "dance" between two partners that "take turns leading" (*Understanding* 156). Earlier in the work he describes the image/word relationship as "a language all its own" (17). Varnum and Gibbons refer to both of the above definitions for support, understanding them to be contradictory: "To say that comics is both an integral language and a partnership strikes us like having one's cake and eating it too, but there are merits to each point of view and each allows us to see features of comics we might otherwise overlook" (xiv).

While the editors of this volume maintain that both definitions are valuable, they contend that both cannot be argued effectively at once. Critics must choose a side in considering graphic narratives as either a partnership between separate entities or as one medium that fuses aspects of each into an inseparable whole. Varnum and Gibbons fail to observe McCloud's assertion that comics is a "language all its own" in the context of his argument. In the very same panel, he explains the reason for the use of seemingly competing comics definitions. He writes of Rodolphe Töpffer, a 19th century Swiss artist, and dubs him the "father of the modern comic" for the great influence he had on the evolution of the medium: "Töpffer's contribution to the understanding of comics is considerable, if only his realization that he — who was neither artist nor writer —

had created and mastered a form which was at once both and neither. A language all its own" (17). McCloud openly presents the contradictions of defining the comics form, and *Understanding Comics* is a testament to how one can classify comics as "both and neither." How we define comics and the graphic narrative form depends on how we as *readers* interpret the relationship between images and words at any given point in the narrative. The relationship (or lack there of) between the two is not an inherent quality of the medium; no one answer is correct. What is an integral aspect of the medium is its reliance on the participation of the reader. Graphic narrative readers *must* actively read both images and words in order to take meaning from the text. Comics is certainly a medium of "both" individual image and word elements as discussed in this chapter. In keeping with McCloud's "contradictory" philosophy for understanding comics, chapter 3 will turn to a discussion of how comics is "neither" a form of written or visual communication, the ways in which words and images work together to form what McCloud refers to as "a language all its own."

CHAPTER 3

A Language All Its Own

"To say that comics is both an integral language and a partnership strikes us as like having one's cake and eating it too, but there are merits to each point of view and each allows us to see features of comics we might otherwise overlook."
— Robin Varnum and Christina T. Gibbons,
The Language of Comics: Word and Image, xiv

The above quotation represents Varnum and Gibbons' concerns with regard to McCloud's inclusion of seemingly competing definitions of comics in his influential work *Understanding Comics*. In it, McCloud defines comics as a medium that functions as a "dance" or partnership between words and images, where "each one takes turns leading" (156). However, he also describes the relationship as one where words and images fuse into a united whole as a "language all its own" (17). Chapter 2 examined how words and images contribute to the meaning of *Watchmen*'s narrative by considering such graphic-narrative elements as word balloons and narrative boxes, typography, perspective, depth and distance, composition, color, facial expressions, and body language. With a foundational knowledge of these basic elements, this chapter will now examine the ways words and images interact with one another within the panel, how each can function as "text" and "context," and how the reader's interpretive decision-making process affects his or her understanding of the individual panel and beyond.

In *Graphic Storytelling and the Visual Narrative*, Eisner writes, "No one really knows for certain whether the words are read before or after viewing the picture. We have no real evidence that they are read simultaneously. There is a different cognitive process between reading words and pictures. But in any event, the image and the dialogue give meaning to each other — a vital element in graphic storytelling" (59). The meaning-making process is dialectical; words contribute to the meaning of the images and vice versa, regardless of whether this "meaning" is created through a partnership of the images and words or through their fusion into a united, inseparable whole. That is, both elements can function as "text" or as "context" of any given panel, and the relationship between the two media is determined by the reader's perception of how they interact. The *Oxford English Dictionary* defines a "text" as "the body of any treatise, the authoritative or formal part as distinguished from notes, appendices, introduction, and other explanatory or supplementary matter" (entry 1, def. 2b). In the most basic terms, the "text" is the primary source of information, which is explained or supported by any other materials present. This definition is concerned with the written word as a text; however, as chapter 2 shows, an image is an equally viable mode of communication that can be read. The word "text" should not be confused as synonymous with "words"; however, the two are often used interchangeably. Eisner's introduction to *Graphic Storytelling and the Visual Narrative* provides a perfect example of this. He ironically uses "text" as a substitute for "words," although he argues that both are equally worthy of being considered as such:

> The reading process in comics is an extension of text. In text alone the process of reading involves word-to-image conversion. Comics accelerates that by providing the image. When properly executed, it goes beyond conversion and speed and becomes a seamless whole. In every sense, this misnamed form of reading is entitled to be regarded as literature because the images are employed as a language [xvii].

Both words and images function as text because each has the potential to be "employed as a language." The "context" of a text is defined as "the whole structure of a connected passage regarded in its bearing upon any of the parts which constitute it; the parts which immediately precede or follow any particular passage or 'text' and determine its meaning" (entry 1, def. 4a). A context determines or gives meaning to the primary subject matter and is explanatory or supplementary in function. When images and words work together, therefore, it is possible that the reader privileges one medium over the other as the text, while the other seems to provide context; the media are read as working in a partnership where one may take the lead. Alternatively, the reader can interpret the image/word interaction as a "language all its own," where words and images cannot be easily separated or identified as text or context of a given panel.

How we as readers determine which is text and which is context (if at all) is based on how we perceive each element in the panel. Comics artists and writers manipulate the ways in which words and images interact on the page in a virtually limitless number of ways, and there are even more ways that readers may interpret these interactions once set in print. First in *Understanding Comics*, and then again in *Making Comics*, McCloud attempts to define some of the potential relationships between images and words by separating them into seven discrete categories. In *Making Comics*, McCloud labels and explains each in a full-page diagram (130). His defining categories of image/word interactions include word-specific, picture-specific, duo-specific, intersecting,[1] parallel, montage, and interdependent. McCloud writes that word-specific combinations are ones where the words provide "all you need to know, while the pictures illustrate aspects of the scene being described." Picture-specific combinations are the inverse, providing "all you need to know" in the images with words that simply "illustrate" the image. The duo-specific interaction is one where "words and pictures [are] both sending roughly the same message," whereas the words and images in an intersecting interaction are "working together in some respects while also contributing information independently." In an interdependent interaction, "words and pictures combine to convey an idea that neither would convey alone." A parallel interaction is one where the words and images *lack* any interaction by depicting two unrelated concepts; and, as previously discussed in chapter 2, a montage features integrated or imbedded words in an image, such as street signs, billboards, or product packaging and labels.

In his earlier publication *Understanding Comics*, McCloud identifies the "most common" interaction as the interdependent word/picture combination ("words and pictures go hand in hand to convey an idea that neither could convey alone" [155]). However, in his later work, *Making Comics*, McCloud retracts his statement and writes that these interactions "aren't as common" as "intersecting" ones, which "readers could partially make sense of without the words, and partially make sense of without the art" (136–7). Why does McCloud change his interpretation of these previously fixed categories? It is perhaps because the former is an attempt to explain the function of the words and pictures, and the latter explains the function of the reader: his or her interpretation of what is on the printed page. This confusion is also a result of McCloud's attempt to classify interactions that, for the most part, elude concrete categorization because all interactions between images and words are partially dependent upon the reader's interpretation of their juxtaposition.

McCloud's explanation of word-specific combinations elucidates the dilemma. He writes, "Think about it! If everything your readers need to know is in the words, you can put pretty much anything you want in the panels, art-wise" (*Making* 132). What would be the point of putting anything at all in the panel if "everything" the readers "need to know" is already there? McCloud's interpretation of a word-specific panel here is based on his interpretive decision as a reader, viewing the words as the "text" and the images as contributing minimal, if any, context. McCloud rightly explains, "Generally speaking, the more is said with words, the more the pictures can be freed to go exploring and vice versa" (*Understanding* 155). Words may be conveying the majority of information in panels that McCloud labels as "word-specific" by contributing to the narrative development, but the way in which the images color the words (literally and figuratively) will inevitably affect the reader's interpretation by way of juxtaposition, no matter how ridiculous or outlandish the combination may seem.

Categorical Conundrums

By using McCloud's categories to understand ways of reading rather than as ways of classifying word and image interactions, this chapter will address

Varnum and Gibbons' cause for disagreement with McCloud's definition of the medium: how comics can function as both a dance between two discrete partners and as an inseparable union of images and words into a "language all its own." Part of this definition dilemma stems from McCloud's use of "dance" to metaphorically explain the word/image relationship. On the one hand, the dance metaphor quickly and economically explains how images and words can take leading roles when paired in the comics form. On the other, the metaphor quickly falls victim to the limitations of explanation. That is, McCloud is referring to one *specific* type of dancing, like ballroom dancing; the accompanying image for his explanation of the metaphor in *Understanding Comics* even pictures three couples twirling across a ballroom dance floor (156). However, not all dancing is done in pairs, nor are all dances led by one partner while the other follows. The same holds true for the relationship between images and words; the "dance" can take on multiple forms in addition to fusing into an integral whole (even moving beyond that which McCloud's seven categories attempt to explain). The possible relationships are gradational, as each interaction is ultimately based on the reader's interpretation. One reader may privilege a panel's images as text while others perceive them as merely providing context for the words or vice versa.

Of course, some image/word combinations strongly suggest one reading over another. Figure 3.1 exemplifies the potential interactions of the two media. The farther the vertical line moves to the left or right on the scale, the more that one medium seems to take the lead in a partnership with the other. The ratio of images to words in a given panel does not necessarily determine how much each medium functions as text or context. Rather, the reader's interpre-

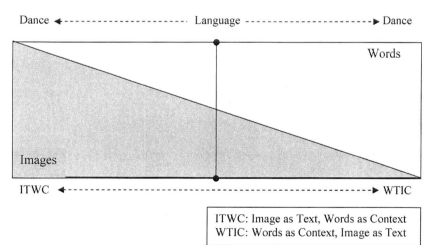

Fig. 3.1. Image/Word Text/Context Scale.

tation is determined by what each signifies. The farther the line moves to the left, the more "is said" through images, thereby increasing the likelihood that the reader will perceive the panel's image as the text (or primary) and the words as context (explanatory or supplementary in nature) because of how each functions within the panel. Conversely, the further the line moves to the right, the reader is more likely to read the words as text and images as context. The center of the scale represents where the relationship between images and words transcends a partnership to become a "language." Images and words function dialectically in roles as text and context, and at times the two media become so inseparable that it may even be difficult for readers to determine where the words begin and the images end.

In his discussion of his seven discrete categories for image/word interactions, McCloud cautions aspiring comics artists to remember that "there's no set rule for when and how to use a given type of word picture combination. Most cartoonists just rely on their instincts and don't get hung up on anyone's nerdy categories. Play around, see what works for you, and build your own instincts through practice. But when those instincts fail — and it happens to all of us — this is a road map [sic] that can help you get back on course" (*Making* 140). Similarly, there are no fixed rules on how each reader will perceive any given panel, and just as McCloud refers to his categories as roadmaps for comics creators, elements in the panel function as roadmaps to guide reading, some more so than others. With some select panels from *Watchmen*, this chapter will examine three different types of panels that strongly guide the reader's interpretation. It will consider those that exemplify McCloud's ballroom "dance," how images and words work together as separate entities with one medium taking the lead; a "line dance," when images and words function as separate but equal conveyers of information; and the language, when images and words unite into an indistinguishable whole.

The Ballroom Dance: Reading Picture- and Word-Specifically

To read a panel picture-specifically is to understand the image as the text, or, to use McCloud's metaphor, as the partner in the dance that is leading while the words play a supportive role by contributing context. At times, *Watchmen*'s narrative transmits information almost entirely through images, strengthening the images' textual pull. In each of the following examples, the vertical line moves close to the left or right side of the scale in Figure 3.1, representing the likelihood that a reader will discern a clear distinction between the leading and supporting roles of the images and words. One such scene is when Rorschach first investigates Blake's murder in chapter 1 (5–8), which includes a total of three word balloons throughout the four-page investigation. As Rorschach pushes against a wall in the back of Blake's closet, his word balloon reads "hunh" (7). Five panels later, the image portrays Rorschach's hand reaching for what appears to be a button located on the back wall of the closet; a word balloon extends from the right side of the panel and reads "ehh." When finally discovering Blake's Comedian costume behind the trick wall, Rorschach stands over the costume that lies on the floor and says, "hurm" (8). In all three of these examples, the images function as the predominant source of information for the reader. They provide representations of Rorschach's actions that lead to his discovery, while the words contribute to the reader's understanding of the nature of his actions. However, this is not to say that the words are any less significant in how the reader makes meaning of the individual panels (they still function as a partner in the "dance"). McCloud would likely categorize this as a "picture-specific" interaction, one where "pictures provid[e] all you need to know, while the words accentuate aspects of the scene being shown" (*Making* 130). Yet, words go beyond simply "accentuat[ing] aspects of the scene." The words and images are dependent on one another to convey a specific message by way of juxtaposition. For example, the word "hunh" in the first panel described above signifies that Rorschach forcefully pushes against the wall instead of gently nudging or leaning against it. The "ehh" sound in the second panel suggests that Rorschach has to strain to reach for the button near the top of the closet's back wall. When Rorschach says "hurm" while lifting his hand to his chin, it suggests a moment of contemplation rather than scratching an itch or coughing, an assumption the reader may make without the supporting words. Although seemingly insignificant, these contextual sound effects are integral to the overall meaning that the reader derives from the panels.[2]

In a similar dance where the images lead, Sally Jupiter's unwanted confrontation with Edward Blake after a Minutemen meeting escalates into an attempted rape. After a struggle, it finally appears as if he will succeed. The image portrays Blake straddling Jupiter as she helplessly lies face down on the floor. With an angry sneer, he unbuckles his belt with one hand as he holds her neck to the ground with the other. Tears stream from her eyes and blood runs from her mouth as she fearfully looks up and exclaims, "Oh, no. Oh, no, Eddie, don't ... oh goddd..." (2.6). Jupiter's compromised position and terrified expression in the image clearly portray her alarm at what is likely about to occur, and her fear prevents her from enunciating much more than a pleading "don't." Similarly, when an assassin attempts to shoot Veidt in the lobby of his high-rise, his secretary seems to notice the assailant first. Her eyes widen and her mouth opens in surprise, but she cannot verbally explain what she sees in time: "Oh, god. Look out, he's..." (5.13). Her words are not only directed toward Veidt, but also to the reader, directing him or her to "look out" into the image to see for oneself what has startled her. In both cases, the images contribute the majority of information for the reader. We see Blake unbuckle his belt while holding Jupiter down,

and the would-be assassin in chapter 5 points a gun toward Veidt and his secretary in the foreground of the panel. The words (and especially each character's
paralyzed verbal ability) provide context for what is pictured in the panels.

Conversely, the words may be read in a panel as taking the lead, functioning as the primary text, while the images function in a more supplementary
role as the context. Here, the words are leading the "dance." In chapter 6,
Rorschach explains his journey from Walter Kovacs to Rorschach in an interview with Dr. Long. Rorschach tells his story orally to Long, communicating
solely through the spoken word. However, some parts of the story are represented visually, which are interspersed in panels between those that picture the
two characters in the interview room of the prison. Word balloons switch to
narrative boxes in these panels to contain Rorschach's words, while the images
correspond to moments from his story. In one such panel, Rorschach explains,
"In 1965, worked with Nite Owl bringing street gangs under control. Tackled
the Big Figure together. Brought down underboss together. Good team. Until
he got soft, like rest. Until he quit" (15). A large amount of information is con-
veyed conservatively through the words (when Rorschach and Nite Owl worked
together, what they accomplished, and why they did not continue as partners),
while only one moment is represented in the juxtaposed image. Words have
the "ability to reduce big chunks of time and information down to a few tiny
words" (McCloud, *Making* 131), and the moment represented in the image
serves to provide a context for their time as partners.

In the image, the reader takes the perspective of a member of an armed mob.
Hands extend from the bottom of the picture plane with a variety of weapons,
including a wrench, a knife, and a broken bottle. Rorschach and Dreiberg stand
in the center of the midground of the panel facing the gang (and the reader), while
the Owl Ship hovers behind them. Neither Rorschach nor Dreiberg have any visible weapons drawn, and Rorschach even stands calmly with his hands in his
pockets. The team, although clearly outnumbered by the mob (at least five to
two), stand squarely facing the gang. Their body language suggests that they are
strong and confident in defeating their approaching adversaries. In Rorschach's
words, he repeats the word "together" twice and calls himself and Dreiberg a
"good team." The accompanying image emphasizes this duality; Rorschach and
Dreiberg stand side by side, and the two glowing "eyes" of the Owl Ship illuminate the background. The image provides context for how Rorschach positively
perceives their once successful partnership, but then Dreiberg "got soft, like rest"
and "he quit," leaving Rorschach to fight back the mob on his own.

The Line Dance: Reading Duo-Specifically

In a line dance, participants stand in one or more rows and complete a
series of steps individually and in unison. One could certainly break into a

rendition of the Macarena or Electric Slide by him or herself on the dance floor, but without other participants (and the appropriate music) the performance is likely to attract some strange looks. The intention of a line dance is to have a group of people participate, and the intended effect is achieved when multiple dancers work together. If one dancer's interpretation of the steps is slightly different from or out of sync with the others, his or her moves affect the look of the collective group. The relationship between images and words in a panel take on a similar relationship. When neither words nor images take a clear lead, and each seems to contribute similar information, readers are likely to read the panel duo-specifically.[3] Words and images are entirely separate but equally responsible for the meaning of the panel. In figure 3.1, such panels would be represented with two vertical lines placed on each far end of the scale. Both words and images function as texts while providing context for the other medium.

In chapter 4, Dr. Manhattan journeys to Mars where he introspectively narrates his transformation from Jon Osterman to Dr. Manhattan. When he relates the process by which he reassembled himself after the accident, the words of each panel describe one event at a time, and the corresponding images seem to do the same. In one such panel, the narrative box reads, "It's November 10th now. There is a circulatory system walking through the kitchen..." (9). In the next panel, he explains, "November 14th: A partially muscled skeleton stands by the perimeter fence and screams for thirty seconds before vanishing...." The images provide the reader the context of scenery and the ability to see other characters' reactions beyond what the words express. Equally significant, the words provide context about movement ("walking," "vanishing") and sound ("screams"), which the images do not.

The words and images also provide objective and subjective perspectives on each particular event. Even though the words portray Dr. Manhattan's subjective understanding of events that have dramatically affected his life, the tone of the narration is oddly absent and seemingly *objective*. He describes "a circulatory system" and "a partially muscled skeleton" with the indefinite article "a" rather than the possessive pronoun "my," which would suggest that the body parts are his. Instead, the article "a" implies that this could be *any* circulatory system or skeleton, not even a particular one (i.e., *the* skeleton), let alone his own. The information presented in the image is objective in the sense that the reader has the ability to observe the scene for him or herself. Through the images, one sees how these two events affect those who are unfortunate enough to witness Dr. Manhattan's return. In the first panel, smashed dishes and other cookware lie scattered on the floor while three kitchen attendants cower in the background. In the second panel, two guards are startled by the appearance of Dr. Manhattan's screaming skeleton, so much so that one appears to become ill. Readers do not see the image through his eyes, but watch (along with the other witnesses) as his partially reformed body comes to life. Dr. Manhattan exists in the same world as other characters; however, his perspective is entirely different, distant, and remote. The disjointedness of images and words that appear to be conveying the same information here provide the reader with a greater meaning for the panel by highlighting Dr. Manhattan's detachment from human beings.

The Language: Images and Words as Text and Context

Chapter 12 begins with six full-page panels that present a panoramic view of the devastation in New York City after Veidt's psychic squid creation is teleported to the Institute for Extraspatial Studies, the epicenter of the destruction and the exact location where Bernard's newsstand once stood. All six pages are eerily lifeless. The creature's tentacles stretch across the once busy intersection as hundreds of bodies now litter the street. On the last of the six pages, readers face the psychic squid's eye and mouth-like structure as it stretches over the institute and rests heavily on the remaining shell of Bernard's stand. Newspapers and debris fly through the air, and the remains of buildings and personal belongings lie scattered on the ground. In the lower left-hand portion of the panel, Bernard's body lies on top of Bernie's body, frozen in an embrace. Bernard's hand remains tenderly cupped over Bernie's head, his last feeble attempt to protect Bernie right before the impact that killed them both. The only incorporation of words in these panels is through montage, where words are integrated into the details of newspaper headlines, road signs, advertisements, and building signage. Some of the words provide context, others function as texts, and some serve as both simultaneously. The wooden structure on the left side of the panel reads "NEWS," and the building in the background of the panel displays part of the Institute for Extraspatial Studies' sign, both of which signify that readers are observing the current state of Bernard's newsstand. The words also function as texts to be read within the context of the documents or buildings on which they appear: the latest headline of the *New York Gazette* reads "WAR?" and the document fluttering in the foreground of the panel is Bernie's copy of *Tales of the Black Freighter*.

What makes the montage so significant here, however, is how the words function within the greater context of the panel as a whole. The image signifies the result of Veidt's plan. For Veidt, the psychic squid (and the sacrifice of millions of human lives) is the only way to save the world from imminent nuclear war with the Soviet Union. When the world learns of what appears to be an alien invasion, they will unite against a common foe and come together to rebuild and heal. Within the context of the surrounding image, the headlines of the *New York Gazette* function as more than a simple conveyance of the current events. The question mark in the headline reflects the uncertainty of the times but also ironically juxtaposes with the very certain fate that Bernard, Bernie, and the others faced when Veidt decided to unleash the psychic squid on the city. Will Veidt's choice prevent future war, creating a united world, or has he simply changed the mode of devastation? Similarly, a poster advertising a Pink Triangle concert benefiting "GWAR" (Gay Women Against Rape) hangs by one corner from the side of the newsstand. The "G" from the acronym "GWAR" is ripped from the pink page, leaving the word "WAR" intact. The poster also reads "LIVE" in large letters. In the context of the document, the word "live" means that the band will play live at a venue in the city, but in the context of the panel as a whole, the word juxtaposes with Bernard and Bernie's lifeless bodies to show how Veidt takes it upon himself to choose who will "live" and who will die. In the foreground of the bottom right portion of the panel, Bernie's issue of *Tales of the Black Freighter* flutters through the air. The comic's pages spread open away from the reader, making the back cover clearly visible, which includes a full-page advertisement for "The Veidt Method," a self-improvement regimen that alleges to improve the purchaser's physical and mental abilities. Veidt promises that he "will give you [consumers] bodies beyond your wildest imaginings." Within the context of the advertisement, the ad promises consumers bodies in the sense that the product will help them achieve better physiques; however, within the greater context of the panel, the ad's claim becomes a horribly ironic pitch: Veidt's "method" has certainly delivered "bodies," meaning corpses rather than physiques, beyond anyone's "wildest imaginings."

Where this panel represents the way in which words and images fuse into a "language" can be found in the damaged remains of the sign for the Institute for Extraspatial Studies. The words, although not completely visible, are situated prominently in the center of the picture plane. The creature's single eye gazes directly over the visible portion of the institute's sign. Its tentacles, which reach from the background to the foreground of each side of the panel, direct the reader's attention toward the letters on the building's wall. The creature has crashed through some of the letters that once spelled the institute's name, while other letters are partially obstructed by green, blood-like ooze that streams from the creature's damaged appendages. The only clearly visible letters are "OR" from the word "FOR," "AL" from the word "EXTRASPATIAL," and "DIE" from the word "STUDIES." The letters are seemingly insignificant other than providing context for the location of the image; however, this portion of the panel clearly displays how words and images "cross the fence" (McCloud, *Making* 139) into each other's territory, blending into a form where it is difficult to clearly distinguish between the two media. A torn paper flutters through the air and is pictured in its descent directly next to the "AL" from the side of the building. The square-shaped paper has two straight edges, which meet at a ninety-degree angle at the bottom left-hand corner, while the other two edges are tattered and torn. Detail on the inside of the paper forms an "L" shape along the two straight edges, which is approximately the same size and shape as the "L" from the side of the building. Through their close proximity to one another, images and words become one in a message that reads, "OR ALL DIE" (see figure 3.2). The montage letters from the side of the building are altered by the images (the green ooze, the crushed building, the creature's tentacles, etc.), while an element from the image (a scrap of paper) dually functions as the letter of a word ("ALL"). This small scrap of paper is both and neither word and image, text and context, making this element of the panel a language all its own.

The Space Between: Text, Context, and the Gutter

The reader's interpretation of text and context within each panel extends beyond the panel borders to include the spaces between. Each panel is separated from the next by a void, also known as the gutter, and within this space, readers determine how each preceding panel relates to the next. Which panels precede others is determined by page construction and basic reading conventions. For example, Western readers begin reading a paneled page similar to the way he or she would read a page of all words—starting at the upper left-hand corner and following each line of panels (or words) from left to right until reaching the bottom right-hand corner.[4] Gutters function in much the same way as the blank areas between words on a page, and are just as much responsible for the meaning as are the images or words, because without negative space, the images or words may become indecipherable (see figure 3.3). In *Understanding Comics*, McCloud explains, "Here in the limbo of the gutter, human imagination takes two separate images [panels] and transforms them into a single idea" (66). This is achieved through a process called closure, which McCloud defines as the "phenomenon of observing the parts but perceiving the whole" (63). Just as each "whole" panel is comprised of elements that serve as text and context (sometimes working together in a "dance" and sometimes unified into a "language"), so too do all the panels that make the "whole" of the graphic narrative. The reading of each panel is dependent on context derived from the collective meaning of all previous panels. Closure is the process by which a reader recognizes that his or her point-of-view moves up and away from the blood-filled gutter on the first page of chapter 1. Each subsequent panel offers the reader a perspective further away than the last until the final panel on the page provides a perspective above even the window from which Blake fell to his death. In chapters 2 and 5, closure allows the reader to perceive how the Rumrunner's sign outside Moloch's apartment is a neon sign that intermittently blinks on and off (2.21–23, 5.1–6, 23–28). A panel that is dimly

Fig. 3.2. The "OR ALL DIE" panel (Moore and Gibbons 12.6).

lit in violet and blue shades provides context for the next, which
is illuminated in a yellow-orange
glow. This is a continuous transfer
from the context of the previous
panel to the text of the following
panel.

| MACESANDWORDS |
| IMAGES AND WORDS |

Fig. 3.3. The Importance of Negative Space.

   Panels may derive context
from panels other than the ones that immediately precede them. This is a discontinuous relationship between context and text. Any and all panels provide
context for the text of each panel read. This is how the reader recognizes when
and if the narrative returns to a previously introduced location, such as Moloch's
apartment in chapter 2 and then in chapter 5, or the reentrance of particular
characters, such as Dreiberg and Juspeczyk at their homes early in chapter 1
and then at Rafael's restaurant together later in the same chapter. Additionally,
recurrent images or visual motifs unify seemingly unrelated portions of the narrative by providing context for later appearances of the image. Perhaps the most
recognizable visual motif begins in the very first panel on the first page of chapter 1. Images that appear to resemble the Comedian's button are continually
repeated at different points in some of the most unexpected places throughout
the narrative. In addition to the first and last scenes with the smiley-face button, Dreiberg holds the button after dinner with Juspeczyk in the first chapter
(25). Dreiberg tosses the button into Blake's grave at his funeral (2.19). The
image is also seen on the surface of Mars at the end of chapter 9 (27). The
visual motif is even found in the lower right-hand portion of the previously
discussed "OR ALL DIE" panel. In this panel, the top has blown off the public spark hydrant that Bernie leans against for the majority of the narrative. Ironically, Veidt explains that the funding for his plan (including the psychic squid
confronting readers in the background of this panel) came from a patent developed for these hydrants (11.22). The yellow receptacle (with two sockets that
resemble eyes) is stained with blood in the same location as the Comedian's
button.

   In earlier chapters we observe the location around where Bernard's newsstand once stood and meet the characters who frequent the spot. These scenes
subsequently provide discontinuous context for the location of the first six
pages of chapter 12, including the "OR ALL DIE" panel. Additionally, closure
accounts for how the reader is able to recognize the hidden message of "OR
ALL DIE." McCloud explains: "Closure can be a powerful force within panels
as well as between them, when artists choose to show only a small piece of the
picture" (*Understanding* 86). This is also true when the artist and writer manipulate elements of the panel in such a way that it requires readers to decipher a
complex blending of words and images into a "language." If the piece of debris
was pulled away from its position in the panel next to the "AL" in the word

"EXTRASPATIAL," one would probably not recognize its shape as the letter "L": "Sometimes, a mere shape or outline is enough to trigger closure" (McCloud, *Understanding* 64).

Closure not only leads to the reader's ability to recognize the message, but also to the reader's understanding of what the phrase means within the greater context of the narrative as a whole. This is yet another example of the discontinuous relationship between context and text. In chapter 11, Veidt explains to Dreiberg and Rorschach his intention behind releasing the creature in New York City: "Unable to unite the world by conquest ... Alexander's method ... I would trick it: frighten it towards salvation with history's greatest practical joke.[...] I would convince them [humanity] that Earth faced imminent attack by beings from another world" (24–25). In the expository materials at the end of chapter 11, the reader is provided with a 1975 article from *Nova Express* in which Doug Roth interviews Veidt shortly after his retirement from masked adventuring. Roth asks, "What sort of world do you see it being, in the future?" and Veidt's answer eerily draws context from what readers have just learned in chapter 11 while also *providing* context for what follows in the beginning of chapter 12. When Veidt answers Roth's question, readers know that he has already begun his plans to "save" the world:

> That depends upon us ... each and every one of us. Futurology interests me perhaps more than any other single subject, and as such I devote a great deal of time to its study. Even so, technology is progressing at an ever-accelerating pace, and by early next century I would hesitate to predict *any* limitations upon what we might be capable of. I would say without hesitation that a new world is within our grasp, filled with unimaginable experiences and possibilities, if only we want it badly enough [11.31].

By killing half of New York City, Veidt believes that the world would be so shocked by the devastation that they would come together to rebuild and heal, but the characters who die at the end of chapter 11 are not merely part of the statistic. Readers come to know and perhaps even grow very fond of some of these characters. Only moments before Veidt releases the psychic squid in New York, the majority of these civilian characters convene across the street from Bernard's newsstand after noticing that Joey and Aline's argument has turned physical. These characters include Detective Steve Fine and his partner, Joe Bourquin, Dr. Long and his wife, Gloria, Milo, the manager of the Promethean Cab Company, his brother, the Gordian Knot Lock Company worker, and even the man selling bootleg watches out of a suitcase. In a single act, Veidt kills eleven characters readers have come to know. It is the sacrifice of some for what Veidt believes to be the benefit of all. The hidden message of "OR ALL DIE" is the fate from which Veidt believes he is saving the world, but is it worth the sacrifice?

In *Understanding Comics*, McCloud aptly summarizes the special relationship between words and images in the graphic-narrative form. He writes:

> Pictures can induce strong feelings in the reader, but they can also lack the specificity of words. Words, on the other hand, offer that specificity, but can lack the immediate emotional charge of pictures, relying instead on a gradual cumulative effect. Together, of course, words and pictures work miracles [135].

Graphic narratives utilize the strengths of what appears to be two distinct media. However, within the form, words and images simultaneously lead, support, and blend with one another. How words and images contribute to the intricate relationship of text and context is used to its full advantage in *Watchmen*'s complex narrative structure. This structure relies on the reader's participation to draw meaning from what is printed on the page, and asks readers to continue their interpretation beyond the final panel of the narrative. What readers imagine as occurring after the narrative on the page ultimately affects their understanding of the narrative as a whole.

CHAPTER 4

The Watchmen

Who watches the watchmen? Scrawled on walls, in alleyways, and on fences throughout the backgrounds of Moore and Gibbons' novel, the question reflects public unrest over the presence of legal masked adventuring prior to the 1977 inception of the Keene Act. But this question also serves as the novel's epigraph, a quotation that normally appears in the beginning of a literary work, foreshadowing possible themes or ideas to come. However, this epigraph does not appear at the beginning of the novel, but at the end. A final white page in the book reads, "'Quis custodiet ipsos custodies,'" Latin for "Who watches the watchmen?" The source given is "Juvenal, *Satires*, VI, 347," and one last note reads, "Quoted as the epigraph of the Tower Commission Report, 1987," a reference to the Reagan-appointed commission to investigate the Iran-Contra scandal, contemporary to the novel's publication. So, who are the watchmen? To whom does the title of the book refer? In the context of the novel, neither the first nor second generation of masked adventurers refer to themselves as "Watchmen." They were the "Minutemen" and the "Crimebusters." The quote at the end of the novel suggests that the use of "watchmen" for the title also has significance outside of its fictional world, both for a Roman poet writing almost 2,000 years ago and for a contemporary American scandal. That is, the essential meaning of the question is applicable to a variety of situations where one calls into question the authority of those in power: who is responsible for keeping the powers of the powerful in check? A "watchman" by definition is someone who keeps guard, making sure that others are safe while they sleep, a person who is not involved in the daily lives of the people and serves as a quiet observer to ensure that no injustice is committed. Within the context of the novel, this "quiet observer" is the narrator; however, the question still remains: who *is* this watchman?

Included with the first set of expository materials at the end of chapter 1 is a note clipped to the first page of an excerpt from chapter 1 of Hollis Mason's *Under the Hood*: "We present here excerpts from Hollis Mason's autobiography, UNDER THE HOOD, leading up to the time when he became the masked adventurer, Nite Owl. Reprinted with permission of the author" (27). This "we" is the novel's only reference to the narrator. Notes like this one are attached to some of the other expository materials, including two other chapters from

Mason's book, a chapter from *Treasure Island Treasury of Comics* and Dan Dreiberg's article from *The Journal of the American Ornithological Society*, all of which explain the legal rights or permission that have been gained by this unknown authority in order to "reprint" the materials (2.29, 3.29, 5.29, 7.29), but none of these include a reference to the narrator's identity. The documents are merely labeled as "presented here" or "reprinted from" a particular source, giving the reader little indication of the identity of the narrator, other than the fact that he or she is subject to copyright law.

In this first note attached to chapter 1 of Mason's book, the plural pronoun "we" could be a reference to more than one narrator (i.e., a corporate narrator, such as a publishing agency, or a coordinated group of narrators), or one narrator using the *pluralis majestatis*, the "royal we." The "royal we" implies that the narrator is in a position of power over his or her audience, and serves as a way of conveying that even though the narrator is only referring to him or herself, he or she also speaks for all of his or her "subjects." Based on this one note, the reader knows that regardless of the narrator's identity (or plurality), this figure is responsible for the entire presentation of the narrative, and is ultimately in control of what the reader sees, when he or she sees it, and how it is presented. If the narrator is the agent of control over the presentation of some of these documents (suggested by the paper-clipped notes), then one can assume that he or she is also presenting the information contained within the panels and the other private expository materials, such as the contents of Sally Jupiter's scrapbook or the paperwork that Rorschach and Dreiberg find on Veidt's desk (9.29–32, 10.29–32). In essence, the reader is at the mercy of the narrator's representation of events, which makes the usage of the *pluralis majestatis* just as likely a possibility as the presence of multiple narrators. In other words, the narrator's "subjects," for whom he or she is speaking, are not only all characters but also all readers.

Any light that these paper-clipped notes shed on the mysterious identity of the narrator or narrators concurrently obscures it. What need would an omniscient or all-seeing narrator have for adherence to copyright permission? Perhaps there is more than one narrator functioning in different roles, such as the narrating "author" and the narrating "editor," but the omniscient or all-seeing narrator still controls everything that is presented to the reader, regardless of agenda. At times, the narrator presents events as seen from the memory or perspective of particular characters, as in chapter 2, which includes a number of daydream sequences, including Sally Jupiter's memory of when the Comedian attempted to rape her, Veidt's memory of the first Crimebusters meeting, Dr. Manhattan's memory of the Comedian killing a Vietnamese woman, and Dreiberg's memory of the riots that spawned the 1977 Keene Act (4–18). These glimpses at the world are mediated by the narrator's representation of a character's first-person point-of-view.

Regardless of the narrator's identity (and there are quite a few possibilities for this identity), it is important to remember that there is always an agenda behind the narrative's presentation. Readers may draw conclusions about a character's actions or reactions based on how the narrator presents portions of the story from a character's perspective, but it is important to remember that this is *only* possible through the narrator's juxtapositioning of various subplots embedded within the overall or main narrative. The narrator determines when and if to allow the reader access to the inner workings of characters, the order in which to present various strands of the story, and even what portions of other characters' written and oral narratives to include. In a sense, the narrator has a super-human perspective, or at least the appearance of one, and he, she, (or they) are in control of every facet of the presentation. Readers do not have the same super-human perspective as the narrator, so this narrator must explain the narrative in terms that readers can follow. That is, the narrator presents the panels in a deliberate sequence to achieve a desired effect. Eisner notes in *Graphic Storytelling and the Visual Narrative*: "To whom are you telling your story? The answer to this question precedes the telling because it is a fundamental concern of delivery. The reader's profile — his experience and cultural characteristics— must be reckoned with before the storyteller can successfully narrate the tale" (47). The narrator assumes that readers have basic "cultural characteristics" (such as reading from left to right and top to bottom of each page) that would allow them to follow the narrative in the way the narrator intends. The narrator also assumes that the reader is able to successfully interpret the text and context of each panel's images and words, and the ways that they interact; and a narrator's ability to successfully tell a story hinges on his or her ability to relate information to the reader "in an easily absorbed manner" (Eisner, *Graphic* 5).

Narrative Frames

Watchmen is a story of storytellers. Rorschach narrates his perspective in his journal; Bernie reads a story, while readers peer over his shoulder into the latest issue of *Tales of the Black Freighter*; Mason and Dreiberg swap stories of times-gone-by during their weekly beer sessions; and Veidt tells an abridged history of his life to his lifeless assistants in chapter 11. Contained within the pages of the book (ultimately presented by the elusive narrator) are multiple stories within the main story. According to Dino Felluga, a frame narrative is defined as a "story within a story, within sometimes yet another story ... the form echoes in structure the thematic search in the story for something deep, dark, and secret at the heart of the narrative. The form thus also resembles the psychoanalytic process of uncovering the unconscious behind various levels of repressive, obfuscating narratives put in place by the conscious mind" ("Terms"). Structurally, *Watchmen*'s narrative contains many stories within other stories or "frames." Thematically, it is also a "search in the story for something deep, dark, and secret," as the narrative begins with the murder investigation of Edward Blake's death.

As discussed in chapter 3, images and words combine in an infinite amount of ways to tell a story within the confines of a single panel. At times, the narrative of the image and the narrative from the words are distinct, revealing their own stories while also revealing a story through their juxtaposition.[1] These micro-stories are arranged in a sequence, creating larger stories that hinge on the reader's use of closure, the way the reader interprets how each subsequent panel relates to the last. Additionally, characters may tell or remember stories throughout the sequence of panels, which represents yet another level of framing or storytelling, stories-within-the-story. Much like the interaction of images and words in a single panel as text and context, the juxtaposition of past and present events within a sequence provides a basis for interpreting both, regardless of the chronological order of events. Flashbacks or stories of past times provide context for subsequent events, while coloring the reader's interpretation of events that precede it in the narrative progression.

Because the reader is unable to clearly identify the narrative voice, it is not always evident in *Watchmen* which narrative is the frame and which is the story-within-the-story. There is some ambiguity on where frames begin and end, what exactly constitutes the frame, and which story houses which, especially with regard to elements that may be overlooked. Some of these elements include the vertical bar designating the chapter number and full-page "cover" design in the beginning of each chapter.[2] Chapter titles such as "At Midnight All the Agents..." (chapter 1) or "A Brother to Dragons" (chapter 7) are embedded between the sequential panels near the beginning of each chapter. These titles are not word balloons or even integrated into panels, provoking readers to determine the meaning of the words in relation to the narrative as a whole. Additionally, the last panel in each chapter is solid black with white lettering, which gives the reader some insight as to the source of the chapter title. These sources are wide-ranging and include everything from the Bible to contemporary song lyrics to Romantic poetry to quotes from prominent intellectuals such as Albert Einstein and Carl Jung. Where do these sources fit in with the presentation of the panels? The same question must be asked of the expository materials. With the exception of chapter 12, a section of expository materials follows each chapter, most of which are referenced within the panel format. These references are both direct and indirect. Characters may actually discuss the contents of particular documents or be seen holding them in the chapter. Juspeczyk talks about her mother's scrapbook in chapter 9, and Hector Godfrey and Seymour work on the October 31, 1985, edition of the *New Frontiersman* in chapter 8 (9.23, 8.10). Professor Milton Glass' *Dr. Manhattan: Super-Powers and the Superpowers* is not directly mentioned in chapter 4, although Glass is introduced earlier in the chapter and is seen with Dr. Manhattan prior to and after his transformation (4.4, 7, 13, 14). Finally, the last page of each chapter concludes with an image of a clock. Blood drips from the top of the page, covering more of the page with each chapter. It is an allusion to the symbolic clock maintained by the *Bulletin of the Atomic Scientists*, which represents the threat of total world destruction. The closer the Doomsday Clock moves toward midnight, the greater the threat of global thermonuclear war. Likewise, in *Watchmen* the clock begins at eleven minutes to midnight and advances minute by minute with each passing chapter. With an unidentifiable source for the narrative, one must ask where does each chapter begin and end? Does the vertical bar designating the chapter's numerical order count as part of the chapter? What about the Doomsday Clock page or the expository materials? The answers depend on how readers read each chapter or see individual units within the narrative structure, thereby determining slight differences in how one perceives the overall narrative, the identity of the narrator notwithstanding.

During the early 1980s, Gérard Genette, French critic and rhetorician, developed a schematic for understanding levels of narration. Genette developed a series of critical categories based on "diegesis," one of the "Platonic categories," along with mimesis, which can be defined as "pure narrative" (30). Jane Lewin, translator for Genette's text, quotes Genette in explaining his use of the term: "With the same meaning ['story'], I will also use the term diegesis, which comes to us from the theoreticians of cinematographic narrative" (27n). Likewise, the *Oxford English Dictionary* defines diegesis as "the narrative presented by a cinematographic film or literary work; the fictional time, place, characters, and events which constitute the universe of the narrative" (def. 1b.). Most simply, Genette's diegesis is a "story," the "signified or narrative content" of a work (27). In addition to exploring other narrative elements, Genette uses diegesis to explain the different complexities of frame narratives. There are three basic narrative categories that are subunits or levels of this primary category of diegesis. These include diegetic, metadiegetic, and extradiegetic narratives. Felluga explains that for Genette, a "diegetic narrative" is "the primary story told," and the terms with the prefixes "meta" and "extra" allow for disambiguation between the narrative levels. Metadiegetic narratives are "stories told by a character inside the diegetic narrative," and extradiegetic narratives are "stories that frame the primary story" (Felluga, "Terms"). Imagine the levels in terms of three boxes, each smaller than the next so that they are able to nest inside one another. The first and largest box is the frame story or "extradiegetic narrative." Inside this box fits the story or "diegetic narrative," and within this box is the story-within-the-story or "metadiegetic narrative."

Who Are the Watchmen?

Genette's static critical categories are intended to classify different levels of narration; however, for purposes of understanding *Watchmen*, these categories can be applied as ways of reading, rather than fixed rules governing each of the narrative levels. Depending on what a reader determines to be the frame of the narration (extradiegetic), and what narrative strands are framed (diegetic) or within this second frame (metadiegetic), the reader's interpretation of the story as a whole is directly affected. To answer those deceptively simplistic questions of where the story begins and what constitutes a "chapter" in the narrative, readers classify (consciously or not) parts of the narrative into different levels in order to make meaning of the narrative as a whole. To show how a reader assigns narrative levels to the text and how this affects reading, this chapter will examine some of the potential identities for the elusive extradiegetic narrative voice in *Watchmen*. The chapter will examine how one is likely to interpret the narrator upon first reading and then will examine two other possible interpretations that are only possible *after* a first reading.

The Omniscient "Other"

As explained earlier, readers have access to very little information about the identity of the narrator in the novel. At first, readers are likely to assume that the omniscient (or extradiegetic) narrator is a disconnected "other," completely separate from the diegesis in which the story takes place. In this scenario, the diegesis of the novel would include any materials that are a part of the world of *Watchmen*, and the dialogue and images in most panels. All of the stories "told" within and between the panels of each chapter are metadiegetic. These would include selections from the notes of Dr. Malcolm Long, Rorschach's journal entries, the interspersed narrative of *Tales of the Black Freighter*, and the stories told within the expository materials, such as Hollis Mason's stories in his autobiography selections after chapters 1 through 3, and Kovacs' written stories that recount a childhood dream and his memories of his parents in the expository materials after chapter 6. The chapter titles, the quotes from which they are drawn, and the notes clipped to some of the expository materials are "intrusions" from the extradiegetic narrator, reminders of an external frame to the diegesis. Genette refers to this as "metalepsis," and defines it as "any intrusion by the extradiegetic narrator or narrate into the diegetic universe (or by diegetic characters into a metadiegetic universe, etc.), or the inverse ... [this] produces an effect of strangeness that is either comical ... or fantastic" (235). It is true that when a narrator's voice interrupts his or her story that it can create a "comical" or "fantastic" effect; however, it also serves a function beyond the effect. The narrator's intrusion directs the reader's interpretation.

Examining chapter 1 with the assumption that the extradiegetic narrator is an omniscient outsider to *Watchmen*'s world reveals that this narrator does not participate in the action of the story but has access to the characters' actions and inner thoughts. The first verso page (left-side page in a page spread) of the chapter includes a full-length vertical black bar with the numerical designation for the chapter. In the upper left-hand corner of this black space a small iconic clock reads eleven minutes to midnight. To the right of this chapter designation is the chapter's cover design, a close-up image of a blood-spattered smiley face button. Only half of the button is seen here at the lower portion of the page. The recto page in this spread begins the panel format for the chapter, the first panel of which shows this same smiley face button in a similar position to the cover design on the verso page, but more background is now seen. This first panel on the recto page also includes two narrative boxes. Assuming that the reader is reading with conventional English language standards (giving primary emphasis to the content in the upper-left hand corner of the panel), the first narrative box reads, "Rorschach's Journal: October 12th, 1985," and the second reads, "Dog carcass in alley this morning, tire tread on burst stomach. This city is afraid of me. I have seen its true face."

There are at least two possible ways to interpret the relationship between the large image on the verso page and the smaller image (the first panel) on the recto page. The first of these is to view the cover design on the verso page as the first image in the diegetic narrative, part of the sequence panning out further and further away from the gutter. If this is the case, then the first narrative box ("Rorschach's Journal: October 12th, 1985") represents what Genette refers to as "metalepsis," an intrusion of the narrative voice, which serves the purpose of alerting the reader that a metadiegetic narrative (a story-within-a-story) is about to begin: Rorschach's telling of his story. The second possibility is that the cover design is separate from the panel format, and part of the extradiegetic narrative level or frame. In this case, it serves a thematic purpose rather than as part of a visual sequential progression away from the street corner, and the first narrative box on the recto page is not a metalepsis but simply the last box of the extradiegetic narrative frame. However, both interpretations understand Rorschach's words from his journal to be metadiegetic and the images in the panels to be diegetic, the events of the narrator's story told visually.

A few panels later on the same page, Rorschach's journal entry reads, "The accumulated filth of all their sex and murder will foam up about their waists and all the whores and politicians will look up and shout 'save us!' ... and I'll look down, and whisper, 'no.'" Rorschach sees the rest of the world as separate from himself, and refers to them as "they" in the next panel. Ironically, Rorschach is pictured in this same panel dressed as Walter Kovacs, a disguise that represents the "they." He parades through street with his "The End is Nigh" placard and walks through the blood in the gutter. Rorschach explains that others will "look up" to him for help, but, ironically, he is pictured below at street level. The reader is unaware that Rorschach and Kovacs are one and the same at this point in the novel; however, with this insight, the distinction between the narrator's diegetic narrative (in this case, images only) and the metadiegetic narrative (words from Rorschach's journal entry) are more clearly distinct. The two narratives are not one and the same, as Rorschach is not pictured writing his metadiegetic narrative in the panel, nor could he share the reader's visual perspective from above. The two narratives are associated with one another only through their juxtaposition. As the panels progressively move up and away from the street level, the final panel on this page depicts Joe Bourquin, Detective Steve Fine's partner, looking down to the street through the shattered window from which Edward Blake, the Comedian, fell to his death. Rather than Rorschach's metadiegetic narrative from his journal, speech balloons correspond to the character pictured in the panel, and both words and images now represent the diegetic narrative.

The next moment where the narrator intercedes into the diegesis occurs a few pages into the narrative when the title "At Midnight, All the Agents..." appears between panels (6). The images that immediately surround the title show Rorschach entering the Comedian's apartment, presumably at "midnight." The title's juxtaposition with the images of Rorschach entering the crime scene suggests that Rorschach is an "agent," and that he is probably there to investigate, and this theory is confirmed on the recto page of the spread. There are no other "agents" with Rorschach, but the plural usage of the term in the title suggests that this is the case. It can refer to the "agents" that investigated the apartment prior to Rorschach's arrival, but it also anticipates Rorschach's visits to his former fellow masked adventurers. Again, the extradiegetic narrative voice intervenes into the diegetic narrative in order to direct the reader's interpretation, not just immediately, but for the rest of the chapter and even for the rest of the novel. After the last panel in the chapter, four lines from Bob Dylan's 1965 song "Desolation Row" place the title in context: "At midnight, all the agents and the superhuman crew, go out and round up everyone who knows more than they do" (1.26).

I Leave It Entirely in Your Hands[3]

Readers may be more inclined to understand the narrator to be completely separate from the world of *Watchmen* and omniscient on a first reading; however, there are other interpretations that are just as plausible. One such reading would be to understand Rorschach's journal as the extradiegetic narrative, serving as the frame for the rest of the novel. In order to interpret the journal as such, one would necessarily have to have read to the end (or at least peeked at the last page). The events that build up to this reading begin in chapter 10. After Dreiberg breaks Rorschach out of jail, Rorschach asks him to take him to his apartment to "collect spare uniform and personal effects, so [they] can proceed" (10.4). Rorschach explains that the "personal effects" to which he refers include his "Spare clothes. Spare face. Final draft of journal. Police only found rough notes" (10.6). After collecting his belongings, the team proceeds to investigate what appears to be the most recent "mask killer" attempt. They start at Happy Harry's and then move on to Veidt's office building. Discovering some shocking evidence that reveals Veidt as possibly behind his own attempted assassination, Dreiberg and Rorschach head to Karnak, Veidt's Antarctic retreat.

First, however, Rorschach needs to attend to some business. In his final journal entry he writes, "Tell Dreiberg I need to check my maildrop. He believes me" (10.22). Rorschach's "maildrop" is a trashcan that he is seen occasionally rummaging through during the novel;[4] however, Rorschach does not want to check this "maildrop." Instead, he drops the "final draft" copy of his journal in the U.S. mailbox that stands beside the trashcan, and he sends the journal to the "only people [who he] can trust" (10.22). The envelope in which he places the journal reads "URGENT," but readers are unaware as to where Rorschach has addressed this important document, the contents of which contain entries that track his investigations of his mask-killer theory over the past two weeks, possibly in addition to other investigations, because the cover of the journal reads "1984 to 1985" (10.22). Over the next two pages, the narrative follows the "urgent" package as a mailman picks it up from the mailbox, carries it down the street, and reaches his destination, the "U.S. Mail Sorting Depot" (10.24). From there, the journal is picked up by another mailman and finally delivered to its destination: the office of the *New Frontiersman*.

The *New Frontiersman* is a super-conservative news outlet, helmed by editor in chief Hector Godfrey. The publication makes appearances throughout the novel, such as in chapter 3 where Rorschach (disguised as Walter Kovacs) purchases his copy of the paper from Bernard's newsstand. Bernard remarks that "[he] keep[s] it [Rorschach's copy of the paper for him] every day" (3.3), and one can infer from this that Rorschach is an avid reader of the paper and has similar political views. Multiple issues of the publication are even found by the police in Rorschach's apartment when they search the premises after his arrest (8.30). The *New Frontiersman* is a publication that Rorschach is known to read and trust, thereby explaining why he would send his journal, what he ominously believes to be his final communication with the world, to the news outlet (10.22). Rorschach's trust in and respect for Godfrey and the *New Frontiersman* is reciprocated by Godfrey, who describes Rorschach as a "patriot and American" when interviewed after Rorschach's arrest (7.12). He even defends Rorschach in an article for the *New Frontiersman*, which is included in the expository materials at the end of chapter 8.

Ironically, however, when Rorschach's urgent package arrives at the office, Seymour, the office assistant, opens the mail and reads Godfrey a familiar line from the journal: "'Dead dog in alley this morning; tire tread on burst stomach....'" (10.24). This is, of course, the same entry that begins the novel in the first panel of chapter 1. Upon hearing this line, Godfrey replies, "Jesus, who's it from? Son of Sam? Sling it on the crank file. New year, we'll burn that garbage heap and start over!" Without giving Seymour a chance to respond to the question "who's it from" or even seriously enquiring as to the identity of the author, Godfrey has the journal tossed into the crank file, seemingly forgotten until the end of the novel. However dismissive it may seem, Godfrey's response to Seymour foreshadows how Godfrey would perceive the writer if he were to discover that it was, in fact, Rorschach. Hector Godfrey's name reflects his political values and character: "Hector" is an allusion to the Trojan hero from Homer's *Iliad* and originates from the Greek "εκτωρ," meaning "holding fast" (entry 1, def. 1). "Godfrey" is a homophone for the words "god" and "free." He is a man who "holds fast" to "freedom" and extreme conservative values. His initial reaction to the journal is to believe the author is like the serial killer, but the words "Jesus" and "son of" ironically also suggest the identity of a savior in context; the unknown author is perhaps the only person who can resurrect the truth about Veidt's plan to save the world.

With Rorschach's greatest fears confirmed in Antarctica, he attempts to return to the United States to reveal the truth about the disaster that has recently transpired in New York. He meets his demise in the snow, eerily alluded to in his final journal entry: "He could kill us both there in the snow. Nobody would ever know…. First night in November. I am cold tonight" (10.22). The end of chapter 12 transitions back to the United States. About two months have passed since the attack, evident by the sign on the "Burgers 'n' Borscht" restaurant that reads "Happy New Year to All Our Customers" (12.31). Seymour and Godfrey have survived the attack. Along with them, Rorschach's journal and the narrative contained within its pages survive. Luckily, Godfrey did not "burn that garbage heap," the accumulated materials in the crank file, as he intended with the start of the new year. As a result of the psychic squid, peace has been established between the Americans and the Russians, but it also means that "Nobody's allowed to say bad things about our good ol' buddies the Russians anymore so bang goes a two-page column!" (12.32). Because the news outlet no longer has the freedom to write any negative articles about Russia, Godfrey directs Seymour to "get some filler from somewhere." Among a cluttered pile of white loose leaf papers and unopened letters of the crank file, Rorschach's journal stands out with its dark red leather cover and gold lettering. Prior to reaching for the pile, Seymour splashes some of his lunch across the right eye of the large, yellow smiley face on his shirt. The final panel of the narrative replicates the first, the Comedian's button stained with "human bean juice" (1.11). As Seymour reaches for the crank file, Godfrey says, "I leave it entirely in your hands" (12.32).

Did Seymour pick up the journal? Was it included as part of the issue for the *New Frontiersman*? The narrative is left in "your" (the reader's) hands to interpret the fate of the journal and its contents. The journal functions in a similar way to the bloodstained smiley face in framing the beginning and end of the narrative: the first page of chapter 1 begins with a selection from the journal, and the last ends with an image of it. Entries from the journal are interspersed throughout the novel. A great deal of the narrative that follows Rorschach and Dreiberg during chapter 10 is also following the journal's journey to its final destination in the *New Frontiersman* office. If Seymour did, in fact, pick up the journal, read it, and decide to publish its contents outside of the *New Frontiersman*, it is possible that the graphic novel is told through *Seymour's* perspective: Seymour (with or without the rest of the *New Frontiersman* staff) assembles the pieces of Rorschach's journal to tell the story.

Ironically, Seymour's name, a homophone for the two words "see" and "more," literally sees more in the sense that he may serve as the narrator who uses Rorschach's journal as the extradiegetic narrative and, by using it, is able to construct a story from the narrative in the journal. Returning to chapter 1, this dramatically affects how the reader perceives the narrative. Rather than Rorschach's journal as a metadiegetic narrative, a story told by one character within the larger narrative told by the external "other" omniscient narrator, Rorschach's journal is the narrative frame. Thinking of the narratives in terms of timing may make this concept clearer. Seymour first reads Rorschach's journal, then attempts to create a narrative guided by what is contained within the pages. That is, the journal and other textual "documents" in the expository material sections dictate what Seymour (possibly alone or with others) creates. The end of the novel is actually the beginning: what readers have just finished reading is the narrative that Seymour pieces together after discovering the contents of Rorschach's journal. As Seymour does not have omniscience, nor was he present to view each of the scenes expressed throughout the novel, the contents of the panels are, at most, Seymour's estimations or predictions of what the journal describes through words. The images and dialogue found in the panels of each chapter that do not directly involve Seymour are hypothetical.[5] The journal takes precedence over the pictorial narrative in the panels, thereby reversing the narrative levels: the journal becomes extradiegetic and guides what is pictured in the panels rather than the pictures in the panels guiding what parts of the journal are included, as is potentially the case with a narrator who is an "other" outside the world of *Watchmen* and has the super-human ability of omniscience.

Additionally, Rorschach's journal entries often include ellipses. Sometimes this accounts for the division of a narrative box into two within the confines of one panel. Ellipses are also used during dialogue in the diegetic narrative, which represent pauses in speech. However, when the ellipses are used in what one believes to be a transposed written narrative (Rorschach's journal as the extradiegetic narrative used by Seymour), the ellipses could serve to represent omitted material. Some of the entries in panels are broken into more than one narrative box without the use of ellipses. This break could serve a similar function beyond merely an aesthetic purpose to allow for more of the image to show in the background of a panel. For example, in Rorschach's journal entry from "October 13th, 1985. 8:30 P.M.," he writes, "The first Nite Owl runs an auto-repair shop. The first Silk Spectre is a bloated, aging whore, dying in a California Rest Resort. Captain Metropolis was decapitated in a car crash back in '74" (1.19). Each of these sentences is contained within its own narrative box within one panel. It is possible that there is omitted material about each character or others in between what is included, which would account for the separation. After all, it is plausible that Seymour has not transcribed the contents of the journal word for word. Hayden White explains, "Every narrative, however, seemingly 'full,' is constructed on the basis of a set of events that might have been included but were left out; this is as true of imaginary narratives as it is of realistic ones" (10). Seymour may have omitted material in order to create a desired effect.

The diegetic narrative does not begin until the final panel on the first page of chapter 1, where Bourquin hangs out the Comedian's broken window and says, "That's quite a drop." When one interprets Rorschach's journal as the extradiegetic narrative, it extends further into the panel format for the chapter. The reemergence of the journal throughout the text appears to undermine its ability to be considered extradiegetic; however, if the frame of a narrative can intercede in the diegesis (what Genette explains as metalepsis), then this reading is plausible. Additionally, notes clipped to some of the expository documents that account for permission of "reprints" suggest that the narrator's voice is probably from within the world of *Watchmen* and subject to copyright law, making the expository documents a sort of public record or proof — in that the materials are reproduced in their "original" form. The narrator is aware of the publication process, and that permission must be gained in order to reprint someone else's work. Seymour's involvement in the production of the *New Frontiersman* would privilege him to access the expository materials present at the end of chapter 8, the pre-production copy of the October 31, 1985, edition of the paper. The document present after chapter 11 is an excerpt from the July 12, 1975, edition of the *Nova Express*, the *New Frontiersman*'s biggest journalistic rival. Interestingly, it does not have a "reprinted with permission" note. Perhaps the *Nova Express* and its creator, Doug Roth, did not survive the psychic squid attack, which thereby opened the documents up for free use. Maybe it is missing because the narrative is not "complete" and still in a draft phase, much like the draft version of Rorschach's journal. This would explain why the other notes are haphazardly paper-clipped to the documents rather than more formally labeled.

Obligations to Our Fraternity[6]

The *New Frontiersman* office is not the only location to which the narrative returns after the characters find out the truth in Antarctica. Prior to the final scene, Sam and Sandra Hollis visit Sally Jupiter at her California home on Christmas. The couple is actually Dreiberg and Juspeczyk, disguised in their new non-heroic identities. Jupiter has not heard from her daughter in some time; she exclaims, "I thought you were dead!" when she recognizes her daughter through her newly-dyed hair and name change (12.28). Prior to arriving back in the United States, Dreiberg and Juspeczyk both agree to never reveal the truth behind the psychic squid that killed millions in New York. Juspeczyk realizes, "Jesus, he [Veidt] was right. All we did was fail to stop him saving Earth." But Dreiberg hesitates, "How ... How can humans make decisions like this? We're damned if we stay quiet, Earth's damned if we don't. We ... Okay. Okay, count me in. We say nothing" (12.20). When faced with the decision of whether or not to reveal Veidt as the villain behind the massacre, both Dreiberg and Juspeczyk agree to never speak of the truth. However, almost two months later, they have the new identities of Sam and Sandra Hollis, two characters that have *not* agreed to remain silent or "say" anything. Juspeczyk (or Sandra Hollis) is anxious, explaining to her mother that they cannot stay, and that she "get[s] nervous waiting around..." (12.29). Maybe the two have fled from Karnak in Antarctica against Veidt's will. After the couple realizes the truth, Veidt says, "obviously, you *must* both make yourselves at home" (12.21, my emphasis). Maybe they are planning to do something to undermine their earlier promise, such as revealing the truth through a written report rather than an oral one. While at her mother's, Juspeczyk says, "People's lives take them strange places. They do strange things, and ... Well, sometimes they can't talk about them. I know how it is" (12.29). Her life has indeed taken her "strange places," everywhere from Antarctica to Mars, but just because the couple cannot "talk about" these experiences does not mean that it necessarily stops them from writing about it anonymously, however dangerous it may be, making the team of "Sam and Sandra Hollis" plausible suspects as the narrators of the novel.

After all, near the end of the novel, Dreiberg is still "talking about adventuring" and thinks that "'Nite Owl and Silk Spectre' sounds neat" (12.30). Their "adventuring" could very well extend beyond their costumed crime-fighting to a written report in the name of justice. Ironically, Dreiberg and Juspeczyk take their new last name from another "author": Hollis Mason. He was the first Nite Owl, mentor to Dreiberg, and author of *Under the Hood*, his autobiography, three chapters of which are included as expository materials. Dreiberg even did some writing himself while on hiatus from crime-fighting. His article from the *Journal of the American Ornithological Society* is included after chapter 7.[7] Additionally, readers know that the pair would have access to Jupiter's scrapbook. Juspeczyk is pictured holding the album in the last panel on page 23 of chapter 9. The album can also be seen in the last panel on page 25 of the same chapter inside the protective sphere that Dr. Manhattan creates around himself and Juspeczyk when his glass-like structure comes crashing down. In addition, Dreiberg has access to the expository materials at the end of chapter 10:

Veidt's desktop materials from his office that he and Rorschach grab prior to leaving for Karnak (10.21). Notice too that after the Owl Ship crash-lands in Antarctica, the papers that have been scattered on the floor have the distinctive "V^eidt" logo (10.27), suggesting that the pair left the papers in Dreiberg's Owl Ship before proceeding to Veidt's retreat, and that the papers would still be there when Dreiberg and Juspeczyk return to the ship. Having been to Mars with Dr. Manhattan, Juspeczyk has first-hand knowledge of what transpired between herself and Dr. Manhattan (seen in chapter 9), and the pair could plausibly speculate about Dr. Manhattan's independent musings on the red planet during chapter 4.

If one believes Dreiberg and Juspeczyk to be the narrators for the novel, then a reading of chapter 1 would again be slightly different than the two that have already been explored. Rorschach's journal would serve as the diegetic narrative within Dreiberg and Juspeczyk's story, the metadiegetic narrative. Because both Dreiberg and Juspeczyk participate in a great deal of the narrative, they would not have to rely on Rorschach's journal as a main source for the story in the same way that Seymour and the *New Frontiersman* would. There are two possible scenarios for how the couple gains access to Rorschach's journal. The first scenario (and the more likely of the two) is that Dreiberg and Juspeczyk have access to Rorschach's "final draft" of the journal through consultation with Seymour and the *New Frontiersman*. However, there are two copies of the journal in existence: the rough *and* final drafts. The inclusion of the expository materials at the end of chapter 6 (Rorschach's police file) suggests that the narrator may also have gained access to the "rough draft" copy of Rorschach's journal, which was confiscated by the police during Rorschach's arrest. However, the report also notes that the journal's pages were "filled with what is either an elaborate cipher or handwriting too cramped and eccentric to be legible" (6.29). The writing is too "elaborate" or "cramped" for the police to decipher, or perhaps they dismiss its contents because they believe Rorschach to be mentally ill, but Rorschach's former fellow masked adventurers could likely have taken the time to decode its contents. Additionally, this copy of the journal includes all entries except for the "final entry" that he writes prior to leaving for Antarctica with Dreiberg (10.22). As Dreiberg was with Rorschach when he checked his "maildrop," this journal entry would be hypothetically written, derived from Dreiberg's experience with Rorschach at the scene, thereby flipping the narrative levels (diegetic and metadiegetic) for the journal and the images in the panels.

Continuing to speculate on Dreiberg and Juspeczyk's possible roles as narrators of the novel, the frame or extradiegetic narrative includes the first verso page of chapter 1. The panning images of the smiley face button in the gutter and the police officer's words on page 1 of chapter 1 represents the metadiegetic narrative, hypothetically derived from Rorschach's journal entry (the diegetic narrative) on the same page. After Rorschach's investigation of the Comedian's apartment, the narrative moves to Mason's home, where Dreiberg is visiting. As Dreiberg represents a narrator in this reading, this scene and the next, where Rorschach visits Dreiberg's apartment, represent a return to the extradiegetic narrative or frame (1.9–13). On the following page, Rorschach's journal, the diegetic narrative, frames the metadiegetic narratives of his investigation of Happy Harry's Bar and Grill and his visit to Veidt's office building (1.14–18). Rorschach's next stop, a visit to Dr. Manhattan and Juspeczyk at the Rockefeller Military Research Center, represents a return to the extradiegetic frame when one considers Juspeczyk to function as a narrator along with Dreiberg (1.19–23). Rorschach's final journal entry for the chapter is framed between Juspeczyk's phone call to Dreiberg and their meeting at Rafael's Restaurant for dinner (1.24–26). Finally, the paper-clipped note on the expository materials represents a continuation of the extradiegetic narrative from the end of the panel format to the beginning of the expository material section. Mason's chapter from *Under the Hood* and the other expository materials throughout the narrative are diegetic, functioning on a similar level as Rorschach's journal. Like the scenario in which Seymour is the narrator, these documents offer support and guidance to the narrative contained within the panels, some of which are diegetic and others of which are metadiegetic.

Who Watches the Watchmen?

In order to even arrive at the three narrative scenarios described here, readers need to speculate about events that occur beyond what is explicitly in the text, and two of these interpretations are based on what readers believe could occur after the last panel of the novel. More specifically, readers may speculate on what happens to Dreiberg and Juspeczyk with their intentions of continuing "adventuring," and on what transpires with Seymour's "crank file" investigation. The narrative, by its very structure, creates indeterminacy, and it would be challenging to sustain any one reading of the novel as having a definite or clear narrative voice. This is not to say that this is a flaw in the narrative, nor is it to say that this takes away from the narrative in any way. Rather, the purpose of the narrative's structure as ambiguous is to encourage readers to think. Iain Thomson, author of "Deconstructing the Hero" for the University Press of Mississippi's *Comics as Philosophy*, notes that *Watchmen* is a text that is necessarily reread:

> Perhaps the first thing one realizes upon rereading *Watchmen* is that it *requires* rereading. *Watchmen* was written to be reread; indeed, it can only be read by being reread. That may sound paradoxical, but upon rereading *Watchmen* it becomes painfully obvious that the meanings of almost every word, image, panel, and page are multiple — *obviously* multiple. In *Watchmen*, the meanings are primarily multiplied by the fact — and this is painfully obvious when one finishes

the series and then rereads it — that, from the first panel (a blood-stained smiley-face, looking like a clock counting-down to midnight, floating in a gutter of blood), the parts all fit into a whole one grasps only in the end (although in retrospect the hints are everywhere) [103].

Much like Rorschach and the narrator of the novel (whomever he, she, or they may be), readers need to read the clues to solve a mystery. Who watches the watchmen? Readers are watching, reading, and interpreting the "watchmen," making meaning out of a collection of documents, reading both the characters and the settings, and solving a mystery presented by an anonymous narrator.

CHAPTER 5

Parallel Histories

In DeZ Vylenz's documentary *The Mindscape of Alan Moore*, Moore explains the possible reasons for what he believes made *Watchmen* so attractive to a mid–1980s audience, both in the United States and abroad:

> I think there were probably quite a few things about *Watchmen* which chimed well with the times, but to me perhaps the most important was the actual storytelling, where the world that was presented didn't really hang together in terms of linear cause and effect, but was instead seen as some massively complex, simultaneous event with connections made of coincidence and synchronicity. And I think that it was this worldview, if anything, that resonated with an audience that had realized that their previous view of the world was not adequate for the complexity of this scary and shadowy new world that we were entering into. I think that *Watchmen*, if it offered anything, offered new possibilities as to how we perceive the environment surrounding us, and our interactions and relations with the people within it.

As discussed in chapter 4, *Watchmen*'s cyclical and layered narrative structure invites readers to participate in the meaning-making of the narrative, coaxing them to revisit portions of the work in search of significance, individual characters' motivations, and to create a narrative that extends beyond the end of the novel. *Watchmen* offers its readers a new way of understanding or, in the very least, a glimpse at an alternative way to understand individual connections between characters, places, and times.

Although for many, the basic conception of time consists of a distinct past, present, and future, the present moment is not simply the event occurring at this exact hour, minute, and second on the clock. At any given point, one person can experience what is happening right now, think about what will happen in the future, or remember what has already happened in the past. Diachronic time, represented by the dashed horizontal line in figure 5.1, is most easily understood in terms of a timeline, a linear mapping of the progression from the past to the present and into the future. Synchrony is a moment or "state" (Saussure 81) along this continuum that accounts for when one is able to remember the past or think about the future in the present. Synchronic moments may incorporate multiple times in the present, but can also include different spaces, and these too are describable in three dimensions. One's mind

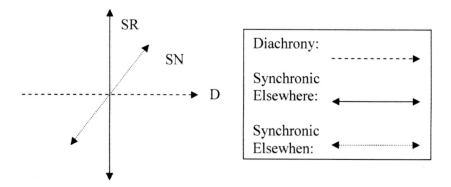

Fig. 5.1. The Three Dimensions of Time.

can inhabit the here and now, a different location (an elsewhere), a different time (an "elsewhen"[1]), or a combination of the two (elsewhere and when). The synchronic moment divides into two separate planes, creating three dimensions.

As discussed in chapter 4, *Watchmen*'s narrator appears to be omniscient, or all-seeing. That is, the narrator represents both diachrony and synchrony for all of the characters, in addition to operating in his or her own understanding of it. All representations of time, regardless of whether they are diachronic or synchronic, or are from third-person or first-person perspective, are mediated by the narrator. The narrative is presented through a set of patterns, a selection from all the narrator knows that directs the reader to experience time as the narrator does. The narrator presents only some of this information, and what is included in the presentation is defined by *how* it is presented. In other words, the narrative's arrangement is neither comprehensive nor random. Readers see only selections from various characters' lives, and there is definite deliberateness to the order in which the narrative is told.

The narrator's presentation highlights the "represent[ation] of (human) events in such a way that their status as parts of meaningful wholes [are] made manifest ... one might be able to explain why and how every event in a sequence occurred and still not have understood the meaning of the sequence considered as a whole" (White 50). This human experience of time is revealed when the narrative shifts from the third-person omniscient perspective to various characters' first-person perspectives: readers see a character's synchronic moment as the third-person narrative perspective continues to fill in pieces of the diachronic progression. The reader becomes a co-conspirator in the meaning-making of the text as the narrator invites the reader to fill in the gaps that have been strategically left open. Within the body of the text, panel size and placement and page layout contribute to the narrator's manipulation of time and space. The narrator also uses various transitional strategies to manipulate time, which ultimately reveal characters' private selves and public images, and their perceptions of themselves and others. All the while, a seemingly objective vantage point reveals the reality beyond appearances.

In Medias Res

In addition to being selective with what is shown to readers, *Watchmen*'s narrator presents the story out of chronological order so as to allow for transhistorical comparisons and parallels. Beginning in the middle, or in *medias res*, the novel opens with Rorschach's journal entry on his observations of the crime scene of Edward Blake's murder. There are many unanswered questions: Who is this masked man who calls himself Rorschach? Who is Edward Blake (the Comedian) and why was he murdered? Why is Rorschach breaking into the crime scene? Rorschach's investigation of the Comedian's murder during the three weeks between October 12 and November 2, 1985, is the primary diachronic line in the narrative, but this diachronic line represents only a small piece of *Watchmen*'s larger narrative. As the narrative continues, the reader pieces together portions of time as experienced by numerous characters (synchronic moments) while sustaining an understanding of the time as represented by the narrator of the present day (the diachronic progression). This story of the present day is mixed with other parallel narratives from different times and places, which span across at least 55 years and two planets and are either interjected into the body of the narrative or presented in short expository materials at the end of each chapter. The narrative moves forward, backward, and sideways (see figure 5.1) in time to complete a "temporality" (Ricoeur 171) to house the narrative: a simultaneous presentation of selections from the pasts, presents, and futures of the characters' private lives, as well as their shared experiences with one another.

Watchmen's fundamental construction exposes what Moore refers to as "an example of the limitations of Western thought." He explains:

> Whereas once there was this great eternal present [for earlier or more primitive cultures], we ... as a species, adopted this different notion of time, [a] rather simplistic and fatalistic idea of past, present, and future.... [Stephen Hawking suggests] that there is this gigantic hyper moment in which everything is occurring. That would mean that it is only our conscious minds that were ordering things into past, present, and future ... we believe we understand the entire Cosmos, but actually we understand the insides of our heads [*Mindscape*].

Watchmen's narrative presentation undermines the "fatalistic idea of past, present, and future," approaching something more analogous to a "gigantic hyper moment." By revealing events of the narrative in a sort of simultaneity, the novel destabilizes readers' previously held beliefs about the ability to neatly confine moments to distinct categories of past, present, and future.

Panels to Pages: Rhetorical Strategies

The basic unit of the page is the panel, the frame that houses each consecutive moment in the narrative. Most of *Watchmen*'s pages are constructed using a nine-panel page in a three-by-three grid pattern. Each of these panels is in proportion to the size of a full-page image (i.e. one-ninth of a page). The panels' uniformity gives the reader a sense of quantifiable time, time as measured by the clock: "A grid of nine uniform panels on each page allows [the reader] to follow the fine-tuned passage of multiple stories moment by moment. Panels tick by like a metronome or a time bomb, counting down to midnight" (Gravett 82). Analogous to the way in which the hours divide the time into twelve equal parts on the face of clock, the panels on a conventional nine-panel page are literally smaller, proportionate units. Additionally, panels' shapes and sizes contribute to the tone of the narrative. *Watchmen*'s oppressive and ominous climate is dominated by the threat of global thermonuclear war, which is reflected through the narrow confines of each uniform panel. As Eisner explains in *Comics and Sequential Art*: "A narrow panel evokes the feeling of being hemmed in — confinement; whereas a wide panel suggests plenty of space in which to move — or escape" (*Comics* 92).

In *Watching the Watchmen*, Dave Gibbons writes that the nine-panel page made "*Watchmen* look different from the super-hero comics of the time" and "lent it a classic look," but it also "allowed Alan a very precise control over pacing and the juxtaposition of story elements" (29). The reason for this control, as McCloud notes, is that "the fixed three-by-three panel grid prepares for the impact of the full-page panel" (*Making* 51) — or for any deviation from this norm, for that matter. Once a convention or standard for the page construction is established, any different construction signals the reader of a change. This can affect the narrative pacing and the reader's perception of time. Eisner observes the close relationship in the reading experience between paneling and the perception of time and space:

> Albert Einstein in his special theory of relativity states that time is not absolute but relative to the position of the observer. In essence the panel (or box) makes that postulate a reality for the comic book reader. The act of paneling, or boxing the action, not only defines its perimeters, it establishes the position of the reader in relation to the scene and indicates the duration of the event [*Comics* 26].

Panels deviating from the norm span the size of two, three, or six conventional panels. Some panels even occupy a full page. The larger the panel, the more time the reader spends with it, and the reading literally slows down. Conversely, narrower panels accelerate the reading. Pages that deviate from this convention contribute to a visual pacing: "The panel shape can actually make a difference in our perception of time. Even though [a] long panel has the same basic 'meaning' as its shorter versions, still it has the feeling of greater length!" (McCloud, *Understanding* 101). As readers becomes more comfortable with a fixed nine-panel page structure, they are more likely to notice deviations from this established norm when they occur, allowing the narrator to manipulate the reader's perception of both time and space.

In chapter 7, Dreiberg and Juspeczyk's unsuccessful first sexual encounter provides a good example of how this visual pacing is established. Juspeczyk remarks, "We've got as long as it takes and don't worry. You're doing fine" (15). A clock in the background of this panel shows the time at approximately twenty minutes to seven. The next panel shows a close-up of the television screen, where talk show host Benny Anger announces the next program, which is the eleven o'clock news, and the following panel portrays Juspeczyk covering Dreiberg's sleeping body with a blanket as the television announces a "break" from the midnight movie (15). This scene is presented in the conventional, nine-panel layout, where each panel represents a moment in time that is separated from the next by a lengthy interval, or maybe better described as an awkward span of silence. Even though a great deal of chronological time passes, very little action takes place.

After unsuccessfully attempting to have sexual relations for over four hours, Dreiberg finally falls asleep. When turning the page, the reader is transported into Dreiberg's mind, where he dreams of an explosive sexual encounter with Juspeczyk. Instead of the conventional three panels to a row, the scene is presented with six panels to each row, accelerating the perception of time in addition to contributing to the excitement or thrill of the scene (see figure 5.2). The two characters unite, and the dream concludes with a mushroom-cloud explosion in the background (7.16). The last row contains four of these thinner panels, and the last panel returns to the conventional dimensions, showing Dreiberg back in reality and awake. These two scenes essentially represent the same sexual encounter, but one is real and one is imagined. The sexual tension between Juspeczyk and Dreiberg builds until this point in the narrative, and both characters and readers are left with unfulfilled expectations, perhaps believing before this point that this moment would be more analogous to Dreiberg's dream for the two characters than the actual reality of the situation. With both scenes presented back to back, each with a different visual pacing, the reality of Dreiberg's position is highlighted even more; his real-life sexual performance does not live up to his imagined expectations.

The uniformity of the nine-panel page layout may give the reader a sense of quantifiable time, but panel size is also a manipulation of qualitative time. Qualitative time is how one experiences time, which is not necessarily analogous to an amount of time as measured by the clock. Mark Bernard and James Bucky Carter's article "Alan Moore and the Graphic Novel: Confronting the Fourth Dimension" explains the interaction of quantitative and qualitative time as the "fourth dimension," which they define as "simultaneous, multitudinous dimensionality deeply entwined in and part of individual experience" (par. 2). It is "a special relationship with space and time wherein the two conflate such

Fig. 5.2. *Watchmen*'s nine-panel page and a deviation from the norm (as seen in Moore and Gibbons 7.16).

that infinite multiple dimensionalities become simultaneously present.... The fourth dimension is bridged by human experience and interaction. The spontaneous, real-time interplay of all these forces at once create an ethereal dimension of its own, also what we refer to as the fourth dimension" (par. 2). Even if the narrator attempts to represent this fourth dimension of time, this representation is necessarily mediated by the use of a two-dimensional medium. Therefore, the placement of the panel on the page and deviations in panel size are critical to the narrator's manipulation of the reader's understanding. The novel evokes quantifiable time in its standard form while also manipulating it through qualification.

A deviation from the nine-panel page layout calls to the reader's attention a change. These are rhetorical strategies based on the convention that "any 'rhetorical' use of variations in framing is only made possible against a 'conventional' background of expectations" (Cohn, par. 5). This is not to say that the events portrayed in these longer and shorter panels will automatically take more or less quantifiable time than those portrayed in other, uniform panels (as is the case with the previously mentioned sexual encounter between Dreiberg and Juspeczyk). Rather, the change in size is a way to change the reader's perception from the quantitative to the qualitative nature of time. The shortening of the panels in Dreiberg's dream is qualitative; the experience is fast-paced and filled with excitement and anxiety, which is portrayed through the panel width. In terms of quantifiable time, the dream could have lasted three seconds, ten minutes, or an hour. If the events were to be portrayed in terms of quantifiable time (in relation to that of the other panels), the panel may be so thin that the reader would be unable to see the events portrayed, or, conversely, the panels may stretch so wide that the reader loses the *feeling* of time (Dreiberg's qualitative understanding of the experience). Even though the novel evokes chronological time with its structured format, the derivation from the norm allows for both qualitative and quantitative time representations.[2]

Filling the Void

Peeters notes that a conventional panel arrangement, such as the nine-panel form in *Watchmen*, "creates the conditions for a regular reading (from left to right and from top to bottom), very close to that of a page of writing" (par. 6).[3] This would suggest that *Watchmen*'s form also stresses a linear understanding of time: the reader moves across and down the page in much the way that one reads a traditional novel composed of all words by following a single, linear path. To an extent, the narrative is confined to a linear representation. Readers do not have the ability to see different times and places simultaneously, as the narrator does, and therefore, the order in which they are presented is far from random if they are to achieve a desired effect.[4] This careful arrangement of panels creates a complex interaction between diachronic time, synchronic time, and various narrative perspectives.

In chapter 7, Juspeczyk descends into Dreiberg's basement to explore the Owl Ship. While looking for the cigarette lighter, she accidentally engages the Owl Ship's flame thrower. In the first panel on the following page, Dreiberg calls down to the basement, "Everything okay down there?" In the second panel, Rorschach says, "Maybe. Or maybe someone's picking off costumed heroes," and in the third panel, Dreiberg rushes to help Juspeczyk (7.3). As discussed in chapter 3, the gutter is the void or blank space between each panel. In *Understanding Comics*, McCloud notes that this space, although small, can "transport us from second to second in one sequence [but] could [also] take us a hundred million years in another" (100). Just think of the difference in time that elapses between panels in Dreiberg's dream in comparison to the panels that represent his actual sexual encounter with Juspeczyk. Comics is a unique medium "where the audience is a willing and conscious collaborator and closure is the agent of change, time, and motion" (McCloud, *Understanding* 65).

The sequence of three panels portraying Dreiberg and Rorschach is dependent on the closure process, which is the reader's interpretation of the space between the panels in relation to what happens within each one (see figure 5.3).

Fig. 5.3 Dreiberg thinks of his previous conversation with Rorschach as he rushes to help Juspeczyk (Moore and Gibbons 7.3).

The first panel in this series pictures Dreiberg calling down to the basement. Panel 2 shows Rorschach's back and a hand that reaches up from the bottom of the panel, holding the Comedian's button. At the present moment in the narrative, Rorschach is in jail, making it physically impossible for him to be in a conversation with Dreiberg. The background behind panel 2 is also much different than the kitchen scene in panel 1, another indication that this is not a conversation between the two characters. This stark shift alerts the reader to something occurring, and in this case, it is a shift in narrative perspective. The narrator's perspective shifts to the narrator's representation of Dreiberg's first-person perspective. By recalling an earlier scene in the narrative, the reader can determine that the second panel in this series is also found on page 12 of chapter 1, but from a different angle.[5] Panel 2 is Dreiberg's memory. Dreiberg's actions are part of diachrony, or time as a "phase of evolution" (Saussure 81). His recollection of his conversation with Rorschach (panel 2) is the synchronic moment, which inhabits an "elsewhere" and "elsewhen." Hearing Juspeczyk scream, his memory of Rorschach, and his flight to help her represents three different moments—in the middle of which there is a shift in narrative perspective. That is, the perspective changes from the narrator's to inside Dreiberg's thoughts and back again. For Dreiberg, his experience of time swerves out of the present to a different elsewhere and elsewhen as he recalls Rorschach's warning. The next moment he is back in the present, where he can react (see figure 5.4).

In order to account for the cause-and-effect relationship between the three moments, they are necessarily represented linearly, panel by panel. The order in which the panels are presented (in this case, diachronic to synchronic and back to diachronic) represent Dreiberg's diachronic experience of hearing Jus-

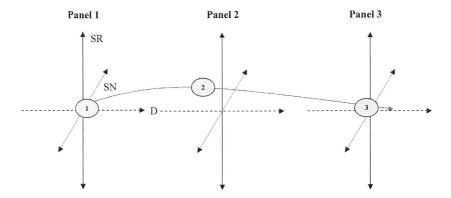

Fig. 5.4. Dreiberg's memory drifts to an "elsewhere" and "elsewhen" while he physically remains in the here and now.

peczyk scream that causes him to mentally shift to a synchronic moment of thinking about Rorschach's mask-killer theory, and this in turn causes him to react as he does. The space between the two panels visually separates them, allowing the reader to recognize the shift from third-person narrative perspective to that of first-person experience. Once the reader establishes that he or she is now viewing Dreiberg's thoughts in panel 2, he or she must then connect the two panels and decipher a reason for the juxtaposition: What is the connection between Dreiberg's recollection of a different elsewhere and elsewhen (the conversation with Rorschach) and his experience of hearing Juspeczyk's scream from the basement? Dreiberg thinks that the "mask killer" has captured Juspeczyk. This prediction is validated a few pages later when Dreiberg, after putting the fire out, says to Juspeczyk, "When you screamed, I thought ... well, y'know. Ever since the Comedian died..." (7.4). Ironically, Dreiberg's "y'know" is directed as much to the reader as it is to Juspeczyk. Readers "know" even better than Juspeczyk to what Dreiberg is referring, as they have just recently finished assuming his perspective. In this particular instance, the reader's experience is similar to that of Dreiberg's in that both are thinking back in time to another "elsewhere" and "when," connecting these thoughts to the present moment, and projecting a prediction into the future. The narrator manipulates this experience for the reader so it is analogous to Dreiberg's experience, a reminder that the narrator is in control of what the reader sees, how he or she sees it, and the order in which the information is presented.

Juxtaposing Time and Space

With thirty-nine different characters in *Watchmen*, twenty-nine of whom are living during the narrative of the present, the narrator is necessarily selective in representing diachronic time while following so many characters. Some characters are as minor as Happy Harry, the owner of a sleazy bar, who appears in chapters 1 and 10, or Benny Anger, the talk show host who interviews Dr. Manhattan in chapter 3. Others appear more frequently, including Dr. Manhattan, Rorschach, Adrian Veidt, Dan Dreiberg, and Laurie Juspeczyk, but all twenty-nine characters are operating in the present day of 1985, and contribute to the overall narrative. The narrator represents the diachrony for multiple characters at once when these characters cross paths and interact with one another in the present. Paul Ricoeur explains this in terms of "public time" or "time common to the actors, as time woven in common by their interaction" (175). These events may be simply presented from the third-person perspective, or may be more complex, involving one or more first-person perspectives.

Many of the events from different times and places are incorporated into the present narrative through flashbacks, memories, and dreams: synchronic moments for individual characters. Chapters 1, 3, 5, 7, 8, 10, and 12 all occur during 1985, but may shift back and forth to synchronic elsewheres.[6] Chapters 2, 4, 6, 9, and 11 all have at least one flashback to an earlier year. Some of these flashbacks are to occurrences in the same locations, and others flash back to an elsewhere and elsewhen. Throughout much of the novel the movements between time and place are rhythmic, integrated smoothly in an almost mechanical fashion. As one can see from the chapters listed above, every other chapter contains flashbacks until chapters 7 and 8, which both take place in 1985. The rhythm then resumes to every other chapter containing one or more flashes into the past, where the reader gains some insight on the workings of the present state of affairs. This oscillating rhythm also emerges within particular chapters, where one can often follow the pattern fluctuating between the past and 1985. The movement between times and spaces functions like clockwork between chapters, within them, and even continues down to the panel level.

One strategy commonly used by the narrator is what we will refer to as "panel-to-panel juxtaposition": the panels flip back and forth between two scenes so that they become interconnected, thereby inviting the reader to draw one or more conclusions from the juxtaposition. Panel-to-panel juxtapositions create strong parallels between two different times or spaces, as is the case when Dreiberg remembers a prior conversation with Rorschach. One type of panel-to-panel juxtaposition is accomplished through the use of a "silent" location by shifting from one "speaking" location (one that contains dialogue) to the other "silent location" (one that has just images). The images oscillate between the two elsewheres, but only one line of dialogue is continued throughout. The speech balloons from the speaking location shift to narrative boxes in the "silent" location's panels to show the absence of a speaker. A word or phrase in the dialogue from the speaking location will connect to the image in the silent one. There are a variety of uses for silent location panel-to-panel juxtapositions, one of which is to show characters operating in different locations simultaneously. For example, in chapter 3, Dr. Manhattan dresses in preparation for a television appearance at the same time that Juspeczyk and Dreiberg are having a conversation in Dreiberg's apartment, each representing the same "when" but different "elsewheres." Juspeczyk and Dreiberg's conversation is continued in the panels that portray Dr. Manhattan (the silent location). The string of dialogue unites the two locations, while the color scheme alternates between warm and cool shades, reinforcing their distinction from one another. Juspeczyk stares into her coffee mug and says, "Y'know, sometimes I look at myself and I don't understand ... sometimes I look at myself and think, 'how did everything get so tangled up?'" (3.10). The words in this panel are Juspeczyk's reflection on her relationship with Dr. Manhattan. The image in the panel displays Dr. Manhattan, who literally looks at his reflection in the mirror as he telepathically ties his "tangled up" necktie.

These two narratives alternate panel by panel for eight pages, strongly reinforcing their connection for the reader. Juspeczyk questions her present state, seemingly unsure of the force that is causing her to feel "tangled up." The juxtaposed panels of Dr. Manhattan suggest that he is responsible for the tangling in her life. In these panels, his mind-control over tying his necktie suggests that he is also very much in control of his present state; he can untie his tie without even lifting a finger. However, Juspeczyk's concerns about living with Dr. Manhattan seem to suggest otherwise. Ironically, Juspeczyk is the one who took control and left her relationship and life with Dr. Manhattan. Conversely, Dr. Manhattan may be able to return to his previous life as Jon Osterman through his memories (he is literally able to see and experience time even before the accident), but he cannot control the process by which he ceased to be Osterman, the accident that transformed him into Dr. Manhattan. He has no power to change his present state and seems to have no control over the change in his now otherworldly view of life on Earth. As Dr. Manhattan became increasingly mentally removed from human life, he essentially caused Juspeczyk to leave. This panel-to-panel juxtaposition invites the reader to consider Dr. Manhattan's and Juspeczyk's perceived levels of control (or lack thereof) over their lives in relation to their actual levels of control, and this is emphasized through the close interwoven structure of the two scenes.

Another example of silent location panel-to-panel juxtaposition is when at Karnak, Veidt reveals that he is the person behind Rorschach's suspected mask-killer plot. As he explains the extensive plan, to both Rorschach and Dreiberg's disbelief, the panels alternate between images of the Comedian's murder and Veidt's present discussion. Word balloons change to dialogue boxes to show a difference between the two locations and times. Again, the color scheme alternates between cool and warm colors; Karnak is predominately colored in blues and greens, and the murder in shades of red. Veidt explains, "Upon learning the creature's intended purpose, Blake's practiced cynicism cracked"

(11.25). These words are shown in a dialogue box with an image of Blake thrown against a window, which has cracked and shattered from the impact. As images of Blake's brutal death flash throughout the scene, Veidt calmly delivers the information about his involvement in Blake's murder. The silent location (Blake's murder) is an elsewhere and elsewhen in Veidt's mind. The reader sees Veidt's memory of the murder, and his allusion to the murder functions as a sick, inside joke. The narrator invites the readers to see this scene as Veidt sees it, thereby making Veidt's words appear even more chilling. Unlike the association between Dr. Manhattan's and Juspeczyk's actions, whose silent location is truly silent (lacking any perceptible noise or speech), this silent location enforces the "silence," alluding to the secrets that Veidt decides not to reveal about his violent (and, more than likely, noisy) encounter with Blake.

The earlier mentioned scene of Dreiberg's recollection of Rorschach in chapter 7 is also an example of a panel-to-panel juxtaposition; however, this scene utilizes a slightly different strategy. This transition is not connected by running narration, as is the case with silent location transitions. Rather, each panel is a separate entity with an image and one or more word balloons that correspond directly with a character or characters in the panel.[7] Another example can be found in chapter 3 when Dreiberg and Juspeczyk are mugged in a dark alley. This scene is woven between Dr. Manhattan's television interview-gone-wrong, which results in his subsequent flight from Earth (3.15–6). This scene comes at the end of the earlier mentioned silent location panel-to-panel juxtaposition between Juspeczyk and Dr. Manhattan. The transition from the use of a silent location to a complete panel-to-panel juxtaposition allows for the lengthy connection between these different elsewheres to begin to, in Juspeczyk's words, "untangle" as each character literally moves to a separate location (Dr. Manhattan to Mars, Dreiberg to Hollis Mason's home, and Juspeczyk to her previous residence with Dr. Manhattan). Other characters in their respective elsewheres are introduced or reintroduced into the chapter (i.e., Rorschach at Bernard's newsstand, Bernie reading from *Tales of the Black Freighter*, President Nixon's deliberation on potential nuclear threats, etc.). What makes the panel-to-panel juxtaposition of Dreiberg's memory of Rorschach in chapter 7 particularly jarring is that it is not connected to any larger panel-to-panel juxtaposition, as is the case with the Juspeczyk/Dr. Manhattan connection. Much like Dreiberg's sudden fearful memory of Rorschach's theory, the panel-to-panel juxtaposition in this case is startling.

Similar Panel Compositions

Similar panel compositions thematically unite one location (elsewhere) or time (elsewhen) to another through a repeated visual pattern or motif. In similar panel compositions, one or more compositional elements (shapes, colors, character positions and body language) join two different locations or times through their recurrence in two consecutive panels. In chapter 5 there are multiple examples of this.[8] One of these examples serves as a transition from Detective Fine's investigation of a murder to Bernie at the newsstand (see figure 5.5). As the detectives are walking out the door of the crime scene, they discuss the case and the possible reasons for why someone would murder their own children. Fine's partner suggests that "these psych-outs are mostly media inspired." A partially-obstructed poster hangs behind his head. The rays of light pictured on the poster seem to illuminate him. Fine responds, "The media inspires boredom not waking up one Monday morning and butchering your kids. That takes something else man" (5.7). The next panel shows the door closed as viewed from inside the apartment, and the poster is now clearly visible. A word balloon represents Fine and his partner's conversation, although they are now unseen: "[A gruesome murder like this one] takes a whole different kind of inspiration," Detective Fine says (5.7). The poster includes a large red triangle that surrounds an image of Buddha, suggesting that this horrible murder may be divinely inspired. A simple, iconic sun (a circle with radiating beams of light) stretches across the poster behind the figure's head. Blood splatters up from the lower-right corner of the panel. An arc of light illuminates everything in the panel starting

Fig. 5.5. A similar panel composition continues from the murder scene to the newsstand (as seen in Moore and Gibbons 5.7–8).

just above the triangle and continuing down to the bottom of the panel. The sun on the poster and the arc of light on the wall reinforce the circular shape. The sun's location in the panel relative to the arc of light seems as if it is "divinely" causing the illumination of the room.

On the verso side of the next page, a Pyramid Deliveries truck pulls close to the curb where Bernie sits, causing the water from the gutter to splash up behind him. This splash mirrors that of the blood in the previous panel. The logo for Pyramid Deliveries, which is pictured on the side of the truck in the background behind Bernie, consists of a violet triangle enclosed in a circle with a lighter shade of the same color. The circle in the logo functions in a similar way to the arc of light in the panel from the murder scene and gives the perception that the circle is illuminating the triangle. Bernie reads from the comic book, "My home and family were doomed, my world reduced to ruin. Fate had dealt its hand casually, despite my bitter protestations" (5.8). The fatalistic attitude of the main character of the story reflects his feelings of hopelessness. "Fate" is responsible for the character's present state, and there was nothing that he could have done to change his present circumstances. Ironically, the suggestive divinely inspired murder is also out of man's control. Some stronger power, whether fate or spiritual inspiration, is in control of the participants who initiate the action.

Another similar panel composition in chapter 5 transitions from Rorschach at the Gunga Diner back to Bernard's newsstand (5.11–2). In the last panel from the diner, Rorschach's hands are pictured at the bottom of the panel holding an unfolded napkin on which he has created a Rorschach test of his own using one of the condiments on the table. From inside the diner he watches his "mail-drop," a trashcan across the street where a group of Knot Tops stand. Turning the page, the location shifts to the newsstand, and the reader sees the same trashcan and group of Knot Tops, but at 90 degrees from the original perspective. Bernard's hands are pictured at the bottom of the panel, holding an open newspaper in the same position as Rorschach's. The two transitional panels have similar compositions, and at the end of this scene (bottom of page 5.12), the same panel composition is used again. In the final panel of the scene, Bernard again holds an open newspaper in the same position. A narrative box from Bernie's copy of *Tales of the Black Freighter* reads, "His eyes, his nose, his cheeks seemed individually familiar, but mercifully I could not piece them together. Not into a face I knew." This narration carries over from the previous panel, where *Tales'* main character is pictured staring at his reflection in the water. The words also comment on what is pictured in the background of this final panel at the newsstand. The Knot Tops are no longer seen standing around the trashcan. Rather, in the background of this panel a man reaches into the can, and his sign that leans against the can reads "The End is Nigh." At this point in the narrative, readers are unaware that the apparent homeless man is, in fact, Rorschach in disguise.[9] Ironically, the narrative from *Tales*, which explains a face as being "individually familiar," comments on Bernard's relationship with Rorschach. Rorschach purchases his daily newspaper from Bernard, but Bernard is unaware that Kovacs and Rorschach are the same person. Additionally, ironic are Bernard's words that also appear in this same panel: "It's our curse. We see every damned connection. Every damned link" (5.12). Bernard does not see "every connection" because he does not realize the man across the street, someone with whom he interacts on a daily basis, is actually Rorschach. The similar compositions and perspectives in these panels join the characters of Rorschach and Bernard through much more than their physically close proximity in space and time. What these two characters do not realize is more telling than of what they are aware. When reading the novel a second time, readers may be able to recognize these associations and relate them to happenings later in the text (i.e., Rorschach's imprisonment and his identity revealed to the world). However, at first, readers are in the same position as Rorschach and Bernard; all three are unaware of some "connection" or "link" other than the ones that are plainly visible on the surface. Readers only have the hint of a connection through the similar panel composition used to transition between the two positions in space and time.

In each of these examples, two elsewheres are united by a similar visual composition, which transcends the time-lapse that the reader experiences between individual pages. The similar compositions construct a continuity between elsewheres for the reader. The parallelisms between different elsewheres are unknown by the characters. Bernie is unaware that his surroundings mirror that of a murder scene. Rorschach and Bernard are not conscious that they are both watching the same scene unfold at the trashcan across the street, and that both are missing a "connection" that will later lead to the former's imprisonment and the latter's revelation of the truth of his daily acquaintance. The narrator's presentation allows the reader to decipher a pattern, to find connections between seemingly unrelated elsewheres and whens[10] that form part of a larger and more meaningful whole.

The Open Door Motif

The last panel on the recto side of one page is a precursor to the first panel on the verso side of the next. Turning the page creates a physical hesitation in the narrative and allows for a certain amount of suspense and surprise. There are many instances in the novel where the narrator moves the reader's perspective to a different time or space by passing through a doorway. With this strategy, which we will call the "open door motif," the reader follows a character as he or she enters a new space (an elsewhere) by opening a door, or when the narrator shifts perspectives for the reader to a different time or place.[11] When the open door motif is combined with the reader turning a page, the reader participates in "opening" the door to the next elsewhere or when. This capitalizes on the potential surprise, and at times, shock value of page-turning as the reader not only confronts a new page spread, but also is immediately transported to a new time and space.

As Rorschach visits many of the old members of the Crimebusters in chapter 1 to inform them of the Comedian's murder, his last stop is at the "Special Talent Quarters" in the Rockefeller Military Research Center, where he manages to elude armed guards and get past locked doors to gain admittance. As he opens the door, an entry from his journal provides narration, and the image in the panel shows Rorschach's back: "Only two names remaining on my list. Both share private quarters at Rockefeller Military Research Center.... I shall go and tell the indestructible man that someone plans to murder him" (1.19). Readers have not yet met the two persons to whom Rorschach refers, but the reference to the later-introduced Dr. Manhattan as "the indestructible man" signals that something is different or special about this him. The next and last panel on the page shows the same scene (Rorschach opening the door), but from the inside rather than the outside of the space. In the previous panel the reader's visual perspective is level with Rorschach, but the visual perspective in the second panel is shifted considerably higher, and Rorschach appears quite small as he opens the door. A word balloon stretches from the top of the panel that reads "Good evening, Rorschach," suggesting that the speaker is much taller than him. This word balloon is blue with a solid white outline, different from any other word balloon previously used. As the reader turns the page, the next panel on the verso side spans the length of the three conventional rows and is double the width of one conventional panel. Rorschach is still in proportion to the size of a conventional panel; however, Dr. Manhattan, who is blue, nude, and has a glow emanating from one of his fingers, fills the space. Readers open the door along with Rorschach to confront Dr. Manhattan, a character whose presence is literally larger than life. Anticipation about Dr. Manhattan's character is built through this transition from one space to another, and the utilization of the open door motif involves the reader's participation as he or she turns the page, opening the door right along with Rorschach.

A slightly different usage of the open door motif in chapter 10 shifts between two different elsewheres, but does not follow a particular character as he or she opens a door. As Bernie reads from *Tales*, Bernard talks to him about the imminent "end of the world" (10.13). The images in each panel shift between what Bernie reads in the comics and the street corner in panel-to-panel juxtapositions, and narration from the comic and dialogue mix into each one. In the comics, Bernie reads about how the main character has just murdered two people. He plans on tying the female victim to her horse and dressing in the male victim's clothes to ride back into Davidstown undetected. Outside of the comic on the street corner, Bernard is visited by two men who try to sell him their newspaper, aptly titled *The Watchtower*, about their belief that "god will shortly end the world" (10.13). The last panel on the page shows the two men riding away from the newsstand on bicycles, and the narration from *Tales* in this same panel relates to the image from the street: "Two figures had ridden here, now two rode back. Soon I would venture amongst evil men, and make them fear me...." As readers turn the page, Rorschach's hand, grasping a door knob, extends across the lower portion of the first panel. Inside the space, readers see the familiar face of Happy Harry (from chapter 1) in the background, who exclaims, "Oh no," and a man is pictured in the mid-ground holding his face in his hands, blood dripping down the front of his shirt. Rorschach and Dreiberg are once again united and working together to uncover information about the attempted assassination planned for Veidt. The "two figures" described in the previous panel from the last page also describe the main character from *Tales* and his female victim, the two men from *The Watchtower*, and Rorschach and Dreiberg, who are "venturing back" to a location that is known to house "evil men." Three different elsewheres and whens are united through this open door motif. The abrupt intensity of this transition is matched by its violence, and shows the dramatic potential of the open door motif when used in conjunction with the turn of a page.

"Coincidence and Synchronicity"

There are numerous ways in which different elsewheres and whens can be directly juxtaposed, and the above described panel-to-panel juxtapositions, similar panel compositions, and uses of the open door motif are just a few of the numerous strategies that the narrator uses to create a sense of simultaneity throughout the novel. The graphic-narrative format — the utilization of both images and words to tell a story — allows for what Paul Gravett calls an "interwoven, multi-tracked storytelling approach" (*Mindscape*), and for interconnections between elsewheres and whens to be created through word-to-word, word-to-image, or image-to-image parallels. Bernard and Carter also refer to graphic novels, or more generally "sequential art," as having a "special artistry ... in the relationship of this metaphorical and literal space-time continuum ... [which makes the medium] unique in its absolute expression of ideals that modernist writers and artists sought independently (and therefore less successfully) in their writings and sketches" (par. 2). The examples mentioned above predominantly use one or more of the strategies over a limited number of consecutive panels; however, some parallels between different times and spaces reveal intricate interactions between images and words from multiple elsewheres and whens over an extended series of panels within one chapter, over multiple chapters, or even throughout the entire novel. Both the strategies already explained and the ones to follow reinforce the concept that the novel's intent is not to simply present a story of past, present, and future, but rather to show what Moore refers to as a new "worldview," that time and space is actually a "massively complex, simultaneous event with connections made of coincidence and synchronicity" (*Mindscape*). Chapter 8 is a direct representation of the narrator's synchrony. Throughout this chapter the narrator represents simultaneous occurrences in eight different locations (elsewheres), and, in turn, presents them to the reader using these various thematic links through related images, words, or combinations of the two.[12]

Different elsewheres and whens are directly connected through the words or images from the last panel of a scene to the words or images in the first panel of the next scene (as is the case with transitions utilizing the open door motif), and also through those details that occur within each scene. One such example from chapter 8, with two locations occurring synchronically, comes when Rorschach sits in his jail cell at the state penitentiary and when Detective Fine visits Dreiberg's apartment. These two scenes are directly juxtaposed. The first scene ends on the bottom of a recto page, and the second begins at the top of the next verso page. As Big Figure leaves Rorschach's cell, he says, "You're alone in the valley of the shadow, Rorschach, where your past has a long reach, and between you and it there's one crummy lock" (8.7). The next panel, one that spans the length of the bottom row, shows Rorschach sitting calmly in his cell, seemingly unfazed by the threats, while Big Figure and his men walk away.

As the reader turns the page, Detective Fine visits Dreiberg's apartment to discuss Edward Blake's murder. The detective questions Dreiberg about his relationship with Blake. Fine pushes Dreiberg about his "past," and makes references to all of the "'heroic figures' in the news lately," insinuating that he knows Dreiberg's alter-ego as the second Nite Owl (8.8). The word "figure" ironically alludes to Big Figure's name from the preceding scene with Rorschach. Dreiberg's apartment has served as his sanctuary and hiding place for his masked-adventurer persona for the past eight years. In the first panel of this elsewhere, the detective is pictured pushing past the "one crummy lock" (previously broken by Rorschach) that the repairman from the Gordian Knot Lock Company now works on for the second time. Earlier in chapter 3, Rorschach even comments on the "crummy" quality of the lock when he breaks it for the second time: "By the way, you need a stronger lock. That new one broke after one shove" (3.24). The recurrent mention of Dreiberg's "crummy" lock and the repairman from the Gordian Knot Lock Company's second appearance allow readers to connect this scene to a few different elsewheres and whens, including when Rorschach initially breaks Dreiberg's lock and when the repairman first fixes it (both different elsewhens), and when Rorschach comments on the lock's poor quality after breaking it a second time (a different elsewhere and when). As the repairman leaves in the present "when," he remarks that Dreiberg now has "maximum security," another allusion to prison systems, as Rorschach is, in fact, locked in a "maximum security" prison. The new lock shines in the light, but, ironically, in the background of the same panel, Dreiberg is continually questioned by Detective Fine. Even a supposedly good-quality, shiny lock cannot protect him.

Another clear example of Moore's "coincidence and synchronicity" also occurs in chapter 8, where three different elsewheres are presented on a single verso and recto page spread. The happenings in the *New Frontiersman*'s office are thematically associated with two different elsewheres: Dreiberg's apartment and the secret island where Max Shea and others work on Veidt's psychic squid creation. In the office, Godfrey says, "Meanwhile I'll get this whole pantomime ready to hit the streets," in reference to getting their latest edition of the paper out for print (8.10). The next panel spans the entire bottom row of the nine-panel grid and shows Dreiberg and Juspeczyk readying themselves to "hit the streets" as they study a map of the state penitentiary, with the intention of breaking Rorschach out of jail. Godfrey's use of the word "pantomime" seems to be out of place in reference to a newspaper, which is mainly comprised of words. A "pantomime" is defined as "an actor, especially in comedy or burlesque, who expresses meaning by gesture or mime" ("Pantomime," entry 1, def. 1). In other words, a pantomime relies on his or her physical appearance and visual cues in order to convey information. Ironically, in the panel depicting Juspeczyk and Dreiberg, Dreiberg is still in the process of literally putting on his "costume" as he holds his cape and goggles in his arms. Godfrey is represented by the narrator as commenting on Dreiberg and Juspeczyk's actions being comedic, but this is the narrator's juxtaposition and not Godfrey's actual commentary on them. The headline that Godfrey pastes down on the newspaper reads, "Honor Is Like The Hawk ... Sometimes It Must Go Hooded," which would suggest that if he was aware of Dreiberg and Juspeczyk's actions, he would think them honorable, not comedic. For the next seven pages, one large panel takes up the bottom third of each page and portrays Dreiberg and Juspeczyk as they travel in the Owl Ship to free Rorschach. No words are used in these panels, only pictures. In a sense, this narrative functions much like a pantomime in that it relies on the reader's understanding of the visuals in order to follow Dreiberg and Juspeczyk's journey.

In addition to the *New Frontiersman*'s office and Dreiberg's basement, the narrator introduces another simultaneous elsewhere, which contributes to the reader's perception of "coincidence and synchronicity" between three seemingly unrelated places, each of which the reader can perceive as commenting on the others through their juxtapositioning. The third elsewhere is introduced and directly associated with the other two through both an image-to-image relationship and an association between an image and a word. In the middle of the recto page, Seymour holds up a picture of Max Shea, the missing writer who mysteriously vanished, along with other "prominent creative figures," some time ago (8.10, 32), and asks if it is suitable to use for a story in the next issue of the paper. The verso page starts at the secret island. The reader is unaware of the location at this point in the novel, but he or she is able to simultaneously

see the picture of the writer on the recto page and the writer in this new location on the verso page. As Seymour holds up the picture, he says, "Will this
picture do of the writer?" Ironically, this transition between the *New Frontiersman* office and the secret island also alludes to Dreiberg and Juspeczyk, who
are also looking for a "missing writer," Rorschach, and whose quest runs along
the bottom of both the verso and recto pages of this spread. Additionally, in
the first panel from the secret island, Shea remarks to Ms. Manish, another
"missing" artist, that he thought "[she]'d be glad to see the back of the damned
thing." She replies, "I am. I just need some final studies of the facial assembly"
(8.11). In the previous panel with Dreiberg and Juspeczyk, Dreiberg's back faces
the front of the panel. In the background, one example of many of his "assem-
bled" faces, his prototype exo-skeleton hangs on the wall. He also holds his goggles and hood in his hands, his usual "facial assembly" when dressed in Nite
Owl's attire. In a single recto and verso page spread there are three locations
moving diachronically in time, but presented synchronically from the narrator's perspective.

Dr. Manhattan and the "Gestalt" of Time[13]

Paul Gravett explains that an element of Moore's work, unrivaled by many
other artists in the medium, is his "great sensitivity to nuance of language and
word, and cue and clue in a page and a whole comic-book storyline. He knows
that when we're reading, we're looking, and when we're looking, we're reading.
He knows how to place cues, both pictorial ones and written ones, that can actually really spark in the brain, and I think that's a very special magic to him, to
his work" (*Mindscape*). As one can see from the numerous examples thus far,
repetition of particular images, words, and thematic connections between the
two serve a mnemonic purpose: the reader is more likely to remember these
details as he or she progresses through the novel. *Watchmen*'s synchronic and
diachronic time includes two different levels: the narrator's own diachrony and
synchrony, as well as his or her presentation of diachrony and synchrony for
the characters.

With the exception of Dr. Manhattan, all of the characters experience time
in a similar way, perceiving some distinction between the past, present, and
future. Dr. Manhattan, however, lives in an eternal present, a sensation that
he describes as forever "standing still" (4.17). Past, present, and future events
all occur at the same time: "He [Dr. Manhattan] is everywhere all the time as
well as where he is presently. He is not most like any other character in the book,
but most like the reader himself in that he transcends transience, simple being,
via not displacement, but *multi*placement, of being many places at once, men-

tally and, in the storyline, physically as well" (Bernard and Carter, par. 20). This is most easily seen in chapter 4, the entirety of which is told from Dr. Manhattan's perspective. After being accidentally locked in the "time-lock test vault" at Gila Flats, Jon Osterman transforms into Dr. Manhattan. He becomes a being who does not age, has powers beyond those ever seen on Earth, and has a unique perspective on the interactions between time and space.

Chapter 4 begins while Dr. Manhattan sits on Mars, which is quite appropriate, as he is literally above and separated from the other Earth-dwelling characters through his perspective on space and time. The title image for the chapter is a torn photograph that we later learn is of Jon Osterman (Dr. Manhattan) and Janey Slater on a trip to the Palisades Amusement Park in New Jersey during the summer of 1959. A photograph literally captures a moment in time, freezing it, and allows the keeper to revisit it in the future; however, once a photograph is taken, the event that has been recorded cannot be altered. Much like this photograph of Osterman and Slater that serves as a recurrent image and symbol in this chapter, Dr. Manhattan's overall perspective is a collection of "photographs." The photographs that are part of Dr. Manhattan's mentality are not just from the past, but also different places in the present and from the future. Even though he is able to see all of these snapshots at once, he is unable to interfere or alter their "contents." Bernard and Carter claim that "Dr. Manhattan can transform the molecular structure of any object, teleport to anywhere in the universe, and is slowing becoming omnipotent" (par. 17). However, as the narrative progresses, Dr. Manhattan expresses his inability to alter the future, questions free will, and has a sense of perversive predetermined conditions: "A world grows up around me. Am I shaping it, or do its predetermined contours guide my hand?" (4.27). All of this points to the limitations of Dr. Manhattan's powers, especially in his perception of the world.

At age 16, Jon Osterman intends to become a watchmaker like his father, but with the dropping of the atomic bomb on Hiroshima, his father refuses to allow him to enter the same profession: "My profession is a thing of the past. Instead, my son must have a future" (4.3). Unlike Dr. Manhattan's later inability to experience events chronologically (as part of a diachrony), his father clearly separates the "past" and the "future," emphasized in the text with bold lettering. Throughout his narration, Dr. Manhattan refers to all events in terms of precise quantifiable time as measured by clocks like the ones his father made for a living. However, he cannot separate the past from the present or future. Most of his narration, therefore, is in the present tense. Early in the chapter he says, "The photograph is in my hand," but it is also "already lying [in the sand]" in "twelve seconds time" in addition to being "still there" at the Gila Flats Test Base "twenty-seven hours ago" (4.1). With Dr. Manhattan's ability to see future events, but no control over changing them, Janey later asks Dr. Manhattan why he did not prevent President Kennedy's assassination if he was aware that it was going to happen. He replies, "I can't prevent the future. To me, it's already happening" (4.16). In the next panel he walks away from Janey toward a painting that hangs on the wall in the background. Appropriately, the painting is a recreation of Salvador Dalí's 1931 painting "The Persistence of Memory." The melting clocks of Dalí's painting that Dr. Manhattan examines prove quite appropriate for his understanding of simultaneity of different times and spaces. He still uses quantifiable measurements related to the seconds, minutes, and hours on a clock to explain time, but they are, in fact, as meaningless or as useless as the melted clocks in the painting due to the fact that he experiences things all at once and has no power to alter their occurrences.

According to Bernard and Carter, "As the audience ingests the comics page as a whole, they are with Dr. Manhattan every step of the way. When the setting turns back to Manhattan at the derelict bar, the reader is there with him, just as the reader is, at the same time, back on Mars with him. After all, while observing the panel that shows Manhattan in the bar, the panel showing Manhattan on Mars is still within eyeshot" (par. 18). While it is true that the interaction of images and words and the paneled format of sequential art allows readers to potentailly see multiple times and spaces at once, readers necessarily have to ingest the information in somewhat of a linear fashion. Dr. Manhattan's experience of space and time differs so greatly from that of the reader that some aspects of his narrative in chapter 4 follow a diachronic continuum in order for the reader to be able to comprehend the narrative (i.e., the chapter and story contained within it has a beginning, middle, and end). Much like the earlier mentioned example of Dreiberg's memory of Rorschach as a cause for his rush to help Juspeczyk in his basement, Dr. Manhattan's presentation, although experienced by him as simultaneous, necessarily has to be presented somewhat diachronically for the reader to understand. The reader recreates Dr. Manhattan's consciousness of space and time, but it is limited by representation.

Readers first learn about Dr. Manhattan's life at home at age sixteen, then about his working at Gila Flats, his relationship with Janey Slater, the accident that transformed him into Dr. Manhattan, his work for the government, meeting Juspeczyk, and his present position and meditation on Mars. Each of these "snapshots" is told in a diachronic progression of two or more panels. However, the reader is able to get a sense of what Dr. Manhattan's experience of time and space is like through his interjected narrative, some of which describe the images from particular panels and others of which mention multiple times and spaces in one panel. For example, after Dr. Manhattan explains the circumstances of when he meets Slater for the first time, the next panel shows the image of the photograph in the sand. Readers now know that the people in the photograph are Osterman and Slater, and they earlier learned on the first page that the photo was taken in 1959, but readers are still unaware of the circumstances surrounding the event during which it was taken. Additionally, three narrative boxes accompany this image, the first of which reads, "It's 1963. We're making love after an argument, our tenderness in direct proportion to its violence...." The second reads, "It's 1966, and she's packing: tearful, careless with anger..." and the third simply states, "The photograph lies in the sand at my feet" (4.5). At this point, readers have just witnessed the two characters' first meeting, which appears positive, but the ominous narrative boxes in the panel described above allude to trouble in the future. Much like Dr. Manhattan's feelings of the lack of control over predetermined conditions (i.e., knowing the future, but not having the ability to change it), readers experience a similar feeling: they are presented with the knowledge of future negative events, but not enough information in order to fully understand. The "argument" and Slater's "tearful, careless" packing of her belongings are both described in the present tense, tempering the positive mood of the first meeting. In one panel, four different elsewheres and whens are referenced: 1963 and 1966 in places unspecified, 1985 on Mars, and 1959 at Palisades Park in New Jersey (literally one elsewhere and elsewhen framed inside another). Together, these different elsewheres and whens create a sense of simultaneity, knowledge of all space and time, but also the negative aspects of Dr. Manhattan's perspective: his inability to do much of anything about it.

Bernard and Carter note that "Moore is deliberate in his utilization of techniques unique to sequential art that deal with space-time, and his calculated interplay provides his own commentary on the possibility of a fourth dimension. Further, he strives to express how the discovery of this dimension affects human existence" (par. 11). Dr. Manhattan's character development and the experiences that he relates to the reader are a direct reflection of how a different understanding of the relationship between space and time can "affect human existence." Dr. Manhattan changes everything, as Slater explains: "I'm scared because everything feels weird. It's as if everything's changed. Not just you [Dr. Manhattan]: everything!" (4.11). Similarly, Hollis Mason says to him, "With someone like you around, the whole situation changes" (4.15). Dr. Manhattan's decision to leave Earth is also seen as a potential catalyst for total world destruction from nuclear war.

In chapter 9, Dr. Manhattan takes Juspeczyk with him to Mars, where he explains to her that they will "debate Earth's destiny" (9.5). The chapter functions similarly to chapter 4 in that it reflects Dr. Manhattan's understanding of simultaneous time, but this chapter also contrasts it with the more conventional understanding of time as linear, represented by Juspeczyk's perspective. As Juspeczyk grows increasingly frustrated with Dr. Manhattan telling her the future before it actually occurs, he explains, "There is no future. There is no past. Do you see? Time is simultaneous, an intricately structured jewel that humans insist on viewing one edge at a time, when the whole design is visible in every facet" (9.6). Ironically, the structure that Dr. Manhattan has created on Mars is jewel-like as it glistens in the starlight, and Juspeczyk's and his reflections appear in its shiny surface. It also resembles the face of a clock; however, this structure is multi-dimensional rather than having only "one edge."

It has gear-like structures at its core and markers around the edges that resemble the placement of numbers around a clock's face. After ascending to the balcony of this clock-like structure, Dr. Manhattan asks Juspeczyk to think about her first memory, which she starts to explain but then replies, "No, no it's gone" (9.6). However it is not "gone," and she even notes that "I can hear them [her parents arguing] *now*" (9.6, my emphasis), suggesting that she can experience the past in the present, and she has the potential to re-member the past, to put the pieces of her memories back together in the present, and to potentially see "the whole design."

Juspeczyk continues to remember episodes in her past as she tries to convince Dr. Manhattan that human life is not meaningless and that he must do something to intervene, but he reveals that their conversation ends with Juspeczyk "in tears," and that he returns to "Earth at some point in [his] future. There are streets full of corpses" (9.17). Juspeczyk erupts, frustrated with Dr. Manhattan and feeling a sense of helplessness in knowing something terrible is going to happen that she cannot prevent. She continues to try to convince him of the importance of human life, but he replies, "Laurie, you complain, perhaps rightly, that I won't see existence in human terms ... but you yourself refuse to consider my viewpoint..." (9.23). What Juspeczyk still does not recognize is that all of her memories that resurface during her time on Mars have something in common: each memory has to do with her father, whom she never knew, or with her frustration toward the Comedian, the man who raped her mother. As her emotions overwhelm her, all of her memories start to collide, mixing together different places and times, which are portrayed through panel-to-panel juxtaposition (9.23). Narrative boxes with dialogue from each of her memories fill the panels as she cries, "I'm through thinking about my life, looking back on all my stupid memories. It's been a dumb life, and if there's any design, it's a dumb design" (9.23). Her emotions climax as she smashes a bottle of Nostalgia perfume against the clock-like structure, causing the structure to crumble. Her literal and metaphorical destruction of "time" as she knew it allows her to finally acknowledge her father's true identity. However, it also allows Dr. Manhattan to understand Juspeczyk's perspective. He realizes that "the world is so full of people, so crowded with these miracles that they become commonplace and we forget ... I forget. We gaze continually at the world and it grows dull in our perceptions. Yet seen from another's vantage point, as if new, it may still take the breath away" (9.27). This experience on Mars takes Juspeczyk's "breath away" because she finally acknowledges the truth, but it also does the same for Dr. Manhattan, who gains a new perspective based on witnessing Juspeczyk's emotional experience. It seems that Dr. Manhattan does for Juspeczyk what the narrator does for the reader, creating a sense of what Moore calls "coincidence and synchronicity"; however, both characters actually offer the other a new perspective, a way of seeing (or valuing) the world in a different way.

CHAPTER 6

Hooded Honor

On March 21, 1983, President Ronald Reagan commended the work of true heroes, battling against America's greatest adversary, the Soviet Union: "To watch the courageous Afghan freedom fighters battle modern arsenals with simple hand-held weapons is an inspiration to those who love freedom.... To the Afghan people, I say on behalf of all Americans that we admire your heroism, your devotion to freedom, and your relentless struggle against your oppressors." Just fifteen years later, President Bill Clinton referred to some of these same Afghanis, members of the Mujahadeen, as "fanatics and killers who wrap murder in the cloak of righteousness." Clinton and Osama bin Laden exchanged bombs instead of encouragement and praise. If the lines from Reagan's speech were uttered after September 11, 2001, they would be construed as unpatriotic or even blasphemous, sympathizing with the enemy. In 2006, just days before the fifth anniversary of the attacks on the World Trade Center, President George W. Bush condemned this group as "radicals [who] have declared their uncompromising hostility to freedom," the very opposite of what one would consider characteristics of "freedom fighters." Are the people to whom President Reagan referred heroes, fighting for justice and the benefit of many, or are they "fanatics and killers," "radicals," or even terrorists?

Heroism is a matter of perspective. Many would like to believe that "the word 'hero' projects to us a kind of spurious solidity, so that we use it, and hear it used, as if it actually referred to a single cognitive image" (Miller 1). However, heroism is far more complex. In 1983, when the Afghans and Soviets were fighting, the Afghani troops were heroes from their perspective, and the Soviet troops were heroes from theirs, but each viewed the other as villains: terrorists or invaders. The uniting factor between all of these definitions is actually a divisive one: heroes to one may be villains to another, or may change designations with changing times. The hero/villain distinction is contingent on individual and social values of what is right and wrong or good and evil.

Heroes and villains function relative to two categories of law: natural and conventional. These categories' definitions and boundaries have been debated for centuries, and the Ancient Greeks even had designations for the distinction in "physis" and "nomos." Natural law remains constant and is unaffected by

101

the conventions of the society (Hooker); these laws "are basic and fundamental to human nature and are discoverable by human reason without reference to specific legislative enactments or judicial decisions" ("Natural Law"). Conventional laws change as social norms and controls change; such laws are "human-made, conditioned by history, and subject to continuous change" ("Natural Law"). For example, gravity functions regardless of whether or not we want it to or how we describe it, while the broken speed limit and the resulting ticket are both conventions agreed on by humans (or at least some of them).

Whether natural or conventional law takes precedent is a matter of perception and perspective. Relative to the system of law under which one operates are good and evil. For the Ancient Greeks, "both nomos and physis may be considered good or bad. Nomos brings progress in society ... but if laws are only valid by nomos they may be changed with circumstances, and may conflict with physis" (Hooker). In figure 6.1, the philosophies of natural and conventional law are represented by the interlocking circles. An arrow radiates from the overlapping portion in each direction, with a continuum of good and evil to each side. The overlap of the two laws contains what is considered "good" in natural law and what is "evil" in conventional law. If visualized in a three-dimensional form, the circles become two sides of a sphere, where the "evil" of natural law meets in an ambiguous overlap with the "good" of conventional law and vice versa.

A natural hero is one who would be affected only by natural law and not the social or political conventions established by the society, whereas a conventional hero abides by the laws of society and the government. The heroes in *Watchmen*'s world find themselves caught in the middle of a divide between these two sets of laws. The 1977 Keene Act, a conventional law created by society, made mandatory the retirement of all costumed adventurers. Whether or not the characters decided to comply with that conventional law is largely based on each of their understandings of law, what constitutes good and evil, and justice. Based on the principles of natural law, the natural heroes ignores the government mandate and continue fighting crime. These heroes are not bound by the workings of conventional law and therefore still view themselves as working for a greater good. From a natural hero's perspective, the heroes limited by conventional law are weak and ineffectual. In contrast, the natural heroes appear to be breaking the law from the perspective of the conventional society. Conventional heroes abide by the laws and view those who do not as evil; among those evil-doers are the natural heroes still in operation after the passage of the Keene Act. With both types of heroes in the novel, *Watchmen*'s world demonstrates that heroism and villainy are all a matter of perspective.

The concept of heroism is further complicated in the novel because it is stated indirectly: a hero in *Watchmen* can be labeled as a "superhuman," "masked adventurer," "vigilante," "God" or "Deity," "the world's smartest man," "crime-fighter," or "legendary being."[1] These are just some of the novel's

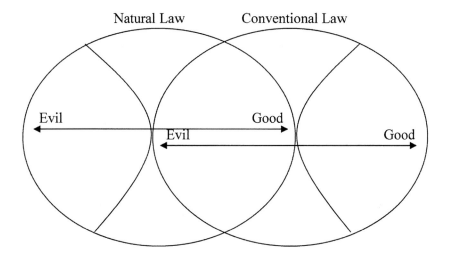

Fig. 6.1. Good and evil represented on continuums within natural and conventional law.

labels under the broader category of "heroism." Each label contributes to the reader's understanding of how the hero defines his or her heroism and how others perceive it. It is almost as if these labels define a conceptual periphery, a series of dots meaningless in and of themselves, but meaningful when connected. Whether or not these labels used to describe the heroes carry positive or negative connotations depends heavily on who uses them, when, and where.

The masked adventurers were at one time accepted by the conventional society as public protectors along with the police officers and other crime-fighting officials. Walter Kovacs (aka Rorschach), Adrian Veidt (aka Ozymandias), Jon Osterman (aka Dr. Manhattan), and Dan Dreiberg (aka the second Nite Owl) were all members of the Crimebusters, a group of masked adventurers who attempted to join forces in an effort against crime, but ultimately did not coalesce due to differences in values and motivations.[2] The Keene Act made clear the divide between the conventional and natural heroes, and this legislation legitimized a new negative connotation for the term "masked adventurer." The novel is set in a tumultuous world where heightening tensions of the Cold War have everyone on edge, looking for scapegoats: "In times of moral crisis, vilification movements tend to arise spontaneously as an urge to find and punish culprits. In such periods, there is a general mood of villain-making ... typically from widespread feelings of moral alarm, resulting perhaps from flagrant crimes, a military threat, or the failure of an institution" (Klapp 60). If not for their conventionally illegal conduct, then for their costumes, *Watchmen*'s natural heroes are conspicuously different from the rest of their society. As a result, these natural heroes have become the villains.

According to Moore, the world in *Watchmen* is a place where there is "increased tension on the streets as the laws become more vague and uncertain and difficult to apply," because the conventional and natural laws are in conflict ("The World"). The "laws [that] become more vague" may, in fact, be conventional laws, especially for the masked adventurers with the inception of the Keene Act. However, even natural laws are destabilized with the arrival of Dr. Manhattan, a being more powerful than any other on Earth. In the absence of clear, certain, and easily-applied laws, it becomes more difficult for the characters to not only define the world around them, but also their own identities and roles. The ways in which each of the four main characters reacts to these ambiguous laws determines how he is subsequently viewed by society. Rorschach, a natural hero, continues his work and disregards the new law, and later becomes widely-known as a "vigilante" (4.23). Veidt, a conventional hero, bows out of the hero business early, at least overtly, and takes full advantage of the marketing potentials of his past work. Dreiberg, a conventional hero, completely fades away and spends his days reminiscing about his past, never revealing his true identity to the public. Dr. Manhattan works for the government and acts as the United States' secret weapon, more or less a god on Earth. Even though Dr. Manhattan works in accordance with the government, they cannot control him or his actions; he works as a natural hero who happens to comply with conventional law, but is not bound by it.

Heroic Motives

A way of organizing the various components of the complex term "heroism" is through the use of Greimas' semiotic rectangle, popularized by Fredric Jameson. With the use of this visual aid, the complex term is divided into smaller parts, making it easier to then understand the larger whole. Each complex term is comprised of two concrete terms and two neutral terms, one of which is positive and one of which is negative in each set. The semiotic rectangle displays the relationships between the respective parts. In figure 6.2, "contraries" are two terms which are direct opposites of each other and are represented by the dotted lines. The dashed lines connecting the corners across the diagonal represent a relation between "contradictories" (Felluga, "Modules"). This relationship links the positive concrete terms with the negative neutral terms. The final relationship between terms is between each top corner to the corner directly below, which is represented by a solid line. This relationship is described as a "relation of implication" (Felluga, "Modules"). This is how neutral and concrete terms are similar but not equal. When heroism is divided among the corners of the rectangle, the aid helps to define each character's heroic perspective and motivation, his relationship to the others, and the ways in which he changes (or stays the same) throughout the novel.

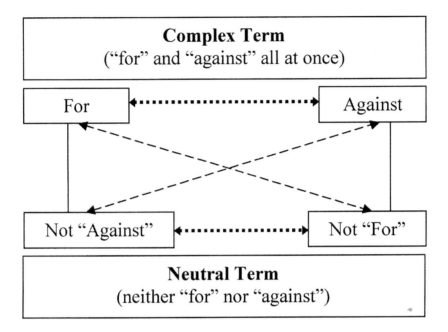

Fig. 6.2. An adaptation of Jameson's illustration of Greimas' semiotic rectangle (Jameson 178).

Heroism is divided between philosophies of natural and conventional law at both "poles of opposition" (Jameson 179), but these two philosophical understandings of the term are insufficient to cover all of the potential labels for heroism in the novel. In figure 6.3, the top two corners of the rectangle represent the conventional and natural ends of heroism, which are "contraries" to each other. The neutral term "non-heroism" is neither for nor against "heroism," and non-heroism is divided into "not conventional" and "not natural," two terms whose relationship is also contrary. One could argue that something described as "not natural" is therefore de facto "conventional." When placed in the rectangle, however, one can see that the two terms are compatible, but not one and the same. The four main character names correspond to each corner in the rectangle: Rorschach represents the concrete term of natural heroism, and Veidt represents conventional. The two characters who represent the neutral terms are Dr. Manhattan and Dreiberg. Dreiberg represents the "not natural" category, and Dr. Manhattan represents "not conventional." These two characters do not fit as neatly into the concrete categories as their counterparts, but do serve as complements. Instead of double-sided arrows to highlight the relationship between the contradictories, there is a one-directional arrow moving from the neutral to the complex. This arrow represents how the neutral

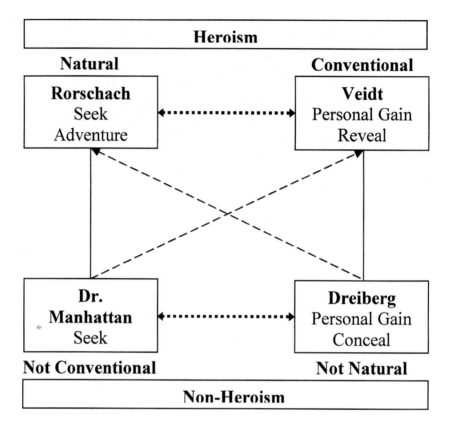

Fig. 6.3. Characters from *Watchmen* on Greimas' semiotic rectangle.

characters, Dr. Manhattan and Dreiberg, develop toward the other end of the contradictories as the narrative proceeds.

Masked Adventuring

At the end of chapter 10 the expository materials reveal the cover for the October 31, 1985, edition of the *New Frontiersman*, which reads, "Honor is like the hawk: Sometimes it must go hooded" (10.29). Why would a hero, someone working for the betterment of others, feel that he or she "must" wear a costume to disguise him or herself from them? The word "masked" implies that the person with this label has some means of hiding his or her non-heroic identity. At some point in the narrative, all four of the main characters are or were considered masked adventurers. Directly related to heroism, the meaning of the label "masked adventurer" dramatically changes depending on if it is used before or after the inception of the Keene Act. The label is made up of two parts, "masked" and "adventurer," both of which have dual meanings. In Ancient Greek theater, masks were used as a way for the actor to take on different personas, to play different roles. Jungian psychology identifies persona as "a set of attitudes adopted by an individual to fit his or her perceived social role" ("Persona," def. 2b). In other words, a person wears a mask or façade to cover up their true identity in order to fit in with others' expectations. Some may consider this dishonest — changing oneself in order to appear a particular way to others. After all, criminals often wear masks themselves to hide their identities from their victims and/or surveilance footage. It is no wonder that some may be distrustful of those who wear masks in order to fight crime: the use of masks by criminals gives masks a negative connotation.

There are many reasons (some more noble than others) why an "adventurer" would feel the need to wear a mask. Some may conceal their identity for protection from those opposed to masked adventuring or even as a way of concealing a public identity. Others may use the mask as a shield to cover personal insecurities, such as feeling uncomfortable in their public identities. Still others may use the mask as a way of defining and revealing themselves as heroes, a personal validation for filling the role of "crime fighter" and as a means of persuading adversaries. Therefore, "masked" implies both the act of concealing *and* revealing, but going "hooded" or wearing a mask is only a means to an end. This is the way in which masked adventurers accomplish their goals— goals or motivations that are determined by each character's decision to be a particular type of adventurer.

While "masked" is relatively easy to separate into two different categories, the term "adventurer" is harder to define. The term has multiple lexical definitions, but two meanings are most applicable to the characters in *Watchmen*. The *Oxford English Dictionary* defines an "adventurer" as "one who seeks adventures, or who engages in hazardous enterprises" (def. 2). There is more than one interpretive possibility for this ambiguous definition, and the term is further complicated with an additional meaning. Another definition of an "adventurer" is "one who is on the look-out for chances of personal advancement; one who lives by his wits" (def. 5). This implies a more self-centered motivation and suggests that one is able to change this status willfully. In contrast, adventurers "engaging in hazardous enterprises" are not necessarily doing so for their benefit.

With two definitions for "masked" and two for "adventurer," there are four potential combinations of meanings for the word "masked adventurer." The first definition for "masked adventurer" is one who uses the mask as a way of concealing his or her identity in the interest of personal gain. The second definition describes a person who also seeks personal gain, but whose costume reveals his or her identity. The third "masked adventurer" conceals his or her identity with a mask, but seeks adventure, and the fourth also seeks adventure, but uses the mask to reveal an aspect of his or her identity. The four under-standings for the term "masked adventurer" correspond to each of the charac-ters in figure 6.3. Each of the four boxes contains the character's name, their motivation or goal, and the function of their mask as a means of reaching that goal. This diagram represents where the characters are at the beginning of the novel. Dr. Manhattan and Dreiberg's positions as heroes change in concordance with their positions as particular types of masked adventurers, and each becomes more like the respective contradictory character. This chapter will examine how Dreiberg, Veidt, Rorschach, and Dr. Manhattan's masks change meaning as their motivations for heroism change, and how their relationships and views of each other are affected by their changing (or static) heroic sta-tuses.

Dan Dreiberg: "The Masked Adventurer"

Dan Dreiberg, once known as the second "Nite Owl," represents the cat-egory of "not natural" heroism, especially at the start of the timeframe in which the action of the novel takes place. Dreiberg gravitated toward "adventuring" in the first place partly because he was seeking a sense of belonging. He explains his motivation for becoming a masked adventurer: "It would have been like joining the Knights of the Round Table; being part of a fellowship of legendary beings..." (7.8). He uses the words "joining" and "fellowship," which empha-size his desire to be associated with these "legendary beings," perhaps because if others view him as a part of this group, he would gain more confidence in himself. Dreiberg goes on to say, "Well I was rich, bored, and there were enough other guys doing it so I didn't feel ridiculous[...] I mean ... I was hanging out with [Hollis Mason, the first Nite Owl] a real hero, being his friend and every-thing" (7.8). Dreiberg refers to Hollis as "a real hero" almost in the same way one would talk about a movie star, famous singer, or sports icon. He entered adventuring not as much for the good of mankind as for his own benefit.

With the imposition of the Keene Act, Dreiberg voluntarily complied with the government's mandatory retirement. He placed his costume, gadgets, and other inventions in an underground lair, beneath his New York City apart-ment, and did not use them for years (4.23). He is apparently unhappy with his present life at the beginning of the novel, especially when Rorschach pays him a visit, which conjures old memories of his past life as a masked adven-turer (1.13). When Rorschach leaves, Dreiberg is pictured with the late Come-dian's button in hand, a reminder of his past crime-fighting days (see figure 6.4). Next to him hangs his unused costume, which appears to be in immacu-late condition. His body, slumped over and shadowed, is directly contrasted to the hollow costume, which ironically stands prominently, illuminated from the front and casting a shadow behind it. The wall behind Dreiberg is stained and

Fig. 6.4. Rorschach's visit brings back Dreiberg's memories of the past (Moore and Gibbons 1.13).

damaged, while the locker that holds his costume is pristine. The railing to Dreiberg's left casts a shadow that descends diagonally away from his body, but the railings in front of the costume ascend with strong vertical lines. Even the costume's belt, which would normally be worn horizontally, instead accentuates the vertical lines of the alcove and locker. In one hand he holds his glasses loosely, and they dangle lifelessly from his fingertips. The goggles around the neck of his costume are horizontal and stable. The image suggests that the empty garments hold more authority than the man who once wore them. Who is really living in the "shadows"— Dreiberg the civilian or the former Nite Owl?

Dreiberg is visibly distraught by the loss of his heroic identity as the Nite Owl, but he continues to deny its effect on his life. He thinks that he "eventually [...] realized the Comedian was right — it's all crap dressed up with a lot of flash and thunder" (7.8). However, his words do not match his obvious demeanor in the previously discussed panel. It is as though he wants to convey that he no longer desires to be a masked adventurer to Laurie Juspeczyk, the former Silk Spectre II, who believes her time as a masked adventurer "was nothing more than ten years running round in a stupid costume because [her] stupid mother wanted [her] to!" (1.25). Dreiberg's weekly visits to see Hollis Mason, the first Nite Owl, as well as his visually evident distress, strongly suggest otherwise. He is denying his natural heroism, constricting himself to following the conventional laws.

Dreiberg continues to downplay the importance of his past as Nite Owl as he and Juspeczyk examine the damage to his Owl Ship: "being a crimefighter and everything. It was just this adolescent, romantic thing" (7.7). He conveys that "adventuring" was merely playing out a childhood dream. Becoming a masked adventurer was not only "romanticized," but also "adolescent." This suggests that he feels that his past life as the Nite Owl was childish, and the mask, costume, and gadgets merely offered some type of fantasy fulfillment. He even admits that the costume, with the drastic effect it has on his actions, makes him feel "so confident it's like [he's] on fire. And all the mask killers, all the wars in the world, they're just cases — just problems to solve" (7.28). Without the mask concealing his true identity, he feels essentially powerless, ashamed of his reliance on the costume. Dreiberg's brief time as a Crimebuster and as Rorschach's partner up through the beginning of the novel is representative of the first definition for the masked adventurer, one who conceals his identity with the mask while seeking some sort of personal gain or fulfillment.

Surely it can be argued that Dreiberg is not a true natural hero because he complied with the government-mandated retirement, but it is apparent that he is regretful for retiring. Even though his original motivations for becoming a masked adventurer were superficial, Dreiberg is not only ashamed, but remorseful for the loss of his past life. He abides by conventional law, but eventually realizes that he cannot suppress his natural heroism. He longs to return to "adventuring" even though he is a man that "sometimes makes mistakes or is uncertain about what is going on, and who sometimes feels afraid" (Moore, "Nite Owl"). Throughout the course of the narrative, readers witness his slow change toward natural heroism, beginning with a period of denial. Along with Juspeczyk, it appears as if his journey closely follows the stages of Joseph Campbell's monomyth, a path that Campbell believes every hero follows in reaching his heroic potential.[3] Eventually, Dreiberg is able to gain the confidence in himself to rejoin Rorschach in uncovering the mask-killer plot, even taking the lead in helping Rorschach escape from jail. During the early conceptualization stages of *Watchmen*'s characters, Moore writes of the influence for Dreiberg's character, the Blue Beetle, and explains that Dreiberg is "the character that will go through the biggest changes ... he will emerge as one of the strongest and noblest characters, although when the strip opens, he's not really at his best. He's not even the [Nite Owl]" (Moore, "Nite Owl").

In the end, Dreiberg does not allow the government to stop him. He only retires temporarily. Moore goes on to say that "maybe [Dreiberg] is even more of a hero in that blind courage does not come naturally to him" ("Nite Owl"). This is not to say that Dreiberg is naturally *less* heroic, but rather that his consciousness of his heroic potential changes through the course of the narrative. By the end, his mask is no longer used as a means to conceal his identity as "Dan Dreiberg," nor is his motivation personal gain (i.e., a relationship with his heroes, such as Hollis Mason). Instead, he even drops the identity of "Dan Dreiberg" for that of "Sam Hollis" to protect his identity as a natural hero. "Sam Hollis" is now his costume that he reveals to the world in order to conceal his dominant identity as "Nite Owl," the natural hero.

Rorschach: "The Vigilante"

Rorschach is a natural hero, as represented by his refusal and inability to retire, as well as his disregard for conventional law. Prior to the present timeframe of the novel (late October 1985), he completes a transformation into a natural hero and remains as one throughout the narrative, which is chronicled in various flashbacks and expository materials. After his arrest, Rorschach (Walter Kovacs) meets with psychiatrist Dr. Malcolm Long for evaluation. During one of their meetings, Rorschach explains his earlier transition into becoming who he is today. Dr. Long wrongly assumes, "Making a mask for yourself, you decided to become Rorschach and..." (6.14). Rorschach quickly corrects him, not even allowing him to finish his sentence. He says, "Don't be stupid. I wasn't Rorschach then. Then I was just Kovacs. Kovacs pretending to be Rorschach. Being Rorschach takes certain kind of insight. Back then, just thought I was Rorschach. Very naïve. Very young. Very soft." Dr. Long's initial thought is to attribute Rorschach's need for vigilantism to his past, which is riddled with disturbing memories. Readers watch as Rorschach remembers when he found his mother engaged in prostitution. He recalls how his mother would physically abuse him, and how other children would taunt him about his unstable home life. After a violent outburst which left a neighborhood boy partially blinded, Rorschach was institutionalized, growing up without the support of a loving mother or father (6.3–8).

Although all of these occurrences are quite traumatic, none of them were the catalyst for Kovacs changing into Rorschach the natural hero. He explains that while investigating the 1975 kidnapping case of a young girl named Blaire Roche, he understood that "this rudderless world is not shaped by vague metaphysical forces. It is not God who kills the children. Not fate that butchers them or destiny that feeds them to the dogs. It's us. Only us" (6.26). In Rorschach's view, mankind's conventional laws are to blame for the evil in the world. He believes that the conventional society did not adequately protect him as a child, nor did they protect Blaire Roche, and Kovacs necessarily changes into Rorschach, a hero upholding the principles of natural law, regardless if they are in opposition to conventional ones. Natural heroes do not stop their fight against evil merely because a conventional law has been established that would make their actions illegal. Rorschach explains, "Once a man has seen, he can never turn his back on it. Never pretend it doesn't exist" (6.15). The natural hero cannot go back once he or she "understands," and for Rorschach this moment was learning of Blaire Roche's horrible fate.

In the first pages of the novel, Detective Steve Fine and his partner Joe Bourquin investigate the murder of Edward Blake, the former adventurer and eventually government-employed crime-fighter whose code name was the Comedian. The detectives do not believe that any of the "vigilantes," formerly "masked adventurers," will get involved if they keep the case concealed from the public, but Fine is skeptical: "Screw them. What about Rorschach? Rorschach never retired, even after him and his buddies fell outta grace. [He's] still out there somewhere" (1.4). The detectives operate under the guidelines of conventional law and thereby view Rorschach through this lens. Within the larger conventional society, Rorschach carries the more negative label of vigilante. Not only is he breaking the law by continuing his masked adventuring, but the detectives also view him as "crazier than a snake's armpit" (1.4). Rorschach never ceased fighting the evil that he saw in the world, and therefore his label as a masked adventurer turned to a more negative association once their work was banned with the introduction of the Keene Act.

At that same moment the subject of the detectives' discussion turns to Rorschach, an apparently homeless man parades past them with a placard reading "The End Is Nigh" (1.4). Both Fine and Bourquin disregard the man, and seem to have no reaction to his presence except Bourquin's ironic "shiver" as he walks by. The reader later learns that the parading homeless man is Rorschach, wearing the disguise of Walter Joseph Kovacs, who the entire time is continuing his work as a natural hero. This costume as Kovacs is not a motivation for fighting crime, but merely serves the purpose of concealing his identity as Rorschach so that he is able to continue his work. Rorschach's "Kovacs" costume functions in much the same way that Dreiberg's "Hollis" costume functions at the end of the narrative. His primary identity is that of Rorschach, the masked adventurer and crime-fighter. Even though others would most likely consider his shape-shifting black and white hood a "mask," Rorschach refers to this as his "face" (5.18, 28). At one point he even describes the transition from Kovacs to Rorschach as "abandon[ing] my disguise and becom[ing] myself" (5.18). When dressed as Walter Joseph Kovacs, he simply blends into the background of the city, exactly what is necessary in order to protect his primary "Rorschach" identity.

In Norman Spinrad's *Science Fiction in the Real World*, he wrongly remarks that Rorschach "comes out of retirement to seek out the murderer of the Comedian" (75). Rorschach never retired, therefore making it impossible for him to "come out" from it. Even though this statement is false, it serves to prove the point that it may *appear* that Rorschach is coming out of retirement because the society in which he lives cannot view him as a hero at all until the story is told from his perspective. The reader is able to see the contents of Rorschach's journal throughout the novel, and by learning his history and reading his words, he or she may just be able to understand why this character has such radical ways of combating crime. Rorschach's methods are indeed extreme and are perhaps impermissible for some readers, but they get results. For example, Rorschach's response to the Keene Act's "compulsory retirement" is leaving the lifeless body of a serial rapist outside of police headquarters with a sign reading "Never!" (4.23). If Rorschach is *too* successful in fighting crime, the police, detectives, and other conventional law enforcement officials potentially could be out of work. Perhaps he will take care of the investigation before the police even have a chance to investigate. Rorschach's natural heroism is a threat to the conventional system of law.

Adrian Veidt: "The World's Smartest Man"

Adrian Veidt — known for his successful business and marketing ventures, including action figures, diet and fitness books, city development projects, and much more — is referred to as "the world's smartest man" (1.17). Veidt is a conventional hero who appears to abide by all conventional rules and laws. He has natural intelligence and unprecedented athletic ability, but this cannot be confused with heroism. According to Moore's character development notes, Veidt is "a superb paragon of humanity in every detail, he has a flawless physique and is in peak condition all the time, and ... is able to use the full one hundred percent of his brain power" ("Ozymandias"). Even though he plots to destroy half of New York City, the plot is never discovered by those who favor conventional society. In fact, Veidt believes that his plan is benefiting the world by alleviating tension between two conventional powers, the United States and the Soviet Union, and thereby helping to uphold conventional law. Veidt is somewhat similar to Rorschach when he says, "An intractable problem can only be resolved by stepping beyond conventional solutions" (11.25). This seems to suggest that conventional law is the problem. However, Veidt sees himself beyond the bounds of conventional law, and upholding the conventional society for everyone else is to his personal benefit. He outwardly conforms to conventional society and wants to uphold its values, chiefly his position on the receiving end of a thriving capitalistic society; his motivation is driven by personal gain.

In addition to sustaining financial success, Veidt is also determined to be remembered in the "hall of legends" with the likes of his heroes. He explains, "I wanted to match [Alexander the Great's] accomplishment, bringing an age of illumination to a benighted world. Heh. I wanted to have something to say to him, should we meet in the hall of legends" (11.8). The *Oxford English Dictionary* defines "legend" as "a person of ... fame or distinction as to become the subject of popularly repeated (true or fictitious) stories" (entry 1, def. 8). Therefore, a "legend" has the potential to be completely fictitious, and the foundation on which Veidt bases his vision could very well be imaginary. Veidt's above statement is similar to what Dreiberg says in chapter 7 about his motivation for becoming a masked adventurer when he explains his desire to be part of a "fellowship of legendary beings" (7.8). Veidt also uses the word "benighted" to describe the world, which curiously resembles the word "knight," again relating to Dreiberg. The Knights of the Round Table form Dreiberg's ultimate concept of the hero, and what he looked toward when dreaming of becoming a masked adventurer before the beginning of the novel. Although the two statements are closely linked, Veidt's statement focuses more on personal recognition. He wants to be remembered as a "legend," whereas Dreiberg simply wants to assimilate into a group. The course of action each man takes in order to fulfill the dream also sets them apart. One continues in the realm of the conventional while the other makes the transition to natural heroism.

With Alexander the Great and Rameses II as idols, Veidt's costume incorporates elements of both Ancient Greece and Ancient Egypt, and the name "Ozymandias" directly refers to Rameses II. Ozymandias' clothing incorporates a color scheme that is predominately violet and gold, colors associated with royalty and wealth. Veidt even reveals that his initial goal in becoming a masked adventurer was to "assume the aspect of kingly Rameses" (11.22). His costume choice reflects that he truly sees himself as nobility or a higher class of man, and that he values both wealth and power. Because he stopped adventuring prior to the imposition of the Keene Act, he also sees himself as a legal form of the costumed hero, or an "unmasked adventurer." Veidt continues being a "hero" in his own mind when he drops the disguise of Ozymandias and adopts that of Veidt. By making both identities public, he is able to make fortunes off the glamour and idealized public perception of the heroic Ozymandias while gaining the public's respect as a business entrepreneur. In doing so, he achieves a sort of celebrity status.

After Veidt retires from adventuring, his costume is the clothing that he wears as "Adrian Veidt." His costume works in a similar way to Rorschach's in that he has no need to conceal his identity when wearing Ozymandias' clothes because this is his primary identity. When in private, Veidt continues to dress as Ozymandias, suggesting that he still associates himself with this regal persona (10.7). Both Veidt and Dreiberg have the potential to change into natural heroes, but there is one distinguishing feature between the two characters that sends them down different paths: Dreiberg is humble about his social position and role, enabling him to transform into a natural hero by the end of the novel; but without the ability to see his fellow man as his equal, Veidt will never be able to make this transition.

Dr. Manhattan: "God exists and he's American"

Jon Osterman, the son of a Brooklyn watchmaker, is transformed into Dr. Manhattan in a tragic accident that everyone presumed to be fatal (4.1–28). When Osterman miraculously returns, he has superhuman abilities and qualities, bringing him closer to the status of a god or deity than a human being. In much the same way that Rorschach did not have a choice in becoming a "vigilante," Osterman did not have a choice in becoming "Dr. Manhattan." In chapter 4 he transports himself to Mars to contemplate human life, and he thinks about how he reached his present state: "Without me, things would have been different. If that fat man hadn't crushed the watch, if I hadn't left it in the test chamber... Am I to blame, then? Or the fat man? Or my father, for choosing my career? Which of us is responsible? Who makes the world?" (4.27). He is not quite sure who or what is responsible for his transformation, but no matter the cause, it does not change the fact that he is now the most powerful being on Earth. Both Rorschach and Dr. Manhattan are natural heroes in that both cannot return to their previous states, nor did they have a choice in becoming who they are today. Dr. Manhattan is more specifically classified as "not conventional" because he is not controlled by the conventional laws, but chooses to act in accordance with them. This places him in a category by himself, possibly better described as a "supernatural hero"— beyond conventional law, but also not created nor destroyable by natural means. After the accident, Dr. Manhattan is perpetually stuck in his present state, and, as he describes it, is always and forever "standing still" (4.17). The feeling of always "standing still" is consistent with the definition of the natural hero, as it would take a natural phenomenon, such as death, for this hero to change, something to which Dr. Manhattan is now immune.

Recognizing the great potential of having such a powerful force, the United States Government took advantage of Dr. Manhattan's new state. They enlisted his abilities and decided to "go public" in 1960 (4.12). The government issued Osterman a costume and the name "Dr. Manhattan." His new name ominously refers to the Manhattan Project, the United States' first big movement toward the development of multiple nuclear weapons during World War II. Transforming into something beyond human, he is described as a "god," a "super-man," and even "the indestructible man," but has no control over even the clothes that he wears (1.19, 4.11–3). The media buzzes with hype surrounding this new being with the code name Dr. Manhattan. They proclaim such things as "We repeat — the superman exists and he's American" (4.13). The government understands the immense power that it has with such a being on their side. According to Professor Milton Glass, author of the expository materials at the end of chapter 4, "It is as if — with a real live Deity on [the United States Government's] side — our leaders have become intoxicated with a heady draught of Omnipotence-by-Association, without realizing just how [Dr. Manhattan's] very existence has deformed the lives of every living creature on the face of this planet" (4.32). Dr. Manhattan drastically changes the world as it was once known.

Arthur Lovejoy's *The Great Chain of Being* demonstrates the dilemma of man's place on the "Great Chain" with the introduction of the otherworldly. Lovejoy cites Giordano Bruno's 1586 *De Imenso*: "Of the endlessly numerous worlds thus demonstrated to exist, some ... must be even more magnificent than ours, with inhabitants superior to the terrestrial race" (118). The superior otherworldly comes to Earth in the form of Dr. Manhattan. His presence on this planet alters the "Great Chain" in that it brings a new life form into the everyday lives of humans, who once believed that they held the highest place in the hierarchy on their own planet. No longer is Veidt, "the smartest man in the world," at the top of the natural "chain of being." Now, "we are all of us living in the shadow of Manhattan" (4.32).

Even though Dr. Manhattan and other humans inhabit the same planet, their worlds and perspectives are very different. A news report comments, "According to Pentagon sources, this astonishing individual can control atomic structure itself" (4.13). Atomic structure is not visible to the human eye, and although it is a part of this world, it is not a tangible element of everyday human life. According to Lovejoy, "The world we now and here know ... seems to the otherworldly mind to have no substance in it; the objects of sense and even of empirical scientific knowledge are unstable, contingent, forever breaking down logically into mere relations to other things which when scrutinized prove equally relative and elusive" (25). Like the atomic structure that Dr. Manhattan is able to break and reassemble, for him, human life and values become increasingly more distant as he evolves into the "otherworldly." The surrounding society has mixed reactions to this new, unknown entity, and much like that of the hero, his role is an ambiguous tightrope walk of good and evil.

In chapter 3 the distinction between Dr. Manhattan's world and man's world is further extended when he and Juspeczyk argue, ultimately leading to the end of their relationship. Juspeczyk feels that Dr. Manhattan has lost his sense of what it means to be human, and she struggles to connect with him. She leaves, but the narrative continues to follow both individuals simultaneously, flipping back and forth from the two locations. Dr. Manhattan has just teleported himself to the television studio when the startled secretary remarks, "They're not paying me enough to handle monsters from outta space!" (3.11). This comment is paired with an image of Juspeczyk speaking to Dreiberg about her frustrations of living with Dr. Manhattan. In the lower left-hand corner of the frame, an image of an alien is seen on an advertisement for the next feature film at the Utopia Cinema, and the creature reinforces both women's feelings. A "monster" is an oddity in this world, and when paired with "outta [outer] space," the "monster" is even further separated in both distance and relationship to that of man. Dr. Manhattan, his worldview, and perspective cannot be fully understood by any human, evoking a sense of fear in most. This label for Dr. Manhattan carries an additional eerie implication upon considering the end of the novel when Veidt's killer monster — presumed by most to be from outer space — lands in Manhattan, taking numerous lives. The label's connection to the most evil force in the novel cannot be ignored, and this further exemplifies how the concept of "heroism" becomes more ambiguous as it is removed from earthly affairs.

At first, "Dr. Manhattan" the mask conceals Jon Osterman, and he holds on to his human perspective, but Osterman loses touch with his previous human existence and transforms into Dr. Manhattan inside and out: he is no longer able to "see existence in human terms" (9.23). Dr. Manhattan's shift toward the "conventional" is evident in chapter 9 when Juspeczyk helps him reconnect with the importance of human life and society, and even more apparent at the end of the novel when he kills Rorschach in an attempt to uphold the conventional society by covering up Veidt's responsibility for the destruction of New York City (12.24). Ultimately comfortable with his now-revealing mask of Dr. Manhattan, he decides to "leav[e] this world for one less complicated" and "create some [life of his own]" (12.27). His motivations shift to encompass his personal fulfillment and gain. His renewed interest in life on Earth is not due to an interest in the welfare of humans, but rather a fascination with the randomness of human creation.

Unlike Dreiberg, who makes a complete transition from "not natural" to "natural," Dr. Manhattan moves in the direction of "conventional" only in understanding; he is not controlled by or even cares for the laws of conventional society when he ultimately decides to leave Earth. Starting as a "not conventional" hero at the beginning of the novel, Dr. Manhattan's subsequent decision to kill Rorschach upholds the structure of conventional society on the surface, shifting him toward conventional heroism; but, in actuality, he has no interest in human affairs. Deciding to leave Earth, Dr. Manhattan moves beyond the status of conventional hero to something entirely beyond our previously defined corners of the semiotic rectangle. In a sense, he becomes the "nonhero" when he completely separates himself from humanity, but this decision is still based on his own personal gain and satisfaction, as well as his comfort level of embodying the persona of Dr. Manhattan rather than Jon Osterman. Dr. Manhattan's end state in the novel is as a "non-hero," one who seeks personal fulfillment and has an outward appearance that is revealing of his primary identity.

Reworking the Hero

Watchmen destabilizes the reader's previous understanding of heroism, and as a concept, heroism becomes more abstract as the characters change and as the appearances of right and wrong give way to their realities. When examining all of the surrounding evidence, the reader may even find him or herself questioning whether or not it is possible that a crazed vigilante is actually the best example of the hero. After Veidt has successfully killed half of the people in New York City, Rorschach views Veidt's actions as an unjust killing of numerous human lives. He is determined to uphold natural law, "even in the face of Armageddon" (12.20). Rorschach's tragic flaw is that he will "never compromise," but this only leads to the end of his natural life (12.20). Rorschach lives on through the writings in his journal, and there is hope that the truth will be revealed when Seymour of the *New Frontiersman* reaches for the copy of the journal on the final page of the narrative (12.32).

Veidt views his actions as upholding conventional order; some must suffer for the benefit of all. The reader is confronted with such a discrepancy between his public image or mask and his true identity that he appears much worse than Rorschach, who perhaps is acting irrationally in wanting to immediately go back to America to reveal what Veidt has done. However, the reader is able to see heroes who choose to operate under both natural and conventional law, whereby he or she gains a double-sided perspective. By the end, the conventional hero does not appear so heroic after all. Rorschach, regardless of his radical ways, emerges as more of a hero. Dreiberg *appears* to uphold conventional law by deciding to not say anything: "How ... how can humans make decisions like this? We're damned if we stay quiet, Earth's damned if we don't. We ... Okay. Okay, count me in. We say nothing" (12.20). With his newfound perspective as a natural hero, Dreiberg questions the validity of conventional law. He agrees to stay quiet, but later reveals that he and Juspeczyk will continue masked adventuring, and both will continue to operate covertly by natural law under the guises of Sam and Sandra Hollis (12.30). Dreiberg's initial decision to keep quiet appears to go against the very growth into a natural hero through which the reader has witnessed him progress, but the reassurance that he will perhaps continue his work, regardless of the Keene Act, leaves him in a more positive light.

Like Dreiberg and Juspeczyk, Dr. Manhattan helps keep Veidt's work a secret. He kills Rorschach, believing that Rorschach's actions would be destructive, but his involvement ends there. His transition from "not natural" to "conventional" occurs at this moment, but Dr. Manhattan then leaves Earth, taking no greater interest in human life, or natural or conventional law. He becomes a "non-hero" whose decision is based on his personal gain. In the end, Dr. Manhattan appears more negatively with his decision to kill Rorschach, a character that has remained consistent throughout the novel and is cast in a more positive light when compared to Veidt.

In the beginning, the readers perceive the characters based on their outward conformity to conventional law. There is no indication that Veidt has any ill intentions nor is committing any wrongdoing. Dreiberg lives alone, has given up masked adventuring in accordance with the conventional law, and is only guilty of what seems to be a mundane existence. Dr. Manhattan works for the government and develops new energy sources, and he too cannot be classified as evil based on a conventional law perspective (in that he works to uphold it). Rorschach, however, in the first chapter alone, breaks into the murder investigation's crime scene, the Rockefeller Military Research Center, Dreiberg's apartment, and breaks fingers in exchange for information at Happy Harry's Bar. All of these acts are considered illegal or against numerous conventional laws, including the Keene Act. By the end, the reader is able to see the characters from the perspective of natural law. The characters make changes, and so too does the reader. Dreiberg and Dr. Manhattan are dynamic characters in and of themselves, but all of the characters are dynamic based on the perspective of the reader.

Reynolds' *Super Heroes: A Modern Mythology* outlines seven basic "laws" of the superhero genre, which further outlines the dichotomy between natural and conventional heroes. Reynolds' third law stipulates: "The hero's devotion to justice overrides even his devotion to the law" (16). The sixth law states: "Although ultimately above the law, superheroes can be capable of considerable patriotism and moral loyalty to the state, though not necessarily to the letter of its laws" (16). Law three essentially describes the natural hero, and, within the context of *Watchmen*, Rorschach. Law six also describes the natural hero, and especially Dr. Manhattan's status at the beginning of the novel. Reynolds goes on to say, "Turning some of these laws on their heads, such as 3 and 6, would give us a good working definition of the superhero's opponent, the supervillain" (16). Ironically, if laws three and six are reversed, they describe the conventional hero in the context of the novel. The conventional hero will put the "law" before "justice" if justice is to be carried out illegally. For this hero, "the letter of [the] laws" is of most value. The "supervillain" in *Watchmen* is hidden among the heroes. By novel's end, Rorschach, the natural hero, lives on as a hero through his journal. Veidt, the conventional hero, is possibly only a hero to himself.

CHAPTER 7

Not So Black and White

Dr. Long places a Rorschach test between himself and his newest patient. He has eagerly awaited this first meeting with the infamous Walter Joseph Kovacs, the recent captive of the New York City Police Department revealed to be the man behind Rorschach the vigilante's mask. Using the inkblot test of the same name, Long hopes to uncover information about what makes this mysterious man psychologically "extreme" (6.32). He asks him to examine the card: "Okay, now I guess you know what this is ... I want you to look at it and tell me what you see. Will you look at it Walter? Will you do that for me?" (6.1). Rorschach stares at the symmetrical black and white pattern intently as Dr. Long pushes him further: "Well, Walter? What is it? What do you see?" The accompanying image reveals the reality of Rorschach's perspective; he sees a German Shepherd, covered in blood, its head split down the center, but he simply responds, "A pretty butterfly." Rorschach knows that his answers determine Dr. Long's analysis of him as psychologically normal or otherwise. He knows what Dr. Long wants to hear, what answers are socially acceptable. Rorschach's predictions are correct; Dr. Long does not see past the pleasant exterior of his answers, and he writes in his notes that he is pleased to find Kovacs' interpretations to be "surprisingly bright and positive and healthy" (6.1). This moment represents a divide between the reader's perspective and Dr. Long's perspective: we can see past Rorschach's "fascinatingly ugly" physical features, beyond his outwardly cheery responses, and into the inner workings of his mind to understand and perhaps even eventually *agree* with his seemingly extreme motivations and actions.

One must ask, however, why we as readers tend to side with a character who Tony Spanakos, author of "Supervigilantes and the Keene Act" in *Watchmen and Philosophy*, depicts as a "psychotically troubled, hideous jingoist, whose use of any means necessary is not employed against superpowered bad guys, but against ordinary people, including the poor and the old" (36). What draws readers to Rorschach, a man wanted by the police for murder and who is described by others as "crazier than a snake's armpit," "sick inside his mind," "nuts," and "a goddamned lunatic"? (1.4, 23, 2.18, 10.10). Even Moore is baffled by the vigilante's popularity among his readers: "I originally intended Rorschach to be a warning about the possible outcome of vigilante thinking. But an awful lot of comics readers felt his remorseless, frightening, psychotic toughness was his most appealing characteristic — not quite what I was going for" (Jensen). Perhaps Moore underestimated the emotional resonance of his dark character in an even darker world, one where both characters and settings as quite different from what they first appear.

Walter Joseph Kovacs, aka Rorschach, and Adrian Veidt, aka Ozymandias, are two characters who come from completely different backgrounds, follow seemingly dichotomous paths through life, and are regarded by the surrounding society as polar opposites. Within *Watchmen*'s world, Veidt is respected for his entrepreneurial spirit, his apparent selfless generosity, and his kindness toward his fellow man,[1] while many despise, fear, or are repulsed by Rorschach's extreme crime-fighting tactics (not to mention his lack of hygiene). However, readers are able to see and judge characters while they are alone, how they differ when in the company of others, and if their inner thoughts are telling a different story than the one that they choose to reveal to those around them. By examining both the appearances and realities of each character, this chapter will uncover the reasons why so many readers are drawn to the "remorseless, frightening, psychotic" Rorschach while finding the well-liked and widely respected Veidt to be the villain of the work.

Monikers, Masks, and Articulation

The names the characters select to represent themselves while in their masked identities reveal much about their respective motivations, beliefs, and values. Veidt selects Ozymandias, a name that appears respectable, prestigious, and is associated with power, wealth, and classical times. However, his motivations for selecting the name are not simply guided by honor and admiration for the one-time conqueror. Of Rorschach, J. Robert Loftis, author of "Means, Ends, and the Critique of Pure Superheroes" in *Watchmen and Philosophy*, writes, "Rorschach is the foil for Veidt in every respect: the unkempt, taciturn, right-wing outsider against the slick, eloquent, left-wing celebrity" (70). Rorschach's name is directly associated with his inkblot mask, but readers later learn that it carries a much deeper meaning, reflective of his worldview and even the way he functions as a character in the narrative.

Throughout chapter 11, Veidt's descriptions of his idols reveal an unhealthy obsession and infatuation with both Rameses II and Alexander the Great. With the recent successful teleportation of his psychic squid creation to New York, Veidt invites his servants to join him for a drink in the vivarium, and without revealing details of his plan, he explains the cause for celebration in his relation to his idol: "Today marks an event especially worthy of such attentions. In many ways, it represents the culmination of a dream more than two thousand years old" (11.7). Veidt is referring to the historical Ozymandias' dream as vicariously continuing through him, not seeing the difference between a long-dead historical figure and himself. Brent Fishbaugh, author of "Moore and Gibbons' *Watchmen*: Exact Personifications of Science," writes, "It seems that Veidt has taken everything into account — everything but the fact that neither Alexander's empire nor the works of Shelley's poetic Ozymandias survived the kings' deaths" (197). Veidt's entire life has become consumed with living through the legend of Ozymandias, a leader dead for over one thousand years and, most importantly, one who did not succeed in making his vision of ultimate control a reality.

Prior to the passage of the Keene Act, Veidt reveals himself as the man behind Ozymandias' mask, shedding himself of the masked adventurer name yet publically profiting from his crime-fighting role. However, in private (and sometimes for public marketing or charity purposes),[2] he still conducts himself as the historical Ozymandias. Later, Veidt explains to Rorschach and Dreiberg his calculated plan behind his early retirement:

> I foresaw that by the late seventies, it [the public status of costumed heroes] would reach bottom. This left ten years to build a fortune and reputation to sustain me beyond that point, allowing me the power and leverage I'd surely need. Developing the basic patent for public spark hydrants, I financed dimensional developments with the proceeds. My plan required preparation for the day when I'd assume the aspect of kingly Rameses, leaving Alexander the adventurer and his trappings to gather dust [11.22].

Veidt's plan is the culmination of more than ten years of calculation, and his reference to Alexander the Great as "Alexander the adventurer" highlights that Veidt believes himself to be superior to others, even exceeding his one-time idol. His tenure as a masked adventurer was merely a way to gain power and recognition. Succeeding as a manipulating adventurer (in the entrepreneurial sense of the word), Veidt pursues greater and more imperial pursuits to become like the "kingly Rameses."

Perhaps Veidt's heroic motivations are better described as hero-worship. According to Bettina Knapp, author of *A Jungian Approach to Literature*, "hero-worshipers and zealots ... seek their goal no matter what the cost, whether murder is to be carried out or another cruel deed. Hitler and Stalin belong to this category" (121). Ironically, Veidt cites Hitler in explaining how he is confident that the public will believe the seemingly unbelievable "alien invasion": "Hitler said people swallow lies easily, provided they're big enough" (11.26). Fueled to reinvent society by his hero-worship, Veidt follows in the footsteps of Alexander the Great and Rameses II, but seeks to excel beyond their accomplishments. He eerily describes how in Alexander's conquests "people died, unnecessarily, though who can judge such things? Yet how nearly he approached his vision of a united world!" (11.8). On the surface, Veidt portrays Alexander as a visionary, sacrificing the lives of a few for the good of many, but Veidt's true concern is not for the benefit of anyone but himself. After all, Moore points out, "It struck the most intelligent being on the planet that there wasn't much point being the most intelligent being on the planet if there wasn't any planet" ("Ozymandias"). The exclamation of the fact that "people died unnecessarily" is quickly brushed off with the question of "who can judge such things?" The words "nearly" and "world" stand apart from the rest in bold lettering, suggesting that unlike Alexander, Veidt plans to *accomplish* this "united world" rather than just "nearly approaching his vision," even if it means that innocent people must die for the cause.

Kovacs' selection of Rorschach as his masked adventuring name is most clearly a reference to his distinctive black and white shape-shifting mask. In chapter 6 he describes the material from which his mask is made to Dr. Long as "very, very beautiful" because of its unique design, with "black and white moving. Changing shape ... but not mixing. No gray" (6.10). In "'Who Watches the Watchmen?': Ideology and 'Real World' Superheroes," Jamie Hughes notes that "the mask not only gives the superhero Rorschach his name; it is also a symbol of his view of society and justice — both of which he perceives in very black and white terms" (552). The mask's patterns are random, but symmetrical, exact, and clear, much like Rorschach's grim worldview: "Born from oblivion; bear children, hell-bound as ourselves, go into oblivion. There is nothing else. Existence is random. Has no pattern save what we imagine after staring at it for too long. No meaning save what we choose to impose" (6.26). Like Rorschach's perspective on the world, an inkblot test has no intrinsic meaning apart from what the viewer sees.

Even though he adopts Rorschach as his masked adventurer identity in 1964, it is not until the 1975 investigation of Blaire Roche's disappearance that he adopts the worldview reminiscent of the test. It is this event that gives Rorschach a Rorschach test-like perspective — when he believes he truly understands the dark and sinister reality of humanity. As Fishbaugh notes, the investigation represents when "Kovacs becomes a mask for Rorschach instead of the converse as it had been. He is no longer 'soft' on criminals" (193). Like the character himself, his mask at times functions as a Rorschach test for the reader, where he or she is able to find meaning in an otherwise meaningless symmetrical black and white pattern. When Rorschach discovers Gerald Grice's two German Shepherds fighting over a large bone in the backyard of an abandoned dressmaker's shop, he realizes that Grice has fed the little girl's remains to his dogs. His shape-shifting mask expresses his shock and dismay at his gruesome discovery (20). The ink pools near the bottom of the mask; the shape resembles a jaw-dropped expression of horror. Two crescent-shaped inkblots look like eyebrows as they mark either side above where his eyes are hidden behind the mask. Two more inkblots dot the forehead of his mask, resembling the wrinkles of a furrowed brow in response to a shocking discovery. Within the context of the scene, readers are able to construe Rorschach's mask as displaying these facial characteristics. Without the context, one may simply see just another symmetrical formation on the ever-changing surface of his mask.

When Grice returns, Rorschach awaits his arrival. After violently subduing Grice with his recently murdered dogs, Rorschach handcuffs him in silence to a cast iron potbelly stove, where he earlier found the remains of Blaire Roche's clothing. He hands Grice a hacksaw and begins to douse the room with kerosene. As he lights a match, Rorschach calmly explains, "Wouldn't bother trying to saw through hand-cuffs. Never make it in time" (6.25). Jacob M. Held, author of "Can We Steer This Rudderless World? Kant, Rorschach, Retributivism, and Honor" in *Watchmen and Philosophy*, notes that although the vigilante's actions are extreme, he may still retain the reader's sympathies: "Rorschach ... exemplifies the *retributive theory of punishment*. He maintains that wrongdoers must be punished for no other reason than that they did wrong; they deserve it. Likewise, the punishment they receive must be fitting" (20). Grice is condemned to burn to death, shackled to the stove used to incinerate the remains of his victim's clothing. Rorschach considers his chosen punishment, although seemingly brutal, as fitting for the crime. Held also contend that, regardless of Rorschach's violent methods, readers may find his actions justified:

> To some degree, we all desire retribution. We are all a little bit Rorschach. We all want to see wrongs righted and wicked people suffering. There is no shame in this, even if retribution often looks shameful. Rorschach, as is befitting of his name, lets us see ourselves. Through him, we see our desire for justice pushed to its limits. With him we see an uncompromising goal of meting out just deserts, its beauty and its horror [20].

His black and white worldview mirrors the way in which he treats the criminals that he sets out to avenge; death is the just punishment for murderous criminals. They cannot be free to exist in the morally ambiguous gray shadows.

Beyond the names that Veidt and Rorschach have selected for themselves, each character's physical presence affects the way in which others perceive them. Readers first meet Veidt while following Rorschach's journey to warn all former fellow masked adventurers of his suspected mask-killer theory. Veidt's high-rise, embellished with a huge Veidt logo, towers over the other buildings in the city (1.17). The next panel portrays the inside of his office, a huge space with shiny, glass-like floors and lavishly gilded décor. He is dressed in a tailored double-breasted suit of the same violet and gold color scheme featured on his Ozymandias attire. His hair is well-groomed, and his facial features are attractive and strong.[3] Veidt appears to have it all: good looks, superior athletic ability, financial success, and a stylish office and attire. When Rorschach brings Veidt the news of the Comedian's death, a clear contrast emerges between the two characters' motivations. Veidt is widely admired for his financial success by many, but not by Rorschach, who believes it was wrong for him to profit off of his reputation as Ozymandias. Rorschach compares Veidt to the late Comedian, who, he explains, "stood up for his country[...] He never let anybody retire him. Never cashed in on his reputation." Clutching one of the many Veidt action figures that lie on Veidt's desk, Rorschach continues, "Never set up a company selling posters and diet books and toy soldiers based on himself. Never became a prostitute" (1.17). Not surprisingly, Rorschach's assertion offends Veidt, but not for the reason that one would suspect. Veidt responds, "Nobody retired me. I chose to quit adventuring and go public two years before the police strike made the Keene Act necessary" (1.18). Veidt's emphasis on the words "nobody" and "chose" suggest that he is offended not by the assertion that Veidt became a "prostitute" by profiting off of his masked adventuring persona, but by Rorschach's implication that Veidt was *forced* to retire. Veidt clearly makes a distinction between himself and the other masked adventurers. Veidt understands his retirement as something that took strength and foresight, but Rorschach simply sees Veidt's decision as a weakness.

Unconcerned with how others perceive him, Rorschach's physical appearance, living space, and eating habits are neither perfected nor polished. His living space, unlike Veidt's, is cramped and cluttered. Dirty dishes, stacks of back issues of the *New Frontiersman*, and open cans litter the nightstand and floor of his room (7.11). His eating habits are quite unconventional; he helps himself to cold beans right from the can before Dreiberg returns home, and slurps down raw eggs from Moloch's refrigerator (1.11, 5.5). His fedora, coat, and gloves are tattered and stained, and they appear as if they have rarely (if ever) been washed. When he retrieves his spare clothes from underneath the floorboards of his apartment after his jailbreak in chapter 10, a large stain darkens the left side of his spare trench coat. The mark curiously resembles the *same* bloody stain from more than ten years earlier when he butchered Grice's dogs (6.24, 10.9). Not surprisingly, other characters frequently make reference to his lack of personal hygiene. In chapter 1, Juspeczyk complains about the "way he smells," and in chapter 5, Rorschach writes in his journal that "on way out of room, met landlady. Usual complaints re hygiene and rent" (1.23, 5.11). Rorschach's trademark stench even has a reputation among common citizens. Early in chapter 1, a patron named Steve at Happy Harry's Bar and Grill remarks, "Hey, you hear that? He's got friends! Musta changed his deodorant!" (15). Aside from his hygiene, cluttered living space, and unusual eating habits, descriptions of Rorschach's appearance as Kovacs are just as negative. In his notes from his first meeting with the vigilante, Dr. Long writes, "Physically, he's fascinatingly ugly. I could stare at him for hours ... except that he stares back, which I find uncomfortable. He never seems to blink." And at the time of his arrest, the police officers refer to Kovacs as an "ugly little zero" and a "runt" who wears "elevator shoes" (6.1, 5.28).

While Rorschach and Dreiberg are submerged underwater in the Owl Ship awaiting nightfall, Rorschach reveals a possible reason for why his personal appearance is not a primary concern. He complains that they are wasting time waiting for dark. In frustration, Dreiberg snaps, "This is no picnic for me, either," which Rorschach construes as yet another attack on his lack of cleanliness. He responds, "Implying something? About coat perhaps? Old. Slightly musty. Apologies. Can't all be fastidious. Can't all keep hands clean" (9). Rorschach knows that he has a reputation for his unsanitary ways, and his defensiveness toward Dreiberg even suggests that this is something that he believes should be *admired* rather than something just to be condoned. He associates time spent on personal hygiene with time wasted. In order to accomplish anything, one must metaphorically (and literally for Rorschach) get one's hands dirty.

Aside from their names and physical appearances, the ways in which Veidt and Rorschach communicate with other characters also reveals a distinction between their public appearances and private agendas. Veidt is an eloquent speaker; his word choice and sentence construction reflect his advanced intelligence, and even alludes to his notions of superiority over his fellow man. He speaks openly to the press, discussing his time as a masked adventurer; however, as Doug Roth's article for *Nova Express* shows, Veidt ensures that his communication with the media is solely on *his* terms. Shortly after Veidt's retirement, Roth phones Veidt, who he refers to as "one of America's best-respected and most consistently left-leaning superheroes," to set up an interview. Veidt "kindly" invites to fly Roth to Antarctica so that the interview can be conducted "in comfort" (11.30). Roth sees this as simply a generous gesture; however, it also conveniently allows Veidt to be perceived within the opulent surroundings of his Antarctic retreat. When Roth arrives, he uneasily recognizes some potential arrogance in the well-liked masked adventurer. He begins his article with a quote in which Veidt refers to President Nixon's advisors and other Washington representatives as "humanoids." At first, Roth is quite shocked. He writes:

> "Humanoids." I'm sitting talking with a retired superhero in a glass dome filled with tropical flowers and hummingbirds, while outside the Antarctic winds build snowdrifts against the glass. I would imagine myself beyond surprise by this point, yet the sudden use of such an odd term is startling. Have I detected a hitherto unnoticed contempt for mere humans behind that eminently likable golden façade? Why "humanoids"? I put this to him and he chuckles [11.29].

Veidt goes on to explain that the term is in reference to a quote by Vice President Ford. His unease assuaged, Roth notes Veidt's laughter as "deep and rich" and "filled with a warmth," but Roth's "liberal sensibilities recoi[l] with a predictable knee-jerk" once more when greeted by three Vietnamese men after his plane lands at Veidt's private airstrip. Roth presumes the men are Veidt's servants, but his apprehension is once again calmed when he finds out Veidt appears to have saved these men from oppression, bringing them to Antarctica, where he "seems to treat them more as respected friends than as lackeys" (11.30).

The extravagance of Veidt's retreat is quite overwhelming, and Roth is unsure of how to perceive the man, who in every way appears to be flawless. For the first page and a half of his article, Roth describes in detail what he observes rather than what he and the former masked adventurer discuss. Veidt could perhaps be *less* well-liked among his lavish display of wealth and power, but like the carefully planned moves of a politician or actor, Veidt molds himself into the humble and modest person that he knows Roth wants to see. Roth looks on as Veidt finishes his morning workout: "He looks like a goddamned god! I can't quite believe he'll submit to being interview by someone so obviously mired in the dregs of the gene pool as myself" (11.30). The setting and timing that Veidt has selected for their interview contributes to Roth's feelings as a lesser man. He literally looks up as Veidt flawlessly flies through the air in his gymnastics routine, and by extension, Veidt appears to be a genuinely giving person for taking the time out of his prestigious and busy life to talk to a lowly reporter. Now in awe of this humble superior, Roth proceeds with his interview, and asks Veidt how he feels about being "referred to in the press as the world's smartest man." He modestly replies, "No, that isn't true, but it's very flattering and I don't mind a bit.... I don't mind being the smartest man in the world. I just wish it wasn't this one" (11.32). Based on context from earlier in chapter 11, readers know that Veidt *does* believe himself to be intellectually superior to his fellow man. He says, "Entering school, I was already exceptionally bright[...] My parents were intellectually unremarkable, possessing no obvious genetic advantages. Perhaps I decided to be intelligent rather than otherwise? Perhaps we all make such decisions, though that seems a callous doctrine.[...] My intellect set me apart" (8). His intelligence distinguishes him as so far "apart" from others that he sees himself as removed from the world in which he lives.

Having no desire or ability[4] to speak publically, Rorschach seldom communicates with others. In chapter 1, his former fellow masked adventurers are surprised at his sudden visit after many years. When he speaks, he rarely uses full sentences. Readers know that he is quite literate from the dark poetic style of his private journal, yet other characters in *Watchmen*'s world are not afforded this perspective. Based on his speech patterns, others are likely to perceive him as cryptic, crazy, or even uneducated. His voice is often described as peculiarly flat and unexpressive, which the lack of bold words in his word balloons reflects. Juspeczyk says she dislikes Rorschach's "horrible monotone voice," and Dr. Long later writes of their first meeting, "He's very withdrawn, with no expression in either face or voice. Getting a response is often difficult" (1.23, 6.1). While most find his manner of speech peculiar or even eerie, Rorschach's minimalist approach suggests (much like his lacking hygiene) that he believes actions are more valuable than words. He wastes little time speaking with others, using only those words necessary to quickly convey his message. Most of the characters are unable to see past his dark exterior to understand the reasons why he appears and sounds the way he does. The reader's perspective is distinct, as he or she is able to read his private journal throughout the narrative; and, in fact, it is the first perspective to which readers are introduced. His journal is his other form of communication, serving as a log or record of his work and actions. Besides, actions prove more useful in obtaining results than words, as Rorschach explains to Dreiberg in chapter 10: "Give me smallest finger on man's hand. I'll produce information" (9).

At times, what Rorschach says is equally as curious as how he says it. His frank and unemotional style is often misconstrued as arrogance or callousness by other characters. In chapter 1, Rorschach's visit to warn Juspeczyk and Dr. Manhattan of the potential "mask killer" turns into a discussion of Blake's involvement with Juspeczyk's mother. She says, "Blake was a bastard. He was a monster. Y'know he tried to rape my mother back when they were both Minutemen?" He asks, "So you support the allegations made in Hollis Mason's book concerning Blake?" It appears as if he is trying to start a confrontation with Juspeczyk (and perhaps he is), as if he knows that the statement will aggravate her. As he casually crunches on some Sweet Chariot sugar cubes, Rorschach calmly responds, "I'm not here to speculate on the moral lapses of men who died in their country's service. I came to warn..." (21). His visit has a particular purpose, and he cannot be concerned with digressions on other matters, especially those that are only based on "speculation." Juspeczyk becomes so angry with the way that Rorschach dismisses rape as a "moral lapse" that she has Dr. Manhattan teleport him out of the facility. But before he does, Rorschach attempts to continue: "With respect Dr. Manhattan, I warned Veidt and Dreiberg and I intend to warn you and your lady friend.[...] Spent a lot of time getting in to see you. Not leaving before I've..." (22). With this unfinished sentence, he suddenly finds himself outside.

Although readers may find Rorschach's dismissal of rape as a "moral lapse" quite heartless at this early point in the narrative, other communication mishaps later in the narrative start to form a pattern, one that reflects his unintentional tactlessness when communicating with his former fellow masked adventurers. In chapter 10, while Rorschach and Dreiberg await nightfall, Rorschach is restless. He says to Dreiberg, "Visit bars. Squeeze people. Been lazing around a long time. Maybe you've forgotten how we do things" (10). There is no clear subject in the third sentence. Is he referring to himself *and* Dreiberg as "lazing around" because they are spending time in hiding, or is he referring to just Dreiberg, a jibe at his compliance with the Keene Act and retirement from masked adventuring? The last sentence suggests that it is the latter, and Dreiberg erupts: "Lazing...? Listen, I've had it! Who the hell do you think you are? You live off of people while insulting them, nobody complains because they think you're a goddamned lunatic.... You know how hard it is, being your friend?" (10). Dreiberg is one of the only characters afforded a perspective on Rorschach beyond his callous exterior. They were partners, and Dreiberg knows Rorschach better than any of the other former masked adventurers. Catching himself, he retracts what he said: "I ... look, Rorschach, I'm sorry. I shouldn't have said all that.... Listen, you're right. We've been down here too long. It must be dark enough to surface by know. I'll take him up" (10). He knows Rorschach is action-driven, and understands that Rorschach believes their time spent underwater is wasted time that they could use fighting crime, something to which Dreiberg knows Rorschach has dedicated his life.

Later in chapter 10, Rorschach attempts to comfort Dreiberg after they learn that Mason, Dreiberg's mentor and father-figure, was recently murdered by a group of Knot Tops (16). As he brings down the Owl Ship for Dreiberg, Rorschach says, "Unidentified gang murders Mason. Supports mask-killer theory...." Dreiberg responds, "Look, I don't care! Right now I don't care about whose theory is best! Just shut up and bring the ship down." Rorschach continues, "Merely suggesting that by finding mask killer, can have revenge for Mason's death. Meant to comfort you." Rorschach's idea of "comfort" is quite unconventional. Most would probably construe his statement as insensitive, but Dreiberg understands Rorschach's unfaltering commitment to retribution, and he once again catches himself in his judgment: "Comfort me? Who in their right mind could take comfort from ... Uh ... Yeah, okay. Thanks, Rorschach. Really. Thank you." Like Dreiberg, readers understand that Rorschach's intensions are not malicious, that he sincerely believes retribution is right and in the name of justice. Held asks, "What compels Rorschach? If it were mere vengeance, a thirst for revenge, or simple hatred, he would be a much less interesting character" (21). Not only would he be "much less interesting," but the reader would be more likely to denounce him for his actions. Held continues, "If all he wanted to do was hurt people out of sadistic urges ... he would be easy to ignore or condemn. But there is so much more to Rorschach. His motives are pure; it is about justice, right, and the moral order" (21).

Veidt's Desktop Materials and Rorschach's File Folder

Aside from daydreams and flashbacks within the paneled format of the narrative, readers are perhaps best able to distinguish between the realities of characters' private lives from the appearances of their public personas by examining their personal documents directly. At the end of chapters 6 and 10, readers gain access to private materials concerning each character: Veidt's desktop materials from his office and Dr. Long's file containing Rorschach's history and police records. When examined closely, the documents provide a clearer understanding of how the characters view themselves, their relationships with others, their pasts, and the implications that their decisions have for the future.

After discovering Pyramid Deliveries as the company behind Veidt's attempted assassination in chapter 10, Rorschach and Dreiberg set out for his high-rise, hoping that this new information will "convince him to help" (16). When they arrive, Dreiberg is impressed with the extravagant furnishings of the office. He remarks, "Heh. Incredible stuff he has here...." However, Rorschach sees something beyond the shiny exterior. He responds, "Mostly reflecting vanity: pictures of self, pretentious Egyptian trappings" (19). They find that Veidt has left his daily planner, which notes he had already left for Karnak earlier that morning. Dreiberg sits at his computer and searches "Pyramid Deliveries." After correctly identifying the password as "Ramases II," Dreiberg makes a shocking discovery: "Rorschach, I think we're in bad trouble. The person behind this, the person we're up against ... I think it's Adrian.[...] He runs it, Rorschach! Runs Pyramid Deliveries, Dimensional Developments, the whole show!" (21). They immediately leave for Karnak in search of Veidt, but they first collect the papers from his desk. Perhaps they will provide some further insight into Veidt's seemingly unbelievable involvement. At the end of chapter 10, the expository materials contain Veidt's personal notes and correspondences with business associates and proposals for new products. At first, the materials appear to be quite standard, documents that one would expect to find on the desk of a highly-successful business executive. However, upon closer observation, readers find that the documents provide some subtle hints of Veidt's plans in the near future, his motivations for doing so, and where his true priorities lie.

The first document included with the materials is a letter from Leo Winston, the president of marketing and development for Veidt's company. The letter concerns the expansion of Veidt's action figure line to include Rorschach and Nite Owl figures. Winston writes:

> Our lawyers seem to think that since the costumed identities themselves are outlawed and illegal, there can be no legal claim to copyright upon their costumed images, leaving us free to register a copyright ourselves. This seems okay to me, but I'm advised that since you may have some personal connection with these individuals, there's a possibility that you'll feel differently [29].

Winston's suggestion is solely concerned with how the company can profit by expanding the line. His only hesitations concern potential legal issues, and, not surprisingly, his suggestions circumvent the possibility that the company would have to share profits with the masked adventurers on whom the figurines are based. That is, if neither Rorschach nor Nite Owl have any "legal claim" to their identities, this means that they will also have no rights pertaining to the marketing, production, or profits earned from the dolls created to resemble them. Readers know from the preceding chapters that both Dreiberg and Rorschach feel that their costumed identities still comprise large portions of who they are, and if Veidt were to market these action figures, he would be — as Rorschach would say — "prostituting" their identities along with his own (1.17).

Winston also recommends that they include a Moloch action figure, but is more hesitant with this recommendation: "Since Edgar Jacobi died recently, there may be a question of taste, but from what our lawyers can determine, Jacobi left no estate likely to oppose such a marketing move" (29). Winston is concerned about how it will appear if they are to market and profit from the identity of a man who was recently murdered. The suggestion becomes even more ironic when readers later learn that Veidt is *responsible* for Jacobi's death, along with many others. Veidt later explains his plan: "Each step was synchronized. Jon, being too powerful and unpredictable to fit my plans, needed removing. Thus, Dimensional Developments hired his past associates[...] Weaver first, Slater and Moloch later. Unwittingly exposed to radiation, they were closely observed, cultivated as weapons against Jon" (11.24). What Veidt does to Jacobi far exceeds the unethical use of Jacobi's likeness to profit from the sale of action figures: he uses him as a disposable pawn, making the last years of the man's life miserably painful.

Veidt's note in response to Winston's recommendations at first *appears* to be concerned with the morality of using his adversary's and former associates' identities. He feeds into Winston's hesitations, making it seem as if he sincerely cares about offending or exploiting Rorschach, Dreiberg, and Jacobi's family. He writes, "Ethically very uncertain about Rorschach, Nite Owl, and Moloch, plus accessories" (30). He goes no further in explaining *why* the company should refrain from this venture, and instead he quickly continues with the assertion that a "More militaristic flavor will sell better. The American public has never really gone in for super-heroes in a big way." In other words, the decision to market military-themed action figures rather than ones derived from super heroes is based on profitability. He proposes: "My study of recorded sales figures in a historical context suggests an increase in the sale of soldiers and action figures in times immediately prior to a period of anticipated war or bloodshed, and we should take advantage of this syndrome for as long as it lasts" (30). The statement may appear suspicious to readers, who, like Rorschach and Dreiberg, have recently learned of Veidt's involvement with both Pyramid Deliveries and Dimensional Developments. Certainly one can study past events or patterns that occurred "prior to a period of anticipation." However, one might ask, how could someone apply this to the present unless he or she had the ability, like Dr. Manhattan, to see the future? Even Dreiberg later remarks, "Those brochures, all that crap we took from his desk ... the tone was wrong, somehow. Not optimistic exactly but ... well, planning for a future" (12.3).

Veidt can foresee a "period of anticipation" precisely because he controls what is to be anticipated. Is Veidt alluding to some forthcoming period of bloodshed of which others are unaware? This document provides the reader with some holes in Veidt's seemingly infallible credibility. When readers later learn of Veidt's involvement in the deaths of millions, it is unclear if the act is for his own personal monetary benefit or for the good of mankind. Veidt certainly conflates the two; he views a fear-stricken society as a viable opportunity to make money, serving his best interest, while also thinking about what can be done to ease global tensions. Jamie Hughes notes, "His wealth, intelligence, and concentration on past societies have already well removed him from the ideological trappings of the world and into one based on his own system of belief, and with each step back in perspective, Ozymandias is still further removed. The murder of three million people is nothing more than a means to an end for Ozymandias" (553). On the surface, Veidt's plan appears to be a "means to an end" solely for the good of mankind; however, it is clear that he considers his personal profit margin, as he continues business as usual. If his associates survive his planned "alien invasion," it will appear that Veidt simply has impeccable foresight about market trends.

Also included in these expository materials is a letter from Veidt to Angela Neuberg, the director of Veidt Cosmetics and Toiletries, concerning the marketing of Nostalgia Perfume and Cologne. An advertisement, which is paper-clipped to the letter, portrays a woman in a bedroom. She wears a suggestively sheer nightgown, and coyly glances at the viewer. Veidt writes, "The sexual imagery is obvious, the woman adjusting her stocking being overtly erotic, yet layered with enough romantic ambiance to avoid offense.... It seems to me the success of the campaign is directly linked to the state of global uncertainty that has endured for the past forty years or more" (31). Earlier in the chapter, Veidt views his wall of televisions and, based on his observation, decides that his company should invest in "the major erotic video companies. That's short term. Also we should negotiate controlling shares in selected baby food and maternity goods manufacturers" (10.8). His emphasis that this is only a temporary investment is curious. What gives Veidt any impression that world affairs will dramatically alter in the near future?

He makes a similar assertion in his letter to Neuberg. Of the Nostalgia product line, he writes, "I feel we must begin to take into account the fact that one way or another, such conditions ['the state of global uncertainty'] cannot endure indefinitely" (31). In the next chapter, readers learn that the "one way or another" to which Veidt refers is actually *his* way, the result of careful planning, which he is clearly anticipating in this letter. He continues, "Simply put, the current circumstances out [sic] civilization finds itself immersed in will either lead to war, or they won't. If they lead to war, our best plans become irrelevant. If peace endures, I contend that a new surge of social optimism is likely, necessitating a new image for Veidt cosmetics, geared to a new consumer" (31). His assertion is frank and straightforward, curiously not reflecting the "global uncertainty" to which he referred earlier in the letter. It is also peculiar that he suggests public attitudes will *change* "if peace endures." The word "endure" implies that the current circumstances will *last* rather than spurring a miraculous new sense of optimism as he predicts. He continues his letter with specific plans and a precise timeframe: "starting next year" the company will replace the Nostalgia products with a Millennium product line, and "The imagery associated with it will be controversial and modern, projecting a vision of a technological Utopia..." (31). Veidt and his company are clearly concerned with preserving a wholesome public image; Winston's suggestions for expansion of the action figure line are concerned with questions of "taste," and Veidt's letter to Neuberg notes that the erotic imagery of the Nostalgia advertising campaign is careful so as not to "offend." Therefore, it may seem peculiar to Neuberg, other associates, and the reader that he suggests using a "controversial" marketing strategy for the new Millennium products. Veidt knows that the imagery that he suggests will not be controversial after his plans are implemented; however, he anticipates how his suggestion for a radical change in the company's direction will be perceived by Neuberg before any world event occurs that would suggest otherwise.

The final document in the expository materials is a revised copy of Veidt's self-improvement program, the Veidt Method. The program is designed to help one achieve his or her ultimate potential. It promises a "better body," "increased confidence and magnetism," and "advanced mental techniques" by simply investing in the program and following the "step by step guide" (32). Veidt appears to truly believe that everyone can willfully cultivate both body and mind to operate flawlessly. In the 1975 interview with Doug Roth of the *Nova Express*, which readers are able to view after they learn of Veidt's world-altering plan, Veidt says, "The disciplines of physical exercise, meditation, and study aren't terribly esoteric. The means to attain a capability far beyond that of the so-called ordinary person are within reach of everyone, if their desire and their will are strong enough" (11.30–31). The statement draws context from this previous document; however, one might question Veidt's sincerity. He clearly does *not* perceive anyone else to have a "desire" or "will" that is "strong enough" to save the world from imminent global nuclear war, so he becomes a self-appointed god-like figure, deciding to sacrifice over three million lives for what he believes to be a positive and permanent change in the world. Does he really believe *anyone* can attain his level of success, power, and intellectual ability when he secretly plots as the sole person able to save the world?

J. Keeping's "Superheroes and Supermen: Finding Nietzsche's Übermensch in *Watchmen*" suggests, "More so than any of the other characters, Veidt consciously sets out to create himself.... Of all the characters, he gives the strongest impression of having ordered his body and mind into an 'artistic plan.' He even creates and markets the Veidt Method as a means of doing so" (57). However, marketing a product for profit and believing in its claims are not necessarily one and the same. The Veidt Method could simply be another product aimed at taking advantage of people's vulnerabilities in the current uncertain global climate. The booklet even promises that the Veidt Method "can turn YOU into a superhuman, fully in charge of your own destiny" (32). In a world where little is certain, the product's claim is perhaps comforting to potential buyers. The claim also reflects Veidt's flawed understanding of his own ability to control "destiny," his belief that his plan will permanently alter the world, with "Humanity's fate rest[ing] safely in [his] hands" (11.26). As Keeping notes, "Although Ozymandias presents his vast scheme in altruistic terms, it's impossible to overlook a level of megalomania in his words and actions, especially when he compares himself to the likes of Alexander and Rameses II" (58). In order to surpass Alexander's accomplishments to achieve a *lasting* united world, he would have to manipulate more than the appearance of an otherworldly threat. He would have to alter human nature, something which Veidt cannot possibly control.

Whereas Veidt's desktop materials suggest how he creates appearances for the surrounding society so as to cover up mass murder and ensure personal profits, Rorschach's file folder suggests that he is a *victim* of society's created appearances, which unjustly mark him as a malicious and psychotic killer. Throughout chapter 6, a yellow file folder labeled "W. Kovacs" appears in panels on nearly half of the pages of the chapter. It is seen on the table in the prison interrogation room, on Dr. Long's desk, or directly in his hands. As the chapter closes, Dr. Long (and readers) are left to contemplate Rorschach's past, which has just been revealed over the last 28 pages. The significance of the file is alluded to throughout the chapter, and the expository materials finally allow the reader to observe its contents directly. Aside from providing basic information pertaining to Rorschach's identity (name, address, birth date, parents' names) and belongings, the majority of information in the first document concerns the two police officers injured at the time of his arrest and the three people the police believe he murdered. Of the officers, the report reads, "Kovacs, who was on the premises at the time, injured two police officers while resisting arrest. Officer Shaw was admitted to the hospital with minor burns, while Officer Greaves, who was shot at point blank range with a gas-powered grappling gun, has a shattered sternum and is still on the hospital's critical list as of this writing (10/22/85)." In chapter 5, readers see Rorschach's attack on the two officers, providing context for the contents of the police report (26–7), but the presentation of the document in the expository materials greatly differs from the reader's original encounter with the material.

Throughout chapter 5, readers witness the events that lead up to Rorschach's arrest. After checking his maildrop, Rorschach discovers a note, presumably from Moloch, that reads, "Call tonight, 11:30PM. Have information. URGENT. Jacobi" (18). When he arrives at Moloch's apartment as directed, the police receive a phone call from an anonymous tipster revealing the current whereabouts of "Raw Shark" (22), and upon discovering Moloch's lifeless body, readers know that someone has framed Rorschach. Rorschach fearfully scrambles around the apartment: "No. No, no, no. Framed. Set up. Walked right into it. Stupid. Stupid. Stupid" (25). Through the context of previous chapters, readers understand that his intentions for visiting Moloch pertain to his investigation into a seemingly connected series of attacks on his former fellow masked brethren. His intentions are seemingly good, and the reader has no indication that he is there to harm Moloch (other than to possibly resort to some coercive finger-breaking). Descriptions of Rorschach and his actions liken him to a frightened and cornered wild animal ready to defend his life. One police officer notes, "Man, I don't like this. The guy's an animal..." and Detective Fine says, "It's okay. It's okay, we've got him trapped. We must have" (26–7). Moments later, Rorschach leaps from the window with a bestial growl: "Rraaaarrl" (27).

By becoming acquainted with Rorschach and his motivations over the course of the first five chapters, readers are more likely to sympathize with him than they are with the police who have surrounded him in Moloch's home. Resisting arrest appears to be more like an act of self-defense rather than one of cold-blooded calculation. Readers approach chapter 6 with the context of Rorschach's violent arrest lending him some sympathy, and as they learn of his troubled past, the gravity of his dark journey toward becoming Rorschach weighs as heavily on readers as it does on Dr. Long by the end of the chapter. The chapter provides context to better understand his actions, but its juxtaposition with the first document in the expository materials suggests a disjointed and jarring reality of two opposing perspectives of Rorschach and the police, who ironically work toward the same goal of eradicating crime. In chapter 5, the two police officers whom Rorschach was responsible for injuring were simply nameless adversaries, but the police report gives the men identities. The report reveals the extent of each man's injuries, confronting the reader with the moral ambiguities of Rorschach's crime-fighting ways. The disconnect between text and context unsettles the reader's complacency and perhaps even his or her desire to side with the vigilante. However, accusations of Rorschach's involvement in three murders reveal the negative implications and power of society's perception, lending him some sympathy. The report reads:

> Although Kovacs has denied the murder of Jacobi, given his previous history of violence against other criminals and his location in the murder house at the time, few other conclusions seem possible. Curiously, Kovacs has not denied the two other murders attributed to him, those of Gerald Anthony Grice, unemployed, in the summer of 1975, and of wanted multiple rapist Harvey Charles Furniss two years later in the summer of 1977, immediately following the passage of the Keene Act into law.

The report reveals that it is unlikely that Rorschach will be able to prove his innocence in relation to Moloch's murder. He has certainly broken the law, but readers are likely to feel sorry for him as he is unfairly pinned with a homicide he did not commit. Most notably, however, is what the document *fails* to say about Grice, whom readers memorably meet in chapter 6. By simply labeling Grice as "unemployed," it appears as if Rorschach is responsible for an innocent man's death, but readers know of Grice's horrific crime through Rorschach's story of his investigation into Blaire Roche's disappearance. Once again, Rorschach's story and experience in relation to that of the police report reveal two sides of the same story. Does the reader side with a supposedly murderous and crazed vigilante, whose intentions and dedication to justice are admirable, or does he or she side with the police, who are the lawful protectors of citizens, but who clearly color Rorschach's crimes in an unjust way?

Paper-clipped to the file folder with this first document, Rorschach's mug shot further complicates the reader's ability to untangle the ethically ambiguous standings of both parties. The image shows Rorschach with a large gash above his right eye and a swollen left eye. During his interviews with Dr. Long, Rorschach is pictured with a badly bruised cheek and a bandage over this gash. Readers know the source of at least one of the injuries from the end of chapter 5, when he leaps from the second floor of Moloch's apartment in a final attempt to evade police. When he crashes to the ground, an officer kicks him squarely in the left eye even though only a few moments earlier someone indicates that "he's down!" (5.28). Another officer taunts, "You like that? You like that, you goddamned queer?" as he beats him with his nightstick. When they pull his mask from his face, the gash above his right eye is not visible, suggesting that this injury occurs *after* the police take him into custody but before he is photographed for his mug shot. Based on how the police treat him at the time of his arrest, readers can assume that the injury is far from accidental. One might ask whether Rorschach's interrogation methods are that much different from the methods used by the New York police during his arrest. Early in chapter 6, Dr. Long's notes read, "The police have beaten on him pretty badly. During the police strike of '77 he made several inflammatory anti-cop statements, and they've never forgotten. The cops don't like him; the underworld doesn't like him; nobody likes him" (2). This first page of these materials alone is rife with morally ambiguous mixed messages. Readers are likely to sympathize with Rorschach's plight; however, there is no clear moral or ethical compass by which to gauge either the police or Rorschach.

In the character development notes included with the 2005 *Absolute Watchmen*, Moore explains that there are two possible interpretations of such a questionable character: "Depending on which way you look at him, [Rorschach] is either the one incorruptible force at large in a world of eroded morals and values or he is a dangerous and near-psychotic sociopath who kills without compassion or regard for legal niceties" ("Rorschach"). In a world filled with "eroded morals and values," is Rorschach really all that different from the society in which he works if he does not regard "legal niceties?" Even though the reader may see beyond Rorschach's extreme methods and adherence to retribution, the law-abiding members of the society in *Watchmen* cannot, and therefore he becomes just another criminal targeted by the police officers and other government sanctioned crime-fighters. Chapters 5, 6, and the expository materials unsettle any stable ground on which readers can judge the characters, and they are left alone to navigate what they believe to be right and wrong for themselves.

Also included in Kovacs' file is an "Early History" from the New York State Psychiatric Hospital (30–31). In much the same way that the police assume that Rorschach must be guilty of Moloch's murder based on circumstantial (although seemingly convincing) evidence, this document makes similar assumptions: "In July of 1951, the boy [Kovacs] was admitted into care after viciously attacking two older boys in the street, partially blinding one of them. When questioned, Kovacs refused to talk about what had caused him to attack the boys, so it must be presumed that it was an unprovoked assault." Based on context from chapter 6, readers know that the attack was, in fact, provoked. The two boys would not let young Kovacs pass, and instead smash a half-eaten piece of fruit into his face and taunt him with a barrage of insulting comments about him and his mother (6–7). At first, the boys elicit little response from Kovacs, who fearfully looks up at the two older and much taller boys. One boy asks, "Whatsa matter? Ya deef [sic] or what?" Kovacs' body language suggests that he is not speaking because he is nervous rather than defiant, and one can easily extrapolate the same fearful disposition to when the hospital interrogated Kovacs about the circumstances of the attack.

There is no question that Kovacs "viciously" attacked the two boys, but what is troubling is that everyone around Kovacs (including the New York State Psychiatric Hospital) sees him as an animal and assailant when readers know that he is just as much a victim as the two boys. When Kovacs leaps onto the two boys, word balloons fill the panels, overlapping one another as onlookers shout: "Oh, God, look, that filthy little animal. Look." "Hold his arms! Hold his arms!" "htta [sic] be locked up. See him biting that" "Like an animal. Like a mad dog...." "Blame the parents." "Exactly like a mad dog..." (7). As the contents from previous chapters become context for the documents of Kovacs' police file, readers decipher gross differences between the realities of Kovacs' past and the way he appears to the outside world both as Kovacs the convict and Rorschach the masked vigilante.

The report continues to explain that Kovacs was admitted into the care of the Lillian Charlton Home for Problem Children after the state discovered that he frequently witnessed his mother's prostitution and was subjected to regular abuse. He was admitted in 1951 and stayed until 1956. In a photograph attached to the document, a young Kovacs stands in front of the sign for the Charlton Home. The image seems to merely give readers a glimpse of Kovacs' appearance around 16 years old. However, a careful look reveals that the image functions much more than as context for the "Early History" document. The suit Kovacs wears in the picture is too big; it hangs awkwardly off his shoulders and the material drapes around his small frame. When using context from previous chapters, readers may recognize the suit in the photograph as the same pinstriped suit, now tattered and worn, that he wears today at 45 years old (see

5.4–6). This small detail is just another testament to the difficult circumstances of Kovacs' life that may lend him sympathy with the reader.

The "Early History" document concludes with a statement which passes judgment even before the hospital fully investigates his circumstances: "Very little physical evidence existsthat [sic] gives a clear insight into the psychology of this troubled man" (31). The reader must ask, however, if there is "little physical evidence," then on what is the hospital making their assumptions that he is "troubled"? The word "troubled" here is used in the psychological sense to refer to Rorschach as somehow psychologically ill or unstable. Even though the report states that the investigation is still in an "early stage," it appears as if the hospital (and the collective society in general) has fastened Kovacs with a label of mental instability without substantial proof. Certainly, Rorschach is an intense character whose crime-fighting ways bypass the conventional system of government, and as Fishbaugh rightly notes, "Rorschach was created entirely by his environment, and it is that environment which has driven him to the extreme behavior he so often demonstrates" (192). It is true that traumatic events from his past may correlate with his extreme vigilante ways, but they are not necessarily cause for "troubled" psychology.

The next document in the file is Kovacs' essay entitled "My Parents" that he wrote at age eleven while in the care of the Charlton Home. He begins with a heartbreaking declaration: "I have two parents, although actually, I don't have any" (31). Young Kovacs does not miss his mother's abuse, but wants terribly to believe that the father he never met loves him and would come for him if he could. He writes, "I have never met my dad and I would sure like to.... Most probably he was out of the country during the war when I was growing up on some sort of mission.... Maybe he got killed fighting the Nazis and he's with God now and that's how come he never managed to find me" (31). His writing is simple and innocent. Readers know from the "Early History" document that his mother and Peter Joseph Kovacs divorced long before he was born, and the name of his biological father is unknown. He was conceived from a "semi-permanent relationship" after his mother had already "drifted into prostitution" (30). Sadly, the young boy's understanding of his father is a complete fantasy, used to soothe the harsh reality of his traumatic past.

With the next document in the file, readers find that his traumatic past continues to haunt him while in the care of the Charlton Home. In a typed document titled "Dream," thirteen-year-old Kovacs dictates a dream (perhaps more aptly labeled a nightmare) to an associate at the home. Also included is a tattered drawing, where Kovacs draws the horrific image from his dream, what he describes as a man and his mother, joined like "Siamese twins" and "dancing" without "any clothes on." The dream's description and his drawing closely resemble Rorschach's memory from earlier in the chapter (6.3). From the "Early History" document, readers know that he was frequently subject to his mother's prostitution as a child, but this dream occurs almost two years after being admitted into care, suggesting that his abusive home environment had long-lasting effects.

Although seemingly insignificant, the two dark ring-shapes that mark the "Early History" documents also contribute to the reader's perception of the file's contents (6.30–31). The stains resemble those left by a dripping mug or a perspiring glass. Earlier in chapter 6, readers see Dr. Long sitting at his desk and examining Kovacs' file late into the night (13). According to the clock on the desk, it is close to midnight, and a steaming pot of coffee stands nearby to keep him awake. Gloria, Dr. Long's wife, even complains, "Mal? You're never gonna sleep with all that coffee inside you" (13). The last panel on the page is a bird's eye-view from above the desk, with Dr. Long resting his freshly-filled mug on top of his papers. The coffees stains on the documents from the expository materials draw context from this moment, but also allude to Dr. Long's seemingly endless nights coping with what he once believed to be a simple case. The documents' arrangement in the expository materials also speak to this; the chaotic display of overlapping papers spread across a desk suggest that Dr. Long is in search of some meaning or pattern by looking at them all at once. Witness to the same information as readers, Dr. Long's final words in his notes for chapter 6 fatalistically read, "We are alone. There is nothing else" (28).

What leads Dr. Long to this pessimistic conclusion after he began the chapter with such optimism for Rorschach's recovery? He confidently begins his sessions with Rorschach noting, "I'm convinced I can help him. No problem is beyond the grasp of a good psychoanalyst, and they tell me I'm very good. Good with people" (6.1) He does not see that Rorschach's initial answers to the inkblot tests are blatant lies. One might question why a character who is so adamantly dedicated to the truth would lie to Dr. Long. Like all of Rorschach's actions, they are driven by a particular goal; he initially lies to Dr. Long about his interpretations of the inkblots in order to ensure that Dr. Long "understands." In one of their later interviews, Rorschach expresses his admiration for the Comedian, who "understood man's capacity for horrors and never quit. Saw the world's black underbelly and never surrendered. Once a man has seen, he can never turn his back on it. Never pretend it doesn't exist" (6.15). But to Dr. Long, Rorschach says, "Fat. Wealthy. *Think* you understand pain" (6.9, emphasis added). Dr. Long "thinks" he understands, believing that he can make his patient well. Ironically, however, these assumptions are based on what others ("they") tell him. On the surface, Rorschach's initial responses give Dr. Long the confidence that he understands his patient. However, this is only an appearance; Rorschach intends to show him a reality that will ultimately change Dr. Long's life.

Uncovering the cause of the infamous vigilante's apparent mental illness would make Dr. Long widely known and well respected among other psychoanalysts. At the end of their second session, Rorschach directly addresses Dr. Long's jaded perspective. Rorschach asks, "Why are you spending so much time with me, doctor?" He responds, "Uh ... well, because I care about you, and because I want to make you well..." (6.11). Rorschach senses his insincerity, and confronts him: "Other people, down in cells. Behavior more extreme than mine. You don't spend any time with them ... but then, they're not famous. Won't get your name in the journals. You don't want to make me well. Just want to know what makes me sick" (6.11). Dr. Long's notes from his first meeting allude to such feelings ("A success here could make my reputation" [6.1]), but readers later learn that Rorschach's prediction is eerily accurate. In the final document from the expository materials, a note printed with "From the desk of: Dr. Malcolm Long" provides the reader insight on what he anticipated before meeting with Rorschach. He writes that he believes the case will be "complex," but is excited to begin working with Rorschach because he can probably use the materials for "future publication" (32).

Dr. Long searches for meaning in the coffee-stained and scattered documents, and the investigation affects him more deeply that he first anticipated. After his second meeting with Rorschach, Dr. Long writes, "My earlier optimism was obviously unfounded. He's getting worse. So am I. Just read back what I've written above. Sixth line down should read 'Kovacs spoke to the other inmates.' Kovacs. Not Rorschach" (6.13). In essence, Rorschach has given Dr. Long a new perspective, one that has led his wife to leave him and later compels him to intervene in a fight between Joey, the driver for the Promethean Cab Company, and her girlfriend, Aline (11.20).[5] Gloria meets Dr. Long near Bernard's newsstand. She wants to come home, but only on certain conditions: "I can't live with someone who feels driven to help hopeless cases, then lets their misery affect our lives.[...] I'm not going to share you with a world full of screwups and manic depressives. I'm not going to share my life with them" (11.20). Gloria's conditions emphasize her personal comfort. She is unwilling to allow her husband to help anyone but herself. Her self-centered motivation is similar to Dr. Long's motivation when he first began work with Rorschach, but now he "can't run from [the world]" (11.20). He asks Gloria, as Rorschach has done for him, to "understand": "I mean, it's all we can do, try to help each other. It's all that means anything ... Please. Please Understand" (11.20). For Dr. Long and the reader, Rorschach's file and his stories of his childhood traumas, Kitty Genovese, and Blaire Roche's murder resonate long after the evaluation sessions end. As a result, Rorschach's harsh crime-fighting tactics and his adamant adherence to honor and justice become, in the very least, understandable.

The Truth in Black and White

When Dreiberg, Juspeczyk, Dr. Manhattan, and Rorschach learn of Veidt's responsibility for killing millions in New York in chapter 12, the discrepancy between Veidt's appearance and the reality of his twisted worldview is revealed to those around him. After unsuccessfully attempting to destroy Dr. Manhattan, Veidt reaches for a remote control to turn on his massive wall of television screens. Dr. Manhattan asks, "What's that in your hand, Veidt? Another ultimate weapon?" And he responds, "Yes. Yes, you could say that" (18). As they face the televisions, Dreiberg's mouth hangs open in utter shock, and tears stream from Juspeczyk's wide and fearful eyes. A swarm of word balloons fill the following panels with messages coming from the simultaneous television broadcasts from news stations around the world. Dreiberg, Juspeczyk, Dr. Manhattan, and Rorschach witness messages such as "Scene here, utterly horrible, I can't describe..."; "[d]eath toll in the millions"; and "The dead. The insane. There are children, children, children ... I can't go on. I'm sorry. I'm so sorry" (19). However, in the final panel portraying the messages from the broadcasts, Veidt watches the same wall of televisions and hears much different messages than the other characters: "Immediate end to hostilities until we've evaluated this new threat to"; "An immediate summit in Geneva"; and "End the war" (19). Tears fall from his eyes as he whispers, "I did it." Are these tears of joy or are they tears of sorrow, like the ones that stain Juspeczyk's cheeks?

In the next panel, Veidt closes his eyes, raises his hands above his head, and shouts, "I did it!" (see figure 7.1). Based on his perceptions of the television broadcasts in the previous panel, his exclamation is one of accomplishment. He triumphantly raises his hands above his head, a sign of victory, with a celebratory shout of his perceived accomplishment. A yellow aura surrounds him. The glow highlights his grand achievement, which he perceives to be analogous to Alexander's cutting of the Gordian Knot, pictured in the painting behind him. This, however, is not what the other characters see as they look on. Based on the negative television broadcasts to which Juspeczyk, Dreiberg, Rorschach, and Dr. Manhattan are reacting, Veidt's declaration of "I did it!" is a *confession* rather than an accomplishment. He raises his hands in surrender. The front of his body is darkened in shadows, and rather than a victorious aura, the yellow glow that surrounds him resembles a police searchlight as it illuminates the guilty party. Loftis notes that this is one moment in the narrative that solidifies Veidt's position as the "villain" of the work: "He may say that the purpose of his plan is to 'usher in an age of illumination so dazzling that humanity will reject the darkness in its heart.' But we know the first thing he thinks about when he sees his crazy scheme succeed is his own glory. 'I did it!' he shouts, fists in the air. And he immediately begins planning his own grand role in this utopia" (67).

The appearance and reality of his motivations unite as the truth is finally revealed, but the discovery is at first hard to believe for some. Even before confronting Veidt at Karnak with their newfound information, Dreiberg hesitates, noting that Veidt is "such a caring, conscientious guy. He's a pacifist, a vegetarian..." (11.15). He cannot possibly fathom Veidt's involvement in any plot to murder, let alone hurt, another human being. Rorschach is not nearly as tol-

Fig. 7.1. Is Veidt's exclamation one of triumph or surrender? (Moore and Gibbons 12.19).

erant, seeing past Veidt's perfected appearance. He responds, "Hitler was a vegetarian. If bothers you, leave Veidt to me." Rorschach never trusted Veidt's seemingly perfect appearance, but "None take Rorschach's assumptions very seriously, since he has a reputation as a paranoid rebel" (Fishbaugh 192). In the eyes of the other characters, Rorschach never gains any credibility, even after his assumptions are discovered to be right. Instead, his adherence to the truth ultimately costs him his life. Even though Dreiberg, Juspeczyk, and Dr. Manhattan may not agree with Veidt's actions, they appear to be too afraid or simply unwilling to reveal the truth to the public for fear that even more damage will be done. Veidt is responsible for the death of millions in New York City and is the mastermind behind numerous other murders that ensured the successful coordination of his plans. Loftis notes:

> According to the standard comic book formula, Rorschach is the hero of the story and Ozymandias is the villain (though, of course, nothing is really that simple in *Watchmen*). Rorschach is the first person we see, and the plot is structured around his investigation of several murders. The audience uncovers the truth behind the murders as Rorschach does. Ozymandias, on the other hand, is behind the murders, and when he is found out, he reveals his elaborate plot involving the further death of millions [67].

When it appears as though Veidt will never be discovered by the public, Rorschach poses a threat to Veidt's well-formed plan. He is alone in believing that the truth should be revealed. In response to Dreiberg's reluctant willingness to "say nothing" of the truth, Rorschach says, "Joking, of course.[...] No. Not even in the face of Armageddon. Never compromise" (12.20). The other characters do not perceive Rorschach as heroic for his adherence to the truth. In fact, they see his actions as irrational. Dreiberg pleads, "Rorschach, wait!

Where are you going? This is too big to be hard-assed about! We have to compromise..." (12.20). At this moment, the other characters (and perhaps the reader) find Rorschach's decision to be wrong, that revealing the truth will serve no benefit other than to accomplish public recognition of Veidt's guilt. After all, we cannot know for sure what the outcome would be if Rorschach succeeded in revealing the truth.[6] However, the reader can be certain of Veidt's confidence even as Rorschach leaves to return to America. Veidt brazenly remarks, "Hmm. Now what would you call that, I wonder? 'Blotting out reality' perhaps? Ah well ... in all likelihood it's of no consequence. As a reliable witness, Rorschach is hardly ... how shall we put it ... 'without stain'?" (12.21). He flaunts the fact that in the public arena, Rorschach, who is considered a crazed criminal, is of no match to his status as a highly-respected and well-liked upstanding citizen. He has killed millions, and it looks as if he is going to get away with it.

As Rorschach walks out into the Antarctic evening, he knows that Dr. Manhattan will not allow him to live and return to the United States. Rorschach lifts his inkblot mask, revealing the face of Walter Joseph Kovacs as he says his final words: "Of course. Must protect Veidt's utopia. One more body amongst foundations makes little difference. Well? What are you waiting for? Do it. Do it!" Dr. Manhattan evaporates Rorschach's body. In the next panel, vapor rises from where Rorschach stood moments earlier. This panel's composition furthers the smiley face motif in the narrative and symbolically links the recurrent image with each character's public perceptions. Veidt, like the plastic, glossy face itself, presents a pleasant exterior to the public, while the blood that stains the face represents Rorschach. Veidt lives in a superficial world of created appearances, while Rorschach is representative of a gritty reality. The smiley face pattern is seen near the circular tunnel to enter Veidt's ornate palace. It glows bright yellow, like the surface of the button. A black shadow of an icicle, back-lit from the glow of the tunnel, hangs down on the left hand side and forms the left eye of the smiley face. On the right, one of the hover scooters serves as the right eye. In the foreground of the panel, pink smoke, all that is left of Rorschach's physical body, cuts across the background image of the tunnel. The bloodstain in the snow is marked with a thick red outline of the same comet-like shape as the blood on the button. Rorschach's remains, the reality of death, literally smear the front of the entrance to Veidt's lavish retreat.

In the end, the novel poses the same question for the reader that Dr. Long asks Rorschach in their first session: "I want you to look at it and tell me what you see" (6.1). The rhetorical presentation of Veidt and Rorschach's public personas ironically disguise their true motives, but only one of them has something to hide. Veidt's perfected appearance, planned early retirement, his obsessive hero-worship, and even his strategies for future business ventures are all tied to his world-uniting plan. Even if his intentions are good and he truly believes that his plan will bring lasting world peace, one cannot help thinking that his goal is self-serving, and the means by which he achieves his goal — "on the backs of murdered innocents"—are not justified (12.27). While one character's lies allow him to personally benefit from "history's greatest practical joke" (11.24), the other's strict adherence to transparency and truth brands him with a negative public perception, and ultimately leads to his demise.

CHAPTER 8

Faceless Heroes

"If you'd only relax enough to see the whole continuum, life's pattern or lack of one, then you'd understand my perspective."
— Dr. Manhattan to Juspeczyk while on Mars (9.23)

Surrounded by what he once called the "monochrome world and limited opportunities" of Northampton Borough as a child, Alan Moore would escape into worlds where heroes and heroines could accomplish terrific feats, both animate and inanimate objects were alive, and men interacted with the gods (*Mindscape*). An avid reader from a very young age, Moore found the mystical worlds of ancient mythology, fairytales, and fantasy intriguing, but the monthly chronicles of various American superheroes offered his expanding imagination an additional outlet:

> I'd already been attracted to mythology, fairy stories, anything that had people that could fly or become invisible or could lift huge mountains or could perform any of these heroic acts for which gods and heroes are largely famous. And so, having discovered the American superhero, it was a fairly natural transition. Here was something where I didn't have to read the same myths over and over again, but where every month I could read something new about Superman or the Flash [*Mindscape*].

In their primary-colored world, heroes and gods were brought to life in modern, sometimes futuristic societies, and each monthly installment brought more information about characters' lives, histories, and the worlds in which they lived. Richard Reynolds' *Super Heroes: A Modern Mythology* contends that superhero stories embody a mythology that both reflect the current cultural and political trends during which they are written and provide a continuation of traditional heroic ideals from ancient mythology. The superhero's "costume marks him out as a proponent of change and exoticism, yet he surprises us by his adherence to an almost archaic code of personal honour" (83). At first, Moore was drawn to the characters' lives, worlds, and heroic pursuits, but he eventually also became more intrigued by the people behind the masks, the artists and illustrators that brought these characters to life. He explains that these early experiences ultimately became "a very important key to a very important door. It opened vistas of the imagination with which I was eventually able to transcend and escape the limitations of my origins" (*Mindscape*). With both knowledge of and affinity for both ancient mythology and the modern mythology of superheroes, Moore's work would inevitably come to incorporate elements of both.

Allusions to ancient mythology, mysticism, and magic abound in Moore's works, perhaps most notably in the *Promethea* series that he co-created with artists J. H. Williams III and Mick Gray. *Promethea* is the story of Sophie Bangs' transformation into the mythical woman of the same name. Moore's *The League of Extraordinary Gentlemen* series, with artist Kevin O'Neill, is saturated with references to literary giants, drawing the main characters from works such as Bram Stoker's *Dracula*, H. Rider Haggard's *King Solomon's Mines*, H. G. Wells' *The Invisible Man*, and many more. To say the least, Moore is extremely well-read, with a wide breadth of knowledge in the literary history of what many consider to be the classics, mythology, and legend. He additionally has extensive knowledge of comic-book superheroes and is keenly perceptive of the cultural and political climate of the times. Although *Watchmen* does not refer to classical mythology or literature as extensively as *Promethea* or *League*, *Watchmen* is an exemplar of Moore's wide breadth of knowledge. Playing with both heroic archetypes found in classical mythology and those that have transitioned into the fabric of the American superhero narrative, *Watchmen* is littered with subtle (and other not so subtle) references to the archetypal heroic figure. Most overtly, Adrian Veidt has an obsession with Ancient Greek and Egyptian culture, and he spent a portion of his youth traveling the world, following the footsteps of Alexander the Great (11.8–27). His masked-adventurer name is "Ozymandias," a reference to Rameses II's Greek name and an allusion to Percy Bysshe Shelley's poem. Dan Dreiberg is a self-proclaimed Arthurian legend and mythology lover, even naming his Owl Ship "Archie" after Merlin's owl Archimedes from Disney's version of *The Sword in the Stone*. The stories of the "Knights of the Round Table" factored into his decision to become a costumed adventurer, and his contribution to *The Journal of the American Ornithological Society* is aptly titled "Blood from the Shoulder of Pallas," a reference to the Greek goddess Athena (or Pallas Athena) (7.7–8, 29–32).

Beyond the direct references to mythology and legend, the novel utilizes elements of the "hero's journey" or "monomyth," a journey on which, according to Joseph Campbell's 1949 *The Hero with a Thousand Faces*, all literary heroes embark if they are to find their heroic potentials. For Campbell, the monomyth embodies the similarities found in all mythic traditions of the hero figure:

> Whether the hero be ridiculous or sublime, Greek or barbarian, gentile or Jew, his journey varies little in essential plan. Popular tales represent the heroic action as physical; the higher religions show the deed to be moral; nevertheless, there will be found astonishingly little variation in the morphology of the adventure, the character role involved, the victories gained. If one or another of the basic

elements of the archetypal pattern is omitted from a given fairy tale, legend, ritual, or myth, it is bound to be somehow or other implied — and the omission itself can speak volumes for the history and pathology of the example [38].

Three stages comprise the hero's journey. The first stage of the journey, the "separation," is divided into five subcategories, the first of which is "The Call to Adventure," in which the hero receives a message compelling him to begin a potentially hazardous journey. If the hero rejects the message, he experiences a "Refusal of the Call." If and when the hero accepts the call to adventure, he will receive "Supernatural Aid," some type of "unsuspected assistance" to help him along the way (36). The hero is then ready for "Crossing the First Threshold" or "The Belly of the Whale," which may be a physical or mental experience; the hero must leave behind the comforts of the known and travel into an unknown and often dangerous world.

The second stage, "initiation," includes six subcategories: "The Road of Trials" is the series of challenges or battles that the hero faces while in this other world, and at the "nadir of the mythological round," the hero will encounter a "supreme ordeal and gain his reward" (246). This course-altering event may be defined as "The Meeting with the Goddess," an incident in which a powerful or even supernatural maternal figure gives the hero strength to move forward in the journey. The hero may be tested by the "Woman as the Temptress," another influential female figure (or the Goddess may serve two roles). In the "Atonement with the Father," the hero must make amends with the "ogre aspect of the father," the father being an influential male figure for the hero (126). The "Apotheosis" is the hero's realization of his heroic potential, and the hero gains the "Ultimate Boon" to enlighten, empower, or benefit the world upon his return.

The third and final stage, the "return," is also subdivided into six different stages. The hero may experience the "Refusal of the Return," where the hero does not want to leave the other world to return home. "The Magic Flight" is the process by which the hero leaves the other world to return to his own, but if the hero has trouble returning home and is in need of assistance, he may experience a "Rescue from Without." The hero will then undergo "The Crossing of the Return Threshold" and become the "Master of the Two Worlds": "The individual, through prolonged psychological disciplines, gives up completely all attachment to his personal limitations, idiosyncrasies, hopes and fears, no longer resists the self-annihilation that is prerequisite to rebirth in the realization of truth, and so becomes ripe, at last, for the great at-one-ment" (236–37). Finally, the hero has the "Freedom to Live," which is a "reconciliation of the individual consciousness with the universal will," an understanding and acceptance of a universal human condition: the "passing phenomena of time to the imperishable life that lives and dies in all" (238).

Many writers have used Campbell's monomyth structure in their works, perhaps most notably George Lucas in the Star Wars saga, beginning with the

release of *Star Wars* (later *Star Wars Episode IV: A New Hope*) in 1977. However, the reproduction of Campbell's structure for new works is often viewed
as an easy way out, a shortcut or cookie-cutter approach to narrative development. A single journey for all heroes is at risk of becoming cliché, undercut-
ting or subverting any epic or mythic qualities. Moreover, the monomyth is
also clearly biased toward the heterosexual masculine male hero's journey, even
though Campbell does discuss some (though few) narratives that include female
heroes.[1] For example, the most easily recognizable male-oriented elements of
the monomyth are "The Meeting with the Goddess" and "Woman as the
Temptress," based on the Oedipal complex in the initiation stage of the journey. To say that all mythic traditions share similarities is clearly biased to a particular understanding of who can and cannot be considered a hero. The majority
of potential heroes are discounted by the assumption that there is only one
man, likely to be of an elevated status, who is destined to bring salvation to the
world. Not only does the monomyth bar most potential heroes, but it also takes
mythic traditions out of cultural context. Robert Elwood in *The Politics of Myth*
notes that Campbell's understanding of myth, based on connections made
between different cultures and times, may be perceived as "undoubtedly represent[ing] its appropriation by bourgeois consciousness ... [and] tends to sub-
jectivize and aestheticize myths and stories that had their real roots in social
alienation and economic deprivation" (145). That is, Campbell is not objective:
it is impossible to objectively view and categorize the elements of multiple
myths out of context in order to create one grand and unified hero's journey
without overlooking elements of the myth that are indebted to the cultures
from which they were drawn.

In literary criticism, Campbell's monomyth is just as potentially meaningless if critics endeavor to mimic the journey stages in their work. If a critic
attempts to cram a narrative into the pre-determined spaces of Campbell's constructed hero's journey to find, as Geoff Klock phrases it, "the thousand-and-
first, -second and -third faces of Campbell's monomythical 'Hero with a
Thousand Faces'" (8), the resulting work is not critically useful. Instead, it is
my aim to show that the monomyth elements found in *Watchmen* suggest a
way of reading, providing a commentary and even criticism of the established
conventions for the heroic archetype. Those similarities between Campbell's
monomyth and Moore and Gibbons' work do not indicate that they were aware
of or were purposely mirroring the steps that Campbell identifies in his monomyth, but that Moore and Gibbons, as well as Campbell, recognize some common elements of the hero's journey in literature and myth. *Watchmen*
deconstructs the construct that Campbell established in the pages of *Hero* almost
forty years earlier, destabilizing readers' notions of heroism and the heroic
archetype in order to push the reader toward the most difficult task: *reconstruct-
ing* for him or herself what it means to be a hero.

Iain Thomson's "Deconstructing the Hero" in University Press of Mississippi's *Comics as Philosophy* examines how *Watchmen* deconstructs heroic archetypes by "examin[ing] the perhaps surprising conceptual roots of *Watchmen*'s postmodern cynicism in the Enlightenment, then show[s] that the existentialists too deconstructed the hero, but that their deconstructions suggest very different conclusions" (109). Thomson acknowledges that the heroes in such works must necessarily be constructed in order to be deconstructed; however, Thomson fails to elaborate on this process. He writes, "*Watchmen* ... develop[s] its heroes precisely in order to deconstruct the very idea of the hero, overloading and thereby shattering this idealized reflection of humanity and so encouraging us to reflect upon its significance from the many different angles of the shards left lying on the ground" (101). But one must ask, *how* are the heroes constructed? This chapter examines how the character developments of Dan Dreiberg, Laurie Juspeczyk, Dr. Manhattan, Adrian Veidt, and Rorschach all partially conform to Campbell's monomyth theory. By the end of the narrative, however, readers are left with a cast of incomplete heroes—a group of characters who are all "heroic," but not one that achieves monomythic "hero" status.

Dan Dreiberg and Laurie Juspeczyk

Since the inception of the 1977 Keene Act, Dreiberg has lived alone in his New York City home, and has separated himself from anything to do with masked adventuring. Juspeczyk has lived with her significant other, Dr. Manhattan, and is employed by the government, but Dr. Manhattan and Edward Blake (the Comedian) are the only heroes sanctioned to continue adventuring. When the narrative's present begins on October 12, 1985, Rorschach pays an unexpected[2] visits to his former fellow members of the Crimebusters to deliver the news of the Comedian's recent death and to warn them of what he suspects to be a mask-killer plot. From the perspectives of Dreiberg and Juspeczyk, Rorschach resurfaces from an earlier era of their pasts, prompting them to begin to reconsider their decisions that have led them to their present circumstances. His visit serves as the first step in the monomyth cycle for both characters.

In Campbell's monomyth, the hero is first alerted to the quest by a "Call to Adventure," and in this case the call is delivered by Rorschach, a character who never retired from adventuring. Campbell explains that this event "signifies that destiny has summoned the hero and transferred his spiritual center of gravity from within the pale of his society to a zone of unknown. This fateful region of both treasure and danger may be variously represented ... but it is always a place of strangely fluid and polymorphous beings, unimaginable torments, superhuman deeds, and impossible delight" (58). Unlike Rorschach, Dreiberg and Juspeczyk have remained in the "pale of [their] society," pre– and post–Keene Act. While adventuring, their activities were condoned by the government, and after the Keene Act, both willingly retired in compliance with the law. Both surrendered their heroic identities to recede into the shadows— Dreiberg into the shadows of his cavernous New York City home and Juspeczyk into the shadow of Dr. Manhattan. Rorschach, who appropriately wears a "polymorphic" inkblot mask, already crossed over into the other or "unknown" world and, as a result, refused to retire when the Keene Act was enacted. Upon learning of the Comedian's death, Rorschach sets out to call upon all of his former fellow adventurers. Eight years into their retirements, neither Dreiberg nor Juspeczyk are willing to accept the call right away. The visit prompts Dreiberg to contemplate his past as a masked adventurer,[3] but accepting Rorschach's call to adventure means breaking the law and a return to adventuring, something that he truly misses but lacks the self-confidence and assurance to do on his own. Juspeczyk is more indifferent. She sees Rorschach as mentally ill, someone whose conspiracy theories cannot be taken seriously (1.23). She brushes off the vigilante's visit, and instead decides to reconnect with Dreiberg.

The same night after Rorschach's visit, Dreiberg and Juspeczyk meet for dinner, where she expresses her unhappiness with the path that her life has taken. She bitterly describes herself as a "kept woman for the military's secret weapon," as her job is contingent upon her relationship with Dr. Manhattan. Her sole purpose at the Rockefeller Military Research Center is to simply keep him "relaxed and happy" (1.25). Residing in the "special talent quarters" (1.19), she herself does not have any special talent other than her ability to serve her specially-talented boyfriend. Even her mother cruelly describes her daughter's "image" as someone who "sleep[s] with an h-bomb[...] The only difference [between Dr. Manhattan and the bomb] is that they didn't have to get the h-bomb laid every once in a while" (2.8). Her role is a disposable one; after all, Janey Slater was quickly replaced by Juspeczyk when Dr. Manhattan lost interest in her (4.19).

As Dr. Manhattan drifts further from human reality, Juspeczyk turns to Dreiberg, possibly the only person who would understand her position as a retired and second-generation costumed adventurer. She confides to him: "It's just I keep thinking 'I'm thirty-five. What have I done?' I've spent eight years in semi-retirement preceded by ten years running round in a stupid costume because my stupid mother wanted me to! ... The Keene Act was the best thing that ever happened to us" (1.25). Assuming her mother's identity as Silk Spectre even before she had the chance to make the decision for herself, Juspeczyk has spent her life defined by her caretakers, first by carrying on her mother's costumed identity and then by her relationship to Dr. Manhattan. Similarly, Dreiberg's heroic identity is derived from Hollis Mason's legacy as the first Nite Owl; however, Dreiberg appears not as satisfied as Juspeczyk with hanging up his mask and tights. After all, Dreiberg willingly assumed the role of the second Nite Owl out of respect and admiration for his idol, Hollis Mason, the aging retired hero who Dreiberg visits at his apartment, where the two reminisce about times-gone-by. Juspeczyk's seemingly certain assertion that the Keene Act was best for both herself and the others is contradicted by the image in the very next panel on the same page. Dreiberg, with furrowed brow, stares at the Comedian's button, a reminder of his time with the Crimebusters, which Rorschach left at his home earlier that day. Next to him, Juspeczyk absently stares off into the distance. This silent moment certainly tells a different story than the words of their conversation. Both seem to be looking for something that is currently missing from their lives.

Soon after her unsettling visit from Rorschach, her reunion dinner with Dreiberg, and her bitter meeting with her mother in California, Juspeczyk's relationship with Dr. Manhattan reaches a breaking point; she leaves and seeks refuge with Dreiberg. Janey Slater's interview with *Nova Express* is juxtaposed with Juspeczyk's flight from the Rockefeller Military Research Center for two pages, suggesting that their experiences with Dr. Manhattan are quite similar (3.6–7). As Slater explains to the reporter how distant he became near the end of their relationship, Juspeczyk journeys to Dreiberg's apartment. Overlaid on a silent panel while Juspeczyk rides in a cab, Janey Slater explains, "I kept quiet all these years, but then this latest thing happened and I had to let it all out..." (3.6). Juspeczyk too "lets it all out," allowing herself to explain to Dreiberg how isolated she feels living with Dr. Manhattan, but her therapy session is cut short as Dreiberg is late for *his* weekly session with Mason. She decides to walk with Dreiberg on his way to Mason's. As they turn down a dark alley, they are jumped by a knife-toting gang of Knot Tops, who are not-so-pleasantly surprised to find that the duo is more than prepared for the attack. The ensuing confrontation ends with the remaining gang members fleeing as others lie reeling on the ground in pain. Dreiberg and Juspeczyk breathe heavily as they lean against a wall in the alleyway. Juspeczyk's trench coat is suggestively opened, revealing the top of her chest and the length of her right leg. Dan's hair wildly hangs in front of his face; one hand reaches inside his jacket, appearing to clutch his heart, and the other rests on Juspeczyk's shoulder. Their word balloons, at first separate, become one in the next panel as they look at each other in acknowledgement of what they have just experienced together. Words like "aroused," "intimate moments," and "I think it safest not to pursue this line of thinking" (3.15) are interspersed in the juxtaposed scene featuring Dr. Manhattan's failed interview on Benny Anger's television program. As Dr. Manhattan moves further away from Earth and human existence (literally and figuratively), Dreiberg and Juspeczyk make a significant connection while incidentally fighting crime, and their partnership against the would-be muggers not only foreshadows the intimate relationship that develops between them, but also anticipates their mirrored monomythic transformations. Before leaving, Juspeczyk explains, "Once the adrenaline wears off I always feel sorta weird ... sorta empty" (3.16). Both have yet to accept Rorschach's call to adventure, but both suggest that they feel something is missing from their lives; however, neither knows exactly what it is.

With this initial intimate connection to one another, Juspeczyk and Dreiberg each subsequently serves as a "helper" for the other, a part of the monomyth that Campbell labels as "Supernatural Aid." The helper is a protective figure (often a little old crone or old man) who provides the adventurer with amulets against the dragon forces he is about to pass" (69). The aid that each receives is not in the form of physical objects, but serves as the means by which they are compelled to continue the monomyth cycle. She spends the night away from home, only to return in the morning and find that Dr. Manhattan has left Earth due to accusations that he caused cancer in a variety of his past acquaintances. A very annoyed government agent informs Juspeczyk of his flight: "I don't know where you spent last night, Ms. Juspeczyk, but haven't you read the papers? Dr. Manhattan left Earth.[...] Did you place Dr. Osterman under any emotional stress last night?" (3.23). The tone of the conversation implies that Juspeczyk is to blame for "the linch-pin of America's strategic superiority" leaving Earth (3.23), and the emphasis on Juspeczyk's absence suggests that she has shirked her duty of keeping Dr. Manhattan company. Juspeczyk is subsequently and unceremoniously fired from her government position, leaving her without a job or a home: "They said I can't live there anymore, now that Jon's gone. Plus, they suspended my expense account so all I have is my savings. It was just 'okay, we're taking your home and money. Chew on that'" (5.10). Juspeczyk seeks Dreiberg's assistance and comfort, and while at lunch, Dreiberg aptly asks, "So where will you stay? Did you call your mother?" to which she responds, "Oh, she'd love that I'd sooner sleep on a grating" (5.10). Unable to turn to her mother or Dr. Manhattan, the two main "caregivers" that she has had throughout her life, she begins to make an emotional attachment to Dreiberg by accepting his invitation to stay with him.[4]

Although this tremendous disruption in her life moves her closer to Dreiberg, the reconnection between the two characters does not immediately lead to any drastic change for either one. When both characters were still actively adventuring, each was paired off with their respective partners, who helped to both validate and define their masked adventurer roles, Dreiberg with Rorschach and Juspeczyk with Dr. Manhattan. At the time of Dr. Manhattan's flight from Earth, both Dreiberg and Juspeczyk are without these partners, and their reconnection with each other serves as a way that the two can begin the monomyth together. They become partners—or, using Campbell's terminology, helpers—for one another: "What such a figure represents is the benign, protecting power of destiny" (71). Protection and comfort as a person is what Juspeczyk seeks in Dreiberg, and he receives from her the confidence in himself to don his Nite Owl garb once again. That is, Dreiberg reinforces her personal identity, and she reinforces his heroic one.

For Juspeczyk, Dreiberg offers a sympathetic ear as he patiently listens to her rants on Dr. Manhattan's lack of understanding in their relationship. Feeling relieved after the confrontation with the Knot Tops is over, Juspeczyk says, "God, y'know, it feels so much better now it's out in the open. Thanks for listening" (3.16). Juspeczyk probably means for the "it" in this statement to refer to her ailing relationship with Dr. Manhattan, but the "it" that is "out in the open" is also her reunion and relationship with Dreiberg. As she spends more time with Drieberg, she reveals that she is less concerned with her breakup than she is with the immense feelings of isolation that she experienced while living at Rockefeller: she "got the bad side of isolation without the compensations, like privacy. There was nobody to talk to, but I'd always feel like I was under observation" (7.10). Juspeczyk describes her relationship with Dr. Manhattan as simultaneously intrusive and isolating, and disregards the possibility that Dreiberg could feel the same way; however, Dreiberg understands all too well. Throughout their conversation, he at first longingly looks at his Nite Owl suit that stands in the open locker. A profile view of the mask looms in the foreground over three consecutive panels as Juspeczyk explains her feelings of always being under "observation." As the characters begin to ascend the stairs into the kitchen, the costume is still in view in the background behind Dreiberg, and actually becomes the focus of the next panel as they move out of view. Juspeczyk's words that balloon from the right side of the panel ironically juxtapose with the Nite Owl costume: "It must be great for you, having a secret identity, a secret place nobody knows about.[...] Nobody watching you" (7.10). The costume, lit ominously from the front, casts a shadow behind it and to the left that resembles motion lines. This inanimate object looks as if it could move out of the locker and follow the pair (or at least Dreiberg) right up the stairs. Throughout the scene, Dreiberg is being watched, similar to the way that Juspeczyk was watched while living at Rockefeller; however, Dreiberg cannot simply leave to escape as Juspeczyk did. Dreiberg is under observation from within by another aspect of his identity.

Even though Juspeczyk does not yet recognize the similarities between herself and Dreiberg, she serves as a helper for his monomythic journey by doing her own share of listening. As he explains how his interest in costumed adventuring began, he dismisses the time spent as Nite Owl II as an "adolescent romantic thing" (7.7) that seems to embarrass him. At least, this is what he explains to Juspeczyk, but she tries to comfort him, saying, "Wasn't anything good about those years? I mean, all these gadgets you designed.... If that was me, I'd feel proud" (7.9). Juspeczyk again sees a distinction between herself and Dreiberg when it comes to their costumed crime-fighting days. Juspeczyk, having no choice or real desire to participate in the first place, has nothing to show for her time spent as Silk Spectre. Dreiberg, on the other hand, is noticeably distraught about losing this heroic era of his life, and the loss renders him literally impotent (7.19). Juspeczyk provides more "supernatural aid" in her role as Drieberg's helper when she suggests that they suit up in their costumes and take Archie out for a spin, an act that is clearly done for his sake more so than for her own benefit. When they spot a tenement fire on their flight, both agree that they have to help rescue the people trapped inside, but Dreiberg is more enthusiastic about the rescue than Juspeczyk. While Dreiberg announces that they will be serving coffee and that he will put on some music in the cabin for the passengers' enjoyment, Juspeczyk irritably tells the last person to be rescued, "I don't care about your 'allergies' or your 'medicine' just get in the ship, you asshole" (7.25). The incident empowers Dreiberg, evidenced by their successful lovemaking in the Owl Ship. Thinking that this incident was enough to bring down his inhibitions concerning their relationship, Juspeczyk coyly asks, "What shall we do next?" Thinking that he will want to continue their intimate rendezvous, she is instead surprised by his answer: "I've been thinking about that, and I feel we have certain obligations to our fraternity. I think we should spring Rorschach" (7.28). Not only were Dreiberg's sexual inhibitions lowered, but so too were any feelings of doubt related to his costumed adventuring. Juspeczyk inadvertently gives him the assurance that it is acceptable to continue costumed adventuring even though it is against the law.

With the confidence that Juspeczyk gives to Dreiberg, and the comfort that he gives to her in return, the couple is confronted with the reality and danger of freeing Rorschach from prison. On the monomyth cycle, after the hero receives some sort of supernatural aid, he or she is ready for "The Crossing of the First Threshold": "With the personification of his destiny to guide and aid him, the hero goes forward in his adventure until he comes to the 'threshold guardian' at the entrance to the zone of magnified power" (Campbell 77). Juspeczyk and Dreiberg have broken the law; even though they save numerous lives by stopping to help the victims of the tenement fire, their night of adventuring is still illegal. Soon after their return to Dreiberg's apartment, Dreiberg receives a visit from Detective Fine, the detective who is investigating Edward Blake's murder. The visit is supposedly in regard to Blake's death; Fine tells Dreiberg that he knows that he attended the funeral, along with Veidt and Dr. Manhattan, but Fine is clearly visiting for another reason: "Funny ... There's been a lot of 'heroic figures' in the news lately: Rorschach captured, Veidt shot at, Doc Manhattan leaves Earth, damn near kicking off World War Three ..." (8.8). He also mentions the tenement fire from the past weekend: "I mean, rescuing fire victims, nobody condemns that, but if it went any further ... it's like *Nova Express* says: "Spirit of '77" (8.9). He makes it very clear that he knows Dreiberg's identity as Nite Owl, and the visit is supposed to serve as a warning for Dreiberg and any of the other costumed vigilantes to forget any future plans for adventuring.[5] In Campbell's monomyth structure, Fine functions as the "threshold guardian," a representative of the established limits of conventional law and order, and he stands between Dreiberg and Juspeczyk and their continuation with adventuring and their completion of the monomyth. Campbell explains that this is a test of the hero's will:

> One had better not challenge the watcher of the established bounds. And yet—
> it is only by advancing beyond those bounds, provoking the destructive other
> aspect of the same power, that the individual passes, either alive or in death, into
> a new zone of experience.... The adventure is always and everywhere a passage
> beyond the veil of the known into the unknown; the powers that watch at the
> boundary are dangerous; to deal with them is risky; yet for anyone with compe-
> tence and courage the danger fades [82].

For Dreiberg and Juspeczyk, crossing the threshold involves not heeding Fine's
implied warning and breaking Rorschach out of jail. Defying the "threshold
guardian," they literally descend into a world of chaos. A riot has erupted in
the penitentiary, and both the guards in the watchtowers and the unruly prisoners pose a threat to the costumed duo (8.15). Their very existence lies on a
threshold between the criminals that they very likely helped put behind bars
eight years ago and the guards, who uphold the law and order that they are now
breaking in order to rescue Rorschach.

Both have the "competence," as Campbell puts it, to complete the task, but
the extent to which both have "courage" is questionable. Juspeczyk hesitantly asks,
"How did you talk me into this? This is getting scary..." (8.16). Even afterwards,
she explains that the event is of no direct benefit to her: "This whole situation's
grotesque. Dan thought springing you [Rorschach] might help; I played along"
(8.21). As her personal relationship with Dreiberg becomes more intimate, her feelings for him compel her to "play along" with him as a costumed adventurer, even
though such play is illegal. She has crossed the threshold, although she may not
have been ready or willing to do so at first: "The usual person is more than content, he is even proud, to remain within the indicated bounds, and popular belief
gives him every reason to fear so much as the first step into the unexplored"
(Campbell 78). But she still takes that "step," and there is no turning back.

Once back at Dreiberg's home, Rorschach, Dreiberg, and Juspeczyk begin
to ready their things; they know that the police are not far behind. As Juspeczyk
gathers her things, she is surprised by Dr. Manhattan, who appears in her room
and informs her, "Our conversation is going to take place [on Mars]. You're
going to convince me to save the world" (8.23). Juspeczyk leaves with Dr. Manhattan, and Dreiberg leaves with Rorschach. They are about to go on separate
but parallel adventures into unknown worlds:

> Once having traversed the threshold, the hero moves in a dream landscape of curi-
> ously fluid, ambiguous forms, where he must survive a succession of trials.... The
> hero is covertly aided by the advice, amulets, and secret agents of the supernat-
> ural helper whom he met before his entrance into this region. Or it may be that
> he here discovers for the first time that there is a benign power everywhere sup-
> porting him in his superhuman passage [Campbell 97].

Each is "covertly aided" by the confidence and comfort each receives from the
other, but each also receives "aid" from their former partners (Dreiberg from
Rorschach and Juspeczyk from Dr. Manhattan), who will accompany them on
their respective journeys as they enter new worlds.

In chapter 9, with Dr. Manhattan as her guide, Juspeczyk ascends to Mars, the unknown world, for her "Road of Trials" where she will come to a revelation that will transform how she perceives her past and her identity. Campbell's "Road of Trials" may include a number of different tests for the hero, one of which is a "Meeting with the Goddess." If one assumes that Dr. Manhattan functions as a "God," then Juspeczyk's meeting with him on Mars could be identified as such a meeting. However, Juspeczyk has never perceived Dr. Manhattan as a "god." Rather, Dr. Manhattan has served as a surrogate father figure and lover for the majority of her adult life, as she never knew the true identity of her biological father (presumed to be Hooded Justice), nor did she have a bond with her stepfather as a child (9.8). For Juspeczyk, the major trial she endures at the "nadir of the mythological round" (Campbell 246) is an "Atonement with the Father," a realization that leads to a new understanding of both Dr. Manhattan, her surrogate father figure, and Edward Blake, the Comedian, her biological father.

Dr. Manhattan informs her that their purpose on Mars is to debate the "destiny of the world," but the debate seems decidedly unequal. Dr. Manhattan's godlike ability to foresee the future (and, by extension, the outcome of the debate) frustrates her: "I mean, this is ridiculous. Why hold a debate when you already know the goddamned outcome?" (9.6). Finally conceding to carry through with the conversation anyway on the condition that he "help [her] understand," he has her think back to her earliest memory (9.6). Juspeczyk moves through a series of memories that bring her back to different moments in her past, all of which focus on her misconstrued relationship with her biological father. She remembers her mother and her mother's husband fighting: "He was always yelling, probably because he knew I wasn't his" (9.8). She daydreams of a Minutemen reunion at her home when she was just thirteen; Mason mistakenly recommends his new autobiography that discusses her mother's rape. At the first meeting of the Crimebusters, she meets Dr. Manhattan and the Comedian for the first time. In 1973, she and Dr. Manhattan attend a dinner banquet in honor of Blake at which she drunkenly confronted him about the rape (9.10–21). For her entire life, she has viewed Blake as a monster, someone who brutally raped her mother, and has believed that Hooded Justice was her biological father, someone whose true identity was never discovered.

All of her memories come flooding back even though she resists Dr. Manhattan's advice: "If you'd only relax enough to see the whole continuum, life's pattern or lack of one, then you'd understand my perspective. You're deliberately shutting out understanding[...] I think you're avoiding something" (9.23). Finally she is able to "understand" as Dr. Manhattan understands. She sees her "life's pattern," and, in retrospect, sees all of the clues pointing to her biological father's identity. For Juspeczyk, "atonement with the father" is a confrontation of both aspects of the father figure that Campbell identifies as representing the "id" and "superego" of the inner psyche:

> The ogre aspect of the father is a reflex of the victim's own ego—derived from the sensational nursery scene that has been left behind, but projected before; and the fixating idolatry of that pedagogical nonthing is itself the fault that keeps one steeped in a sense of sin, sealing the potentially adult spirit from a better balanced, more realistic view of the father, and therewith of the world. Atonement (at-one-ment) consists in no more than the abandonment of that self-generated double monster—the dragon thought to be God (superego) and the dragon thought to be Sin (repressed id). But this requires an abandonment of the attachment to ego itself, and that is what is difficult. One must have a faith that the father is merciful, and then a reliance on that mercy. Therewith, the center of belief is transferred outside of the bedeviling god's tight scaly ring, and the dreadful ogres dissolve [Campbell 129–30].[6]

Juspeczyk has constructed a reality ("a pedagogical nonthing") of who she believes Blake to be, and she has denied the clues that would have led her to recognize that he is, in fact, her father. She has seen him as a wicked person, a literal embodiment of the "id," a man who brutally beat and attempted to rape her mother. In addition, although Juspeczyk does not see Dr. Manhattan as a "God" or as a representative of the moral conscience of the "superego," Dr. Manhattan represents the other side of this "father spectrum" for Juspeczyk, the father figure that she never had. When she experiences all of these memories related to Blake at once (at-one-*mo*ment), she divorces herself from both constructed realities: Blake is no longer "the monster," and Dr. Manhattan is no longer the guardian or protector on whom she can rely to "straighten everything" (8.21). She at once both acknowledges and divorces herself from reliance on either man, and is surprised to find that she has made a difference in Dr. Manhattan's thinking: she has successfully (although unknowingly) convinced the "God" to return to Earth.

While Juspeczyk ascends to the red planet for her "Road of Trials," Dreiberg *de*scends into the darkness of the underworld.[7] Rorschach and Dreiberg are pursued by the police, and in order take cover, Dreiberg submerges the Owl Ship under the water of a nearby river to wait for nightfall. When they emerge and dock near Rorschach's neighborhood, Rorschach explains that they must proceed by "mak[ing] inquiries amongst underworld" (10.5). Where Rorschach "lives" is mythologically symbolic: while breaking Rorschach out of jail, Dreiberg, referencing the gruesome remnants of the prison riot, says, "All this stuff, this horror and madness, he [Rorschach] attracts it. It's his world. This is where he lives ... in this sordid, violent twilight zone ... under this shadow" (8.18). Rorschach lives in Campbell's underworld. As they climb out of the Owl Ship, Dreiberg is pictured standing on top of the ship as Rorschach reaches for the dock (10.4). The river serves as a border or boundary separating two different worlds, like the River Styx, one of the rivers in Greek mythology that separates the world of the living from that of the dead.[8] They have traversed a body of water to reach their destination, and their time spent under the water serves as a portal between the everyday world (the traditional, law-abiding society) and that of the underworld. After Rorschach retrieves his "personal effects" (10.4) from under the floorboards of his apartment, they re-submerge for the day to wait for nightfall. Once it is dark, Dreiberg agrees to ask questions in the underworld as Rorschach has been recommending: "Let's go up to visit the criminal fraternity ... and really start plumbing the depths[...] Hell, it'll be like coming home" (10.11). Although Rorschach and Dreiberg worked together on investigations in the past (possibly following leads in the same locations), this is not exactly "coming home" for Dreiberg, as he may suspect. Based on the laws that are in place, he is a criminal for both his costumed adventuring and for helping Rorschach, a wanted felon, escape from prison. No longer are his actions condoned, and he essentially occupies the same position as the criminals that he intends to help interrogate; and the fact that he does not think any of this suggests how far beyond the threshold he has come.

The next stop in Dreiberg's road of trials is at Happy Harry's Bar and Grill, where he discovers that Hollis Mason, the first Nite Owl, was brutally murdered the night before in a case of mistaken identity: the gang was actually targeting Dreiberg. When the murderous group of Knot Tops plan their revenge on the "super dupers," they are specifically looking for "some owl character," who they believe to be responsible for springing Rorschach from prison (8.25). The tragic news is the catalyst for Dreiberg's monomythic "atonement with the father." Mason served as a father figure and mentor for Dreiberg. Earlier, he explains to Juspeczyk, "I idolized him.[...] Hollis was my hero" (7.5, 8). As for Dreiberg's biological father, Dreiberg explains that "he always seemed disappointed in me. He wanted me to follow him into banking, but I was just interested in birds and airplanes and mythology" (7.5). Dreiberg sees Mason as much more than the person from whom he inherited his job title; he is a supportive father figure, more so than even his biological father. Dreiberg reacts to the news with brutal force by savagely choking his informant: "Who did it? Tell me who did it, you slime! Who murdered Hollis?[...] You tell them! Tell them they're dead! You know how much fire power I have floating out there? I oughtta take out this entire rat-hole neighborhood! I oughtta ... oughtta break your neck, you ... you ..." (10.16). Not only is Dreiberg on the other side of the law now that he is back adventuring, but his violent threats and actions are at least as brutal as those of his adversaries, the "criminal fraternity." Dreiberg's "atonement with the father" is an ironic twist on Campbell's construct:

> Ideally, the invested one has been divested of his mere humanity and is representative of an impersonal cosmic force. He is the twice-born: he has become himself the father. And he is competent, consequently, now to enact himself the role of the initiator, the guide, the sun door, through whom one may pass from the infantile illusions of "good" and "evil" to an experience of the majesty of cosmic law, purged of hope and fear, and at peace in understanding of the revelation of being [136–37].

Dreiberg is certainly "divested of his mere humanity"; his attitude in the bar is more bestial than humane. He has unknowingly "become himself the father" in the sense that Dreiberg was the intended target of the Nite Owl murder, and his actions have indirectly caused his father figure's death. His passage from "the infantile illusions of 'good' and 'evil'" is not a comforting or peaceful "understanding." In the final panel of the encounter between the Knot Top and Dreiberg, he exclaims in a moment of revelation, "Oh god damn. God damn god damn god damn!" (10.16). His lips part slightly and his eyebrows rise in dismay, making the wrinkles on his brow visible under the cover of his costume. Dreiberg is just as "evil" as, if not worse than, the innocent Knot Top that he physically assaults.

Dreiberg is still in the "underworld" depths of his monomyth voyage, and the allusions to death and the afterlife continue as he and Rorschach move on to seek Veidt's help. As they leave Happy Harry's, Dreiberg ironically remarks, "I remember Adrian once telling me that the Egyptians regarded death as a voyage..." (10.16). While Dreiberg takes "the role of the initiator" in searching Veidt's computer for some answers, Rorschach examines the Egyptian relics that line the walls of the office: "Funny ... ancient pharaohs looked forward to end of world: believed cadavers would rise, reclaim hearts from golden jars. Must be currently holding breath with anticipation. Understand now why always mistrusted fascination with relics and dead kings ... in final analysis, it's us or them" (10.20). Dreiberg reveals the possibility of a terrible truth; the enemy for whom they have been searching may, in fact, be Veidt himself. As he radios up the Owl Ship, the top of the ship and its headlights illuminate the two adventurers, bathing them in a sun-like glow through the plate-glass window of Veidt's high-rise. Although Dreiberg's earlier "atonement with the father" did not accomplish exactly what is expected by Campbell's construct, the two adventurers symbolically pass through what Campbell calls the "sun door" on their way to the next leg of their "long journey" (10.21).

When Dreiberg and Juspeczyk are reunited at Karnak, they experience an ironic variation of Campbell's "Sacred Marriage" or "Meeting with the Goddess." According to Campbell, this event is where the hero unites with a goddess figure, who then leads him to a revelation about the meaning of life beyond mortality. After they discover Veidt to be the mastermind behind not only the Comedian's murder, but also a plot that killed half the population of New York City, they are left alone and decide to find "someplace quiet" in order to think over the devastating reality of recent events. Juspeczyk is overwhelmed as she tells Dreiberg about the scene she witnessed in New York: "It doesn't matter. After New York, nothing matters. That's what I'm trying to say. Dan, please ... sit with me. I need you.[...] Need you now. Dan, all those people, they're dead. They can't disagree or eat Indian food, or love each other.... Oh it's sweet. Being alive is so damn sweet" (12.22). They lie naked together in recognition of both the value and vulnerability of human life: "The meeting with the goddess (who is incarnate in every woman) is the final test of the talent of the hero to win the boon of love (charity: *amor fati*), which is life itself enjoyed as the encasement of eternity" (Campbell 118). *Amor fati* is a Latin phrase meaning a love of one's fate. No matter what positive or negative events happen in one's life, one should love them all because *all* events represent one's movement toward a determined destiny. Juspeczyk's realization that "nothing matters" could be construed as *amor fati*, but also simple nihilism. She loves her own and Dreiberg's "fate" in the sense that they both are still living; they were spared from the tragedy in New York. The couple does not necessarily love life as "the encasement of eternity"; but, rather ironically, the last words between the two before their sexual union is in reference to Dreiberg's cologne, "Nostalgia." Dreiberg and Juspeczyk realize that life is *not* eternal, that they must live life while they are still alive, and the reference to Dreiberg's "Nostalgia" cologne suggests that they wish to forget about the present reality and think back to a time prior to the tragedy in New York. That is, embracing the past is more reliable and satisfying than embracing the future.

Campbell suggests that the goddess is "incarnate in every woman," and that it is the male hero's accomplishment if he is to "win" her. This suggests that Dreiberg would be the hero here, and that Juspeczyk would represent the "goddess figure." However, he does not "win" her. Neither has to convince the other; if anything, Juspeczyk takes a more active role than Dreiberg. He is more concerned with Dr. Manhattan's knowledge of his and Juspeczyk's relationship. Is Juspeczyk operating in the role of hero here or is Dreiberg? Are the roles reversed when she gains some revelation by being with Dreiberg? If one is to consider Juspeczyk as the hero, Campbell explains that the "sacred marriage" is different when the hero is female: "And when the adventurer, in this context, is not a youth but a maid, she is the one who, by her qualities, her beauty, or her yearning, is fit to become the consort of an immortal. Then the heavenly husband descends to her and conducts her to his bed — whether she will or no. And if she has shunned him, the scales fall from her eyes; if she has sought him, her desire finds its peace" (119). Campbell's explanation suggests that it is not *possible* for the female hero to "win" the love of the god or initiate such a revelation; the female hero accomplishes a sacred marriage simply through her "beauty," and the event is contingent upon whether the "god" will accept her. The female's role is a passive one, whether she be the goddess or the female hero. In contrast, the scene between Dreiberg and Juspeczyk is between two seemingly equal heroes.

As we have seen, readers may follow both Dreiberg and Juspeczyk through what appear to be realizations of their respective heroic potentials by closely following the stages of Campbell's monomyth structure in apparently mirrored paths, and by piecing together evidence to show that both characters are "heroes." Other readers may conclude quite differently that, as Juspeczyk reveals, "nothing matters." Additionally, Dreiberg and Juspeczyk's false "sacred marriage" suggests that "nothing matters," not even the reader's understanding of heroism and the characters, who seem to have embodied heroic constructs all along. The end of the narrative provides little comfort. The characters "return" to society after their monomyth-like visits to other worlds, and are "reborn" as Sam and Sandra Hollis. Both discard their civilian identities by changing their names and appearances, as first revealed when they arrive at Sally Jupiter's California home. When Jupiter opens the door, readers are greeted by the Hollises; Jupiter's television provides the narration: "... in which Robert Culp is physically transformed by ... The Architects of Fear!" (12.28). The television program juxtaposes with the couple's new identities, suggesting that they have perhaps changed their identities out of *fear* rather than out of heroism or courage. Juspeczyk even remarks, "I get nervous, waiting around..." (12.29). Even though they have returned to society, they are not considered heroes in the monomythic sense unless they fully complete the hero's journey, which includes distinct action after the return:

> When the hero-quest has been accomplished, ... the adventurer still must return with his life-transmuting trophy. The full round, the norm of the monomyth, requires that the hero shall now begin the labor of bringing the runes of wisdom, the Golden Fleece, or his sleeping princess, back into the kingdom of humanity, where the boon may redound to the renewing of the community, the nation, the planet, or the ten thousand worlds [Campbell 193].

Why does the couple change their identities? Are they afraid of Veidt or of the police, who now know that Dan Dreiberg and the second Nite Owl are the same person? There is evidence that they plan to continue adventuring (12.30), and there is no indication that the Keene Act has changed, which would mean that they plan on covertly engaging in an illegal activity. With this adventuring, the readers are unaware if they will bring any "runes of wisdom" back to society. Even though Dreiberg and Juspeczyk have answered the "call to adventure," challenged the "threshold guardians," and even experienced the "road of trials," neither clearly brings back any boon or restorative property to society. They are living in secrecy, presumably out of "fear," and readers cannot know for sure if they complete their monomythic transformations into heroes. The answers lie beyond the end of the narrative, and it is up to the reader to, as Thomson suggests, speculate based on "the many different angles of the shards left lying on the ground" (101).

Adrian Veidt

For Adrian Veidt, the monomyth is a conscious expedition that results in a created heroic persona. Through his determination to follow and ultimately succeed his hero, Alexander the Great, Veidt manufactures for himself (and for the world) a "hero," someone who appears to conform to the ideal heroic archetype. In chapter 11, Veidt invites his servants to his vivarium, where he tells the story of his journey. He explains how different he was even as a child, and that his parents "were intellectually unremarkable, possessing no obvious genetic advantages" (11.8). Even after his parents' deaths when he was just seventeen, he realized that there was "nobody whose advice might prove useful. Nobody living" (11.8). From the start, Veidt took a condescending attitude toward his fellow man; he saw his intelligence and ability as far superior to anyone else on the planet.

Turning to the only person with whom he could identify, Veidt consciously sets out on a quest to become a hero by following Alexander the Great. According to Campbell, the call to adventure "signifies that destiny has summoned the hero and transferred his spiritual center of gravity from within the pale of his society to a zone of unknown" (58). From what Veidt tells his servants, it appears that his superior intellect and ability have shaped his "destiny" to become a hero; he is simply using his intellectual superiority to its full potential. Ironically, however, Veidt does not undertake his own journey. Instead, he is simply "retrac[ing his] hero's steps" (11.8). By following the existing and known path that Alexander took more than two thousand years before, he never really enters the "zone of the unknown." There is no danger or uncertainty with the trajectory of a journey already mapped out before the adventurer. Veidt even explains, "I followed the path of Alexander's war machine ... imagining his armies taking port after port" (11.10). His quest, and any of the stages of the monomyth to which he might happen to conform, are "imagined," constructed for self-validation. His only trip to an "unknown" world is by way of a drug trip, induced by some Tibetan hashish: "The night before returning to America, I wandered into the desert and ate a ball of hashish I'd been given in Tibet. The ensuing vision transformed me. Wading through powdered history, I heard dead kings walking underground; heard fanfares sound through human skulls" (11.10).

Veidt's faux adventure to the "unknown" even includes an artificial "road of trials." He creates false adversity when he gives away his parents' money to make a challenge for himself: "I gave away my inheritance to demonstrate the possibility of achieving anything starting from nothing" (11.8). But even this supposed fact from Veidt's past is questionable. After all, he certainly has the money to travel the world, following the footsteps of a long-dead hero, with no evidence that he had to work, beg, borrow, or steal in order to make the journey. The story suits his purpose by suggesting that he has been through a series of tests or trials in order to achieve the heroic status he now believes himself to have. Even more ironic is the fact that Veidt's servants, his audience for this tale of adventure, are being poisoned as he speaks. Essentially, Veidt tells his heroic story of accomplishments to himself, validating his belief that he is a hero. His logic is flawed, a variation of Descartes' *cogito, ergo sum*, meaning "I think; therefore, I am." Veidt's hero journey is based on his belief that he is a hero or destined to be one: I think that I am a hero; therefore, I am a hero. In an interview with *Nova Express*, he explains how anyone can become a hero by first simply *thinking* that he or she is one: "You get to be a superhero by believing in the hero within you and summoning him or her forth by an act of will. Believing in yourself and your own potential is the first step to realizing that potential. Alternatively, you could do as Jon did: Fall into a nuclear reactor and hope for the best" (11.30).

After believing himself more than capable of being a hero, Veidt sets out to *surpass* Alexander the Great, his heroic father figure, seeing himself as better able to complete what Alexander failed to do. As Campbell explains:

> The traditional idea of initiation [atonement with the father] combines an introduction of the candidate into the techniques, duties, and prerogatives of his vocation with a radical readjustment of his emotional relationship to his parental images. The mystagogue (father or father substitute) is to entrust the symbols of office not only to a son who has been effectually purged of all inappropriate infantile cathexes—for whom the just, impersonal exercise of the powers will not be rendered impossible by unconscious (or perhaps even conscious and rationalized) motives of self-aggrandizement, personal preference, or resentment [136].

For Veidt, Alexander the Great is "the only human being with whom [he] felt any kinship" (11.8). What Campbell refers to as the "radical readjustment of his emotional relationship" with the father figure is, for Veidt, that he understands himself to be superior. The only "atonement" that occurs is a self-fulfilling ego-boost that validates Veidt's drive to continue with his journey, which is now guided by a blinding determination to outdo Alexander's accomplishments: "Where he'd turned back to quell dissent at home, I travelled on, through China and Tibet, gathering martial wisdom as I went.[...] I saw at last his failings" (11.10). He is driven by what Campbell calls "self-aggrandizement," not necessarily publicly recognized, but by his personal goals of succeeding where Alexander failed, and by surpassing his hero, who at one time seemed unsurpassable. After all, he has no need for an audience or any public recognition because he feels he is superior to his fellow man by having had the self-discipline and perseverance to complete (at least, in his mind) a monomythic transformation.

Upon his monomythic "return" to society, he vows to fight crime as a costumed adventurer, bringing the "boon" of his superior intelligence and ability back to society for benefit of the greater good. Beyond "self-aggrandizement" as a motivation for uniting the world, Veidt is also motivated by what Campbell refers to as "resentment." At the first and only meeting of the Crimebusters, the Comedian calls attention to Veidt's naiveté when dealing with the problems facing America and the world. The incident left an indelible impression on Veidt. He was determined to "deny his [the Comedian's] kind their last black laugh at Earth's expense. I also swore that when next I met Blake or any other foe, though perhaps not on my territory ... it would certainly be on my terms"

(11.19). Veidt wants revenge, but Veidt covers for this motive by failing to mention that the Comedian's "black laugh" was directed at him and his actions. The Comedian makes a fool of Veidt at the Crimebusters meeting, and the event motivated Veidt toward his plan, or else he *would* end up, as Blake explained, "the smartest man on the cinder." He suddenly realizes that he must do more than simply fight the "symptoms" of society's ills: "I despised myself; my sham crusade. Knowing mankind's problems, I'd blinded myself to them" (11.19). Veidt acknowledges that his "crusade" against crime was a "sham," but not the means by which he has become a hero—his constructed monomyth-like journey. Without uniting the world, Veidt would be unable to surpass Alexander the Great's accomplishments, and without "trick[ing the world]; frighten[ing] it towards salvation with history's greatest practical joke," he would not get his much-desired revenge on Blake (11.24).

Veidt sees himself as superior to others, bearing the burden of fixing mankind's problems when no one else is capable. Campbell would perhaps label Veidt's self-appointed hero status as a false invention: "one may invent a false, finally unjustified, image of oneself as an exceptional phenomenon in the world, not guilty as others are, but justified in one's inevitable sinning because one represents the good. Such self-righteousness leads to a misunderstanding, not only of oneself but of the nature of both man and the cosmos" (238). Veidt even markets a program that enables buyers to learn the step-by-step approach on how to become heroes: "The Veidt Method is designed to produce bright and capable young men and women who will be fit to inherit the challenging, promising, and often difficult world that awaits in our future.... If followed correctly, [the Veidt Method] can turn YOU into a superhuman, fully in charge of your own destiny" (10.32). Veidt sells the do-it-yourself faux monomyth that he himself completed; as long as one follows the steps of his or her purchased Veidt Method and believes that he or she is a hero, the person then becomes a hero.

Having completed the steps of his monomyth-like journey, Veidt believes that he is best suited to bring Campbell's "ultimate boon" back to society because of his intellectual superiority and his self-confirmed heroic status. With his plan accomplished, Veidt believes that he has succeeded in achieving his goal to permanently unite the world based on all of humanity's common fear of invasion by an otherworldly force. He asks Dr. Manhattan, "I did the right thing, didn't I? It all worked out in the end." And Dr. Manhattan replies, "'In the end?' Nothing ends, Adrian. Nothing ever ends" (12.27). In his blinding determination to surpass Alexander the Great and to take revenge on the Comedian, the smartest man in the world overlooks the fact that a utopian society simply cannot last. The only certainty is the uncertainty of the future, and without this knowledge the hero is flawed: "The hero is the champion of things becoming, not of things become, because he *is* .... He does not mistake apparent changelessness in time for the permanence of Being, nor is he fearful of the next moment (or of the 'other thing'), as destroying the permanent with its change" (Campbell 243). The news broadcasts ironically foreshadow that the present world peace cannot last forever: "Could further attacks be imminent? We think not. Imagine an Alien bee, not very intelligent, that stings reflexively on death" (12.25). The emotional shock of the event will eventually subside. In time, people will become less fearful of another alien attack, reopening the potential for human conflict, aggression, and war. Veidt's false monomyth and "ultimate boon" have not accomplished anything more than temporary peace.

Dr. Manhattan

Whereas Veidt creates his own hero's journey to substantiate his status as a hero, Dr. Manhattan has a heroic status created for him. In 1959, Jon Osterman is accidentally locked in a test chamber for intrinsic field separation experiments. The accident transforms him into Dr. Manhattan, a super-powered being who slowly becomes more super and less human. In his musings on Mars in chapter 4, Dr. Manhattan relates the story of the accident. As the scheduled experiment begins for the intrinsic field separation of concrete block fifteen, he explains that the "air grows too warm, too quickly" and how "the light is taking me to pieces" (4.8). On his way to becoming a "hero," Dr. Manhattan is never called to adventure, and never has the chance to accept or refuse the call. Instead, an accident has forced him to his departure. Rather than confronting a "threshold guardian," as did Dreiberg and Juspeczyk in their monomyth journeys, Dr. Manhattan's departure on his adventure begins with a symbolic journey into what Campbell refers to as "The Belly of the Whale": "The idea that the passage of the magical threshold is a transit into a sphere of rebirth is symbolized in the worldwide womb image of the belly of the whale. The hero, instead of conquering or conciliating the power of the threshold, is swallowed into the unknown, and would appear to have died" (90). Locked inside the "womb" of the test chamber, Jon Osterman's body is literally dissolved, a process that is consistent with Campbell's "belly of the whale" motif: "The physical body of the hero may be actually slain, dismembered, and scattered over the land or sea" (92). Osterman's colleagues have no reason to believe that he has survived the accident; they hold a ceremony in honor of his life.

But over the course of approximately ten days in November 1959, Osterman is miraculously "reborn" as something more consistent with a "god" than a human being. He recreates himself, and Jon Osterman's nude blue form appears for the first time in the Gila Flats cafeteria. The panel is double the width and height of a normal panel in the nine-panel page format. An aura of light surrounds his outstretched body; his arms slightly extend away from his sides, and his palms face outward. As he levitates above the heads of terrified onlookers, his form is reminiscent of many artistic renditions of the Resurrection of

Christ, and his blue skin resembles many artistic renderings of the Hindu deity Krishna. Wally Weaver appropriately exclaims, "Oh, holy god. Willya look at that..." (4.10). Jon Osterman has become a god on Earth, and has changed everything. Janey Slater later explains: "I'm scared because everything feels weird. It's as if everything's changed. Not just you: everything! I mean, I don't know what you are. Nobody does. You were disintegrated, you put yourself back together.... They say you can do anything, Jon. They say you're like god now." He denies the association, saying, "I don't think there is a god, Janey. If there is, I'm not him" (4.11). He may choose to believe that his existence has not altered the world, but the ensuing media coverage and marketing of "Dr. Manhattan" as "the American superman" prove otherwise.

His potential as a lucrative instrument against adversaries is quickly noticed by the American government, who christen him "Dr. Manhattan" and market him as their personal weapon against invasion and attacks by foreign countries. They choose his costume, his "symbol," and even his name: "They're shaping me into something gaudy and lethal.... It's all getting out of my hands..." (4.12). A television reporter announces that the arrival of Dr. Manhattan is "possibly the most significant event in recent world history": "The superman exists, and he's American" (4.13). Even though Dr. Manhattan complies with government mandates and works as a government operative, one must question what sincere interest he truly has in human existence. As time goes on, his emotional connections to human beings dissolve, and any interest that he may have sincerely had in human affairs diminishes. Even though he is "reborn" in the sense that he returns to Earth as a new being, Jon Osterman never really returns. He only completes half of the monomyth, experiencing what Campbell labels the "refusal of return": "The responsibility [of return] has been frequently refused. Even Buddha, after his triumph, doubted whether the message of realization could be communicated, and saints are reported to have passed away while in the supernatural ecstasy. Numerous indeed are the heroes fabled to have taken up residence forever in the blessed isle of the unaging Goddess of Immortal Being" (193). Dr. Manhattan exists in the "isle of the unaging Goddess of Immortal Being" while surrounded by a world that does not. No one else can understand the way that he experiences timelessness. No one else around him can fully grasp what it is like to have the immense powers that he now possesses. He comes back no longer able to relate to anyone in his world, ultimately leading to his final exit from Earth: "Human affairs cannot be my concern. I'm leaving this galaxy for one less complicated" (12.27). This is perhaps the first time that Osterman or Dr. Manhattan has actually made a decision for himself; by his very nature, Dr. Manhattan is the exact opposite of the determined and decisive heroic figure that emerges from Campbell's monomyth. He is and always has been dependent on others making his decisions for him. He is literally "caught in the tangle of their [humans'] lives" (4.25). People, with whom he can no longer relate and from whom he is separate, shape "Dr. Manhattan" into the hero that he does not see himself to be.

Rorschach

In addition to serving as the messenger who delivers Dreiberg and Jus-peczyk's "call to adventure," Rorschach embarks on a monomythic journey of his own; however, his journey starts long before the beginning of the present-day narrative. In chapter 6, Dr. Malcolm Long is appointed to psychologically evaluate Walter Joseph Kovacs, aka Rorschach. Presuming a "classic case of misdirected aggression," Long believes the case to be "perfectly simple" (11). He gives Rorschach a series of inkblot tests to which Rorschach responds with blatant lies, visible by the narrator's juxtaposition of what Rorschach *really* sees in the images. It appears that it is not Rorschach who is "misdirected," but Long, who jumps to the hesitant conclusion that Rorschach "might be getting better" after spending only moments with him (6.1). Over the course of four sessions Long discovers how Walter Joseph Kovacs was "reborn" as Rorschach in his monomyth transformation, and the horrific past that led to where he is today. Kovacs never knew his father, and his mother verbally and physically abused him as a child (6.3–4). At ten years old, Kovacs was taken away from his mother and committed to the Lillian Charlton Home for Problem Children after brutally attacking two other children (6.6–7). At sixteen, he began work in a garment factory, where he became acquainted with the material that would later become his shape-shifting mask — the material was from an unwanted dress ordered by Kitty Genovese, the real-life woman who was murdered in 1964 as many of her neighbors watched (6.10). All of these events helped color Rorschach's worldview in terms of black and white; however, one investigation in particular changed Walter Joseph Kovacs into Rorschach forever.

After learning of the Kitty Genovese murder as an influential event in Rorschach's life, Dr. Long asks, "After the murder of Kitty Genovese you decided to vent your hostility upon the underworld?" (6.14). But Rorschach explains that at this point he was only "pretending to be Rorschach" (6.14). Kitty Gen-ovese's murder was only his "call to adventure" on Campbell's monomyth. It is the event that started his career as a vigilante crime-fighter. His actual descent into the "underworld," where he crosses the threshold of adventure, does not occur until he investigates the 1975 kidnapping case of Blaire Roche. He explains that he "visited the underworld and began hurting people. Put fourteen in hos-pital needlessly"; the fifteenth person gives him an address in a "bad neighbor-hood," to which he arrives at "dusk" (6.18). He discovers two German Shepherds fighting over the bones of the deceased Blaire Roche. He raises a butcher knife to hit the dog and closes his eyes as he lets the cleaver drop: "It was Kovacs who said 'mother' then, muffled under latex. It was Kovacs who closed his eyes. It was Rorschach who opened them again" (6.21). In Rorschach's monomyth, this moment serves as both his transition (crossing of the threshold into the under-world) and an "atonement"— not with a father figure, but with his mother. Killing the dogs is his "atonement" in the sense that it serves as a symbolic reparation for the emotional and physical trauma that she caused him. Thus he passes into the underworld, a place in which he remains for the rest of his natural life.

Upon killing the dogs and leaving Gerald Grice, their murderous owner, to fend for himself, handcuffed in a burning building, Kovacs is "reborn" as Rorschach; but his rebirth does not signify a "return," as is the case with Drieberg and Juspeczyk. Kovacs' rebirth into Rorschach is more analogous to Osterman's rebirth into Dr. Manhattan; both remain in the other world, and neither feel as if they had a choice in the change. Rorschach narrates to Dr. Long his rebirth: "Streets stank of fire. The void breathed hard on my heart, turning its illusions to ice, shattering them. Was reborn then, free to scrawl own design on this morally blank world. Was Rorschach" (6.26). The first three panels of the page are filled with the fire and smoke from the burning building. The hellish imagery alludes to Rorschach's position as fixed in the underworld. As the building burns to the ground, he explains his bleak outlook on humanity: "Born from oblivion; bear children, hell-bound as ourselves, go into oblivion. There is nothing else" (6.26).

Blake, although not close to Rorschach,[9] shared his dark worldview. Blake's death is significant for Rorschach, serving as the initial event that leads to his mask-killer investigation and his subsequent "call to adventure" for Dreiberg and Juspeczyk. Kovacs never knew his biological father, and while at the Charlton Home, an eleven-year-old Kovacs wrote an account of the kind of person he believed his father to be:

> My mom told me she threw my dad out because he was always getting into political arguments with her because he liked President Truman and she didn't. I think perhaps my dad was some sort of aide to President Truman, because he liked him so much. Most probably he was out of the country during the war when I was growing up on some sort of mission. I think he was the kind of guy who would fight for his country and what was right [6.31].

Without a biological father or even a living surrogate father figure to guide him, Rorschach finds a role model and father figure in the Comedian. He explains to Dr. Long how he admired him more than his other masked brethren: "No staying power. None of them. Except Comedian. Met him in 1966. Forceful personality. Didn't care if people liked him. Uncompromising. Admired that. Of us all, he understood most. About world. About people. About society and what's happening to it. Things everyone knows in gut. Things everyone too scared to face, too polite to talk about. He understood" (6.15). Rorschach projects onto the Comedian the kind of person whom he wants to believe his father was. Like the father he describes in his writing, the Comedian is a government "aide," was frequently away on "some sort of mission," and "was the kind of guy who would fight for his country and what was right." The Comedian is the only other costumed adventurer whose commitment to justice Rorschach admires, and Rorschach's intense interest in uncovering information about the

Comedian's murder suggests that he is seeking "atonement" with this father figure, who perhaps never knew that Rorschach admired him.

At the end of the novel, it appears as though Rorschach is incapable of completing the monomyth, making a "return" from the underworld, because he meets his demise in the snow. According to Campbell, without the return to society, the monomyth is incomplete, and the adventurer cannot be considered a hero: "The returning hero, to complete his adventure, must survive the impact of the world" (Campbell 226). However, even though Rorschach's physical body does not "survive the impact of the world," his journal certainly does. Prior to leaving New York for Veidt's Antarctic retreat, Rorschach wraps his journal in a package marked "urgent" and sends it to the *New Frontiersman* (10.22). The narrator meticulously traces the journey of this package from mailbox to recipient.[10] In the final panels, as Seymour reaches for the journal in the crank file of the *New Frontiersman*'s office, the reader can easily extrapolate the possibility that the journal will be read. Could Rorschach's journal be what Campbell refers to as the "ultimate boon" that saves the world? Is this the artifact that finally brings to light the truth behind the atrocities in New York and "restores the world" (Campbell 246)? Much like the fate of Veidt, Dreiberg, and Juspeczyk, readers cannot be certain what happens to Rorschach's journal. Rorschach dies as a mortal being, and it is up to the reader to decide if his heroic journey ends like the rest of the failed heroes in defeat or if he lives on and is "reborn" in the pages of his journal.

Where Are All the Heroes?

Returning to Campbell once more, let us examine what happens to the hero if he or she does, in fact, complete the monomyth and achieves archetypal heroic status as the "Master of Two Worlds":

> The individual, through prolonged psychological disciplines, gives up completely all attachment to his personal limitations, idiosyncrasies, hopes and fears, no longer resist the self-annihilation that is prerequisite to rebirth in the realization of truth and so becomes ripe, at last, for the great at-one-ment. His personal ambitions being totally dissolved, he no longer tries to live but willingly relaxes to whatever may come to pass in him; he becomes, that is to say, an anonymity. The Law lives in him with his unreserved consent [236–37].

The hero must complete the full round of the monomyth journey in order to be considered a hero, but with no positive examples of characters who clearly embody a heroic archetype, where does the reader turn after the end of the narrative? No matter how one defines heroes, whether it be through Campbell's monomyth or by other means of establishing the heroic conventions, it is virtually impossible to call any one of the characters in the narrative purely heroic without ignoring contrary or incomplete evidence that questions a definitive answer. Dreiberg and Juspeczyk become what Campbell refers to as "anonymous," but it is not clear that all of their "hopes and fears" are dissolved. In fact, they still live in fear, suggested by their new identities, but their joint decision to return to adventuring also suggests that this may change. Veidt fiercely "resist[s] the self-annihilation," and his personal ambition never "totally dissolved"; in fact, it is enhanced by the end of the novel. He "tries to live" rather than "willingly relax[ing] to whatever may come to pass in him." He attempts to *forcibly* unite the world. Jon Osterman does not willingly give up his "attachment" to anything, but when transformed into Dr. Manhattan, he gives up *all* attachments; he simply checks out and never returns. As for Rorschach, he accepts his own mortality, and even welcomes this "annihilation" by Dr. Manhattan, but only with the knowledge that there is the potential for his words to live beyond his physical body, vowing to "never surrender." In the end there are no heroes, only those who display heroic traits.

CHAPTER 9

Measuring Up:
Zack Snyder's *Watchmen*

"The book is always better. Seeing a movie made from a favorite novel, or even an ordinary one, the reader-viewer invariably finds something missing, lacking, overstressed or just plain wrong, because it was changed. When we read the book, we make the movie: we cast it, visualize it, control its pacing. We own it. Any other version of the book — say, Hollywood's — competes with our original experience and simply can't measure up."

— Richard Corliss, *Time* magazine[1]

The Unfilmables

"Who watches the watchmen?" asked David Hughes in his 2008 revised edition of his book *The Greatest Sci-Fi Movies Never Made.*[2] The answer to that question, until 2009, was no one: no one could watch *Watchmen* the movie because no one could figure out how to bring it to the big screen. In his book, Hughes depicted the long and seemingly unending journey to when the movie that was "never made" became the movie that actually was. Interest in the prospect of a *Watchmen* film started well before Zack Snyder and company took the helm in 2006 to create the major motion picture *Watchmen*, first released in March 2009. Twenty years earlier, and not long after Moore and Gibbons' *Watchmen* was written and published, Lawrence Gordon Productions obtained the rights for Twentieth Century–Fox for the film adaptation, with Joel Silver slated to produce (A. Thompson). This, however, was only the first of a long list of unsuccessful attempts by different production companies, writers, directors, and producers to bring *Watchmen* to theaters. The project seemed to be doomed from the start. Moore had always adamantly believed that *Watchmen* belonged in the medium in which it was created. There was no reason to adapt, modify, translate, or re-imagine it as a film. In an interview with *Entertainment Weekly*'s Jeff Jenson in October 2005, Moore clarified his feelings for those who believed in the lucrative prospect of *Watchmen* the movie: "My book is a comic book. Not a movie, not a novel. A comic book. It's been made in a certain way, and designed to be read a certain way: in an armchair, nice and cozy next to a fire, with a steaming cup of coffee. Personally, I think that it would make a lovely Saturday night." In *The Mindscape of Alan Moore*, he discussed his work and the relationship that is frequently drawn between graphic narratives and the film medium:

> I feel that if we only see comics in relationship to movies, then the best that they will ever be are films that do not move. I found it, in the mid–80s, preferable to try and concentrate upon those things that only comics could achieve. The way in which a tremendous amount of information could be included visually in every panel, the juxtapositions between what a character was saying and what the image that the reader was looking at would be. So, in a sense, I suppose that you could say that most of my work from the '80s onward was more or less designed to be unfilmable, which is what I had to explain to Terry Gilliam when he was originally selected as the director on the touted *Watchmen* movie that was being discussed at that time.

When the "unfilmable" graphic novel was finally filmed and released in theaters, reviews ranged from masterpiece to muddled mess, and as Lev Grossman of *Time* magazine aptly pointed out, fans of *Watchmen* were "as divided about the movie as they are unanimous about the graphic novel." Many reviewers, intentionally or not, analyzed the value of the film based on its relation to other artifacts, including the original graphic novel and other superhero films; however, these materials were contextual, merely tangentially related to the film. Other critics fell into the trap of a classic *ad hominem* fallacy, attacking graphic novel fans and even Alan Moore himself rather than addressing the text. They imprecisely attempted to quantify the film's value as too much or not enough of what they expected. Some noted what the film should or could have been, and made arguments based on personal preference rather than on specific details innate to the film's construction and presentation. Over the years, the graphic novel was praised and admired by many. It was lauded by filmmaker Terry Gilliam as "the *War and Peace* of graphic novels" (D. Hughes, 148); graphic novelist Brad Meltzer called it the "*Citizen Kane* of comics" (Boucher); and *Lost* co-creator Damon Lindelof said it was "the greatest piece of popular fiction ever produced" (Jensen). Even before the film's release, it looked as though *Watchmen* the film would have a hard time freeing itself from the massive weight of *Watchmen* the graphic novel, its history, and fandom.

From Bad to Worse: Contexts (Mis)understood as Text

Many reviewers had already made up their mind about the quality or value of Snyder's *Watchmen* prior to its theatrical release. If Moore and Gibbons' *Watchmen* was of little value to a reviewer prior to viewing the film, then chances were that he or she would understand Snyder's adaptation to be of even *less* value. Anthony Lane of *The New Yorker* was one such critic, who seemed more interested in suggesting that superhero-themed graphic novels were of little value than in reviewing Snyder's film. The opening sentences of Lane's article suggested his bias: "The world of the graphic novel is a curious one. For every masterwork such as *Persepolis* or *Maus*, there seem to be shelves of cod mythology and rainy dystopias, patrolled by rock-jawed heroes and their melon-breasted sidekicks. Fans of the stuff are masonically loyal, prickling with a defensiveness and an ardor that not even Wagnerians can match." Here, Lane made a clear distinction between works in the superhero genre ("cod mythology" with "rock-jawed heroes") and those such as Speigelman's *Maus* and Satrapi's *Persepolis*, which are graphic memoirs. Certainly, it was reasonable to distinguish between graphic novels and graphic memoirs, but Lane made a genre-based value judgment, dismissing any and *all* works that contained superheroes. He immediately equated the genre with overt sexuality and dark themes ("melon-breasted sidekicks" and "rainy dystopias"), as if the majority of superhero narratives were filled with semi-pornographic material and gore. Lane's review resembled those from more than twenty years ago that perceived *Watchmen* the graphic novel as somehow less valuable than others because of its superhero themes.[3] In other words, Lane posited that one may find value in graphic narratives, but if they also include superheroes, a common genre from their comic-book origins, then they were automatically of lesser value than those that did not.

Lane attacked superhero graphic novels in general, but Philip Kennicott's review in *The Washington Post* was almost entirely based on his disapproval of *Watchmen* the graphic novel specifically. Kennicott considered, "For years, people have wondered if it is filmable. But the real issue is whether the novel is *worth* filming at all." It was a little late for this consideration; the film had already been made, and Kennicott had already begun his review. One may ask how fairly a reviewer could critique the film if he had already dismissed its production upon entering the theater. Instead of critiquing the film's value for what it was worth as a text, Kennicott decided to focus on the inadequacies of the source material: "*Watchmen* [the graphic novel] was fun, but also incredibly pretentious—a word that hardly applies anymore to high culture, but sure comes in handy when dealing with pop culture's more desperate efforts to be taken seriously. By treating the original text as a sacred document, the movie is laughably pretentious, too." Ironically, he disapproved of how strictly Snyder focused on the source material in his adaptation for the film, but his review did exactly that. He even attacked Moore's writing, claiming that it "rarely rises above B-movie fare. It is silly and dated, the faded gibberish of an old-fashioned *noire* stylist (the kind who now works for newspapers). And it is filled with clichés." Not only did Kennicott confuse the text of the film with its contextual literary counterpart, but he also blended his description of Moore's writing in the graphic novel with the film. Moore's writing was never intended for any medium but the one in which it was published, not for a major motion picture nor a "B-movie." He had no part in the film's production or even any control over how Snyder used his material. Without a clear separation between the film and its source, readers were left with film reviews that appeared more like scathing book reviews, twenty years too late.

Whereas some reviewers condemned the film based on their perception of the graphic novel, others attacked the film by unfairly stereotyping fans. These reviews read as if every person who enjoyed the graphic novel or film was a real-life equivalent of *The Simpson*'s "Comic Book Guy" character, and this constructed (and blatantly false) context was argued as somehow reflective of the film's value. Lane was one such critic, who wrote that the film "should meet the needs of any leering nineteen-year-old who believes that America is ruled by the military-industrial complex, and whose deepest fear — deeper even than meeting a woman who requests intelligent conversation — is that the Warren Commission may have been right all along." For Lane, all *Watchmen* fans were ill-adjusted, socially awkward, juvenile, and insecure heterosexual males. Perhaps Lane was projecting his own insecurities as a critic, feeling the need to distance himself from superhero narratives and their fans in order to write a review. A. O. Scott of *The New York Times* also labeled fans with condescending stereotypes. He wrote that the "ideal viewer — or reviewer, as the case may be — of the *Watchmen* movie would probably be a mid–'80s college sophomore with a smattering of Nietzsche, an extensive record collection and a comic-book nerd for a roommate." Scott implied that the "ideal viewer" was perhaps educated, yet certainly immature. Ironically, however, by distancing himself from these viewers, Scott also suggested he was less than an "ideal" reviewer for the film, automatically making his review less valuable for readers. *Watchmen*'s Cold War themes may have been more relevant for an audience twenty years ago, but according to Scott, "shallow nihilism ... has always lurked beneath the intellectual pretensions of *Watchmen*," and both film and graphic novel were "fundamentally immature, self-pitying and sentimental." Scott explained that even if this "ideal viewer" could describe some moviegoers today as they were twenty years ago (that is, *Watchmen* fans circa 1986), they still would probably find the film to be lacking. Any mature adult, even the grown-up version of this "ideal viewer," had no reason to find *Watchmen* (both graphic novel and film) interesting.

Tom Long of *The Detroit News* revealed his opinion of the source material by contending the film could appeal *only* to hardcore comic book fans, a group he too deemed unsophisticated and immature. He referred to Snyder's *Watchmen* as an "adaptation of the highly praised, 12-part graphic novel (read: comic book) from the '80s" that would appeal to "fanboys, geeks, and fantasy hounds." By now, it is perhaps safe to say that the majority of readers know what "graphic novels" are, but Long felt the need to insert the descriptive parenthetical to clarify the "graphic novel" as a "comic book." Why? There is a distinction between the two forms, the least of which is their very presentation and marketing, but Long's clarification of the two forms as being one and the same suggested something about the way in which he perceived *Watchmen* the graphic novel's overall narrative value. He wrote that David Hayter and Alex Tse's script "clings tightly to author Alan Moore's original story," a story which Long tactfully described as "a load" and "clichéd." For Long, *Watchmen* was never a "novel," but rather always a "comic book," a justification for why the film would appeal to "fan*boys*" (immaturity implied) and the like, often a derogatory term if used by someone like Long, who saw himself as an outsider to this culture.

Reviewers were also critical of how *Watchmen* the film did not neatly align with their expectations for a superhero-themed film. This was yet another contextual argument, driven by assumptions about generic conventions confused with value. On a March 9, 2009, episode of National Public Radio's (NPR) *Talk of the Nation*, Neil Conan took calls from listeners about their reactions to and experiences with the *Watchmen* film. Movie theater manager Ryan from Riverbank, California, called in with this experience: "Yeah, I'm actually a movie theater manager who thoroughly enjoyed the movie over the weekend. And I think the biggest issue is really the expectations the customers are having when they come in to see the movie. We've had a ton of people bringing in their three- and four-year-old kids, expecting it to be a *Spider-Man* or an *Iron Man*, and it's just not that at all." For more reasons than one, *Watchmen* was not typical superhero fare. *Watchmen* the film was drawn from a self-contained story, told in only twelve installments with a unique set of characters, making it unlike films that featured Superman, Batman, or Spider-Man, whose narratives contained years of stories and scenarios in which the characters participated. Additionally, *Watchmen* challenged superhero conventions, prodding readers to question their understandings of heroism, power, authority, and justice. Not all moviegoers (or reviewers) were aware of *Watchmen*'s history or its subversion of superhero themes before heading to the theater; and as a result, these viewers were in for quite a surprise.

Because the narrative did not conform to superhero-comic and -movie conventions, Kirk Honeycutt of *The Hollywood Reporter* clearly disliked *Watchmen*. He referred to the basic premise for both the graphic novel and film versions of *Watchmen* as "nonsense" with "back stories [that] owe more to soap operas than to superhero comics." Similarly, Claudia Puig of *USA Today* wrote, "In the canon of comic-book movies, it's [Snyder's *Watchmen*] not as campy bad as *Batman* starring George Clooney, but nowhere near the caliber of the Spider-Man movies or *The Dark Knight*. It may have more style, but it's only a jot more entertaining than *Catwoman*." She measured the film based on her approval or disapproval of other superhero films, and how they fit into her understanding of what a superhero film *should* be. Aside from these imprecise quantitative assessments, she judged the film's narrative quality by its most basic quantitative element: the film's running time. She explained, "Not many stories require 2½ hours to be told effectively, and this is not one of the rare few." Puig noted that the film's narrative is derived from "Alan Moore's cult graphic novel," and that Silk Spectre II's "black-and-flesh-colored latex outfit and thigh-high boots connote dominatrix more than good-natured comic-book heroine." Notice how Puig's assessment not only denounced the film for its noncompliance within the context of other superhero films, but also for its fan base (i.e., the *Watchmen* "cult"). Both critics attempted to define the film by way of comparison to see if and how the movie measured up to other super-hero films, and both were terribly disappointed to find that *Watchmen* the film was not a superhero movie at all.

Honeycutt and Puig neglected to mention that nonconformity was exactly Snyder's intent. He wanted viewers to see a distinction between *Watchmen* and other superhero films, as he explained in an interview with Glenn Romanelli, creator of *WatchmenComicMovie.com*. Snyder noted that *Watchmen* should "constantly remind you of the things that you like about super hero [sic] movies. Whether it's the romance, or the violence, or the costumes. It's asking, 'Do you really like these things? Because if you do let me explain to you what the reality of those things are'" ("Zack"). The "reality" that Snyder showed through-out the film resulted in some very gory and sexually explicit scenes, appropri-ately earning its "R" rating from the Motion Picture Association of America. For films with "R" ratings, children under the age of 17 are not allowed admis-sion without the accompaniment of a parent or guardian, and the MPAA "strongly urge[s parents] to find out more about R-rated motion pictures in determining their suitability for their children." However, some moviegoers seriously underestimated the potential (and maturity level) of the film based on an assumption that it was just another superhero flick, a genre they per-ceived as made for children. On the Monday following the film's nationwide debut, Michael Phillips of *The Chicago Tribune* posted to his blog "Talking Pic-tures" an article detailing instances of mass walk-outs from the weekend screen-ings of *Watchmen*. In addition to providing links to other websites reporting a similar phenomenon, Phillips cited his colleague from the *Tribune*, Chris Bor-relli, who explained that there were a number of people who walked out of the theater during the Saturday showing of the film that he attended:

> The couple behind me argued for 45 minutes about who was who and what was happening and why is that man blue and was this scene happening now or did these events happen in the past and, holy crap, why are we now on Mars; even-tually, they gave up and laughed their way through the exit doors. (And they were not shushed.)
> A father seated in front of me, accompanied by antsy young boys, shifted uncomfortably with every splatter of brain; he sank lower into his seat at the arrival of a nude Dr. Manhattan's fully exposed Little Dr. Manhattan then gath-ered up his stuff and bolted during the fairly explicit sex between Night Owl [sic]

and Silk Spectre in the back of the Owl Mobile — or whatever it's called. (The movie is rated R.)

It's hard to say exactly when the trickle became an exodus — but maybe a quarter of the theater walked.

The confused couple and the squeamish father's reactions to the film were perhaps a result of a misinterpretation about the film's intent. Many moviegoers believed that they were attending an action flick and were lured by stunning visual effects seen in the film's trailer. The father may have brought children to the film thinking that it was going to be a kid-friendly PG–13 superhero film. Phillips concluded his article by asking for readers to respond to the comments section of the page with their perspectives on these stories of mass exoduses from theaters; and these comments proved as informative as Phillip's post, revealing what moviegoers were expecting to find when watching *Watchmen*. A post by Revenant reflected his and his girlfriend's disappointment with the film's violence; they decided to leave during Rorschach's origin story: "The media advertisement gave the perception this was a 'super hero esque' [sic] film. It is true people would've known what to expect if they had read the novel but the movie was not written with that prerequisite in mind." Another post, by Vince, disclosed that he was also lured in by the film's theatrical trailer: "The Smashing Pumpkins trailer was awesome but the movie was pointless." And a post by Wolverine is even more succinct: "It's better to watch the trailer than the whole movie ... haha [sic] I've seen a lot of comic movies and this is different. Waste of time and money."

The distinction between *Watchmen* and other superhero narratives was clear for those in the audience who were familiar with the story and its characters; however, Revenant rightly pointed out such familiarity was by no means a prerequisite. Even if moviegoers had not read the graphic novel, Warner Bros. (domestic distribution) and Paramount Pictures (international distribution) used numerous viral marketing strategies to promote the film and its narrative premise to those unfamiliar with the source material. The first teaser trailer released in July of 2008 ended with "*WatchmenMovie.com*"[4] splashed across the screen, inviting viewers to visit the site where they could learn more about the characters and *Watchmen*'s world. As the release date for the film quickly approached, both companies launched a variety of website tie-ins. One such website was Paramount Pictures' *TheNewFrontiersman.net*, a site based on the newspaper of the same name from the graphic novel. Starting in mid–January of 2009, this site updated every few days to include "declassified" documents from *Watchmen*'s world in chronological order, starting with documents related to the Minutemen and moving all the way up to the present day of the narrative (October 1985) to include a clip from an episode of *World in Focus* about Dr. Manhattan's influence on escalating world tensions. The video even included interspersed Veidt Enterprises commercials and an interview with Hollis Mason. Some of these photographs, videos, and documents were drawn directly from the graphic novel, while others were easily extrapolated from the alternate history it presented (i.e., Dr. Manhattan's presence at the Apollo moon landing). Other websites, such as *6MinutesToMidnight.com*, included an interactive inkblot test, guided by Rorschach himself, who offered his perspective on each of the main characters as the visitor correctly identified images in shifting shapes. *MinutemenArcade.com* allowed visitors to play in a 1980s-style arcade game based on Nite Owl I and Silk Spectre I's adventures. Paramount Pictures' *IWatchTheWatchmen.com* offered *Watchmen* enthusiasts downloadable computer wallpapers featuring the characters, buddy icons, "skins" for various social networking sites, iPod applications, and much more. Even with the creation and marketing of all of these information-packed websites,[5] moviegoers were not necessarily aware of the websites or even the premise for the film prior to attending a show. Moreover, a visit to the website did not guarantee that one would find and read information that would suggest *Watchmen* as something other than simply another comic-book superhero film.

When Romanelli asked Snyder what he believed the response of mainstream audiences would be to his film, Snyder responded, "When we set out to make *Watchmen*, ... I said, 'This is what it is, this is the material, I love the material, I am not going to fuck it up to make it commercial, or cool, or what everyone might want or might like.' I feel like that is what we did. As far as like whether mainstream audiences how they would feel about it, [sic] I have no idea" ("Zack"). After the film's release, mainstream audiences (and reviewers) responded to Snyder's approach to *Watchmen*, and many found Snyder's portrayal of violence in the film to be a flaw. In another interview with Romanelli, producer Deborah Snyder explained the film was "commenting on violence. It's there, it's very intentional. If you look at ... these PG superhero films where people are getting bashed into walls and there's no consequences. There's no consequences to the violence and the violence in this film has a consequence to it. And that's what distinguishes itself. That's what makes it *Watchmen*" ("Producers"). Yet, many reviewers did not see the violence as a commentary on film conventions, but rather as simply excessive.

Bob Mondello of *National Public Radio* writes that Snyder "splatter[s] blood a good deal more liberally than he needs to," and Kennicott of *The Washington Post* viewed the violence as a *change* from the original rather than something that had been maintained: the "most significant change between the movie and the novel is the density and immediacy of the violence. What was merely hinted at, or done off-stage in the book, is seen full on, with buckets of gore in the movie. Too bad." Similarly, J. Hoberman of *The Village Voice* writes, "Social satire is pummeled into submission by the amplified pow-kick-thud of the sub–*Matrix* action sequences; not just metaphysics and narrative are simplified, but even character is ultimately eclipsed by the presumed need for violent spectacle." That is, while the film was *more* violent than other action or superhero movies, the violence contributed *less* to the film's meaning. The distinction between the filmmakers' intention and the viewer's reception was that the former believed it to be a show of realism whereas some members of the latter understood it to be a "spectacle," sensationalism for shock-value.

Christopher Orr of *The New Republic* echoed Hoberman's response. He wrote, "Moore's original was bloody to begin with, but Snyder amps the violence up still further, as if worried the material has lost the ability to shock.... In Moore's comic the blood was plentiful but not beautiful; Snyder's film — like James McTeigue's adaptation of Moore's *V for Vendetta*— strives to make it both." Ironically, this is exactly what Snyder was intending *not* to achieve. As Deborah Snyder explained, the violence was intended to elicit from the audience a negative response in order to make them think about the implications of violence in superhero films more generally. Even more ironic was Dana Vinson's, of *G4TV.com*, response: "Wonderfully choreographed and beautifully executed, no one can say that this film skimps on bone crunching. There are plenty of well-placed and — dare I say — classy moments of blood and gore that will leave you reeling and wanting more." It is not clear if Vinson reflected on the implications of plentiful "bone crunching" in the film as somehow relative to superhero flicks more generally, but she certainly *enjoyed* the spectacle. Like most elements of the *Watchmen* film, there was either too much or not enough. For some viewers, Snyder's *Watchmen* went too far with the violence, turning it into a gore-filled spectacle, and for others he did not go far enough, failing to elicit the response for which the use of violence was intended.

Whatever viewers expected *Watchmen* to be was not necessarily what they got. In his review of the film, James Berardinelli of *Reelviews Movie Reviews* predicted differing reactions from audience members based on their expectations for the film:

> Those who approach the movie with an understanding of the plot and a familiarity with the characters and their backstories [sic] will get more out of the movie than those who are facing their first exposure to the material. For anyone coming to *Watchmen* as a different way to experience something with which they have a link, the film may work in the way Snyder intended. However, for viewers without this background, *Watchmen* has the ability to alternately fascinate and frustrate.

Along with scores of moviegoers, it appeared as though many critics were unable to approach Snyder's *Watchmen* as a separate work. They condemned the film precisely because they were unable to see it as a "different way to experience" that which they already believed they knew, whether that was the graphic novel, comic-book and graphic-novel fans, or superhero films in general.

Blinded by Brilliance

In *Watchmen: The Art of the Film*, Peter Aperlo related Snyder's attempted adamant adherence to the graphic novel when creating the film: "He felt very strongly about respecting the visual style of the graphic novel and handling it as nearly sacrosanct. 'I always say treat *Watchmen* like an illuminated text, like it was written 2000 years ago,' explains Snyder" (26). Snyder was not alone among those involved with the production of the film in his dedication to try and somehow preserve the graphic novel for the screen. In an open letter published on the Web, David Hayter, one of the screenwriters for the film, wrote of his frustration with some of the negative reviews that the film received throughout the media in the first week of its release: "I have listened for years, to complaints from true comic book fans, that 'not enough movies take the source material seriously.' 'Too many movies puss out,' or 'They change great stories, just to be commercial.' Well I f***ing [sic] dare you to say any one of those things about this movie. This is a movie made by fans, for fans" (Llyr). Using the graphic novel as a guide, Snyder sketched out the entire storyboard for the film with painstaking detail; and production designer Alex McDowell noted, "Almost in every set we have a frame or several frames from the graphic novel" (Aperlo, *Art* 42–43). But when Snyder was originally offered the *Watchmen* film project, the script he was handed differed substantially from the story in the graphic novel. In an interview with Romanelli, Snyder explained, "The studio said this is PG13, it's going to be updated to the war on terror where Dr. Manhattan is going to go to Iraq, Adrian gets killed in the end, the Owl Ship crushes him with some cool tag line.... It was just a superhero movie. It was a real franchisable [sic] super hero movie" ("Zack"). However, Snyder was able to convince the studio to abandon this "superhero movie" script in favor of a film that would perhaps be less marketable to a mainstream modern audience:

> Snyder wasn't concerned that this choice might relegate the film to being a period piece; he knew it contained enough universal themes to resonate strongly with the present. "When you take a medium and have it shine light on humanity, that's what *Watchmen* does," says Snyder. "It's something to comment immediately on the pop culture of the moment, and at the same time it has this deep reflective quality that's timeless" [Aperlo, *Companion* 18].

In other words, Snyder envisioned the film as a way of retelling the past in the present as a means of commenting on present-day circumstances.

    Yet, some critics thoroughly disagreed with Snyder's analysis, and in measuring the graphic novel against the film, they found that *Watchmen*'s story no longer carried the same resonance that it did more than twenty years ago. Tom Maurstad of *The Dallas Morning News*, and Devin Gordon of *Newsweek*, found the film to be incongruous with the times in relation to the current global climate. Maurstad explained that today's world is in no way analogous to the one in which Moore and Gibbons constructed the text, and therefore the film has "a distinct whiff of out-of-step, out-of-time datedness.... In a world splintered by terrorism and atomized by the Internet, such black-and-white order can seem simplistic at best, nostalgic at worst. Either way, it's the antithesis of what the original *Watchmen* set out to be." Maurstad was assuming the authorial intent here, transposing his own conception of what *Watchmen* the graphic novel was for him onto Moore and Gibbons' intentions when writing and illustrating the work. Likewise, his analysis suggested that he would have perhaps enjoyed the studio's updated version of the *Watchmen* film, as his argument contends that a film set in the past is less than satisfactory because it portrays the past rather than the current times. Gordon, however, saw *Watchmen*'s Cold War premise as very applicable to 2009, feeling that it reflected current global tensions. However, he wrote, "Onscreen, the original tale's Soviet-era dread feels dated, and it shouldn't — not with religious terrorism offering such an able proxy for anticommunist paranoia." Some viewers were unable to see past the 1985 setting, but others clearly understood and even admired Snyder's decision to keep the film in its original setting. John Ridley, screenwriter, graphic novelist, and NPR contributor, found critical reactions to the 1985 setting like Maurstad's and Gordon's quite "odd." He defended Synder's decision to keep the narrative in its original setting: "It should feel dated. Some of the ideas, of course, are going to feel dated, but that's the world that is set up in..." ("Are Critics"). After all, a disjointed and nostalgic sense of time is one that the source material explores quite extensively. Perhaps the criticism to the 1985 setting was not quite as "odd" as Ridley suggested. Rather, these critics were reacting to Snyder's faithful adherence to the original work, but from their perspective, something was lost in translation.

While Snyder's film prioritized the preservation of the graphic novel's design, setting, and most of its main storyline, some critics faulted Snyder's insistence on staying so true to the text directly; when the trailer for the film dubbed Snyder a "visionary" director, it left him and his film vulnerable to awaiting critics. The title of "visionary" suggests originality and creativity, and prior to *Watchmen*, Snyder had only directed two other major motion pictures — the 2004 *Dawn of the Dead* remake of George A. Romero's 1978 film of the same name, and the hugely successful 2006 film *300*, a cinematic interpretation of Frank Miller's graphic novel. The question was whether a director could be considered "visionary" after only presenting filmic interpretations of classics. For some, his three films did not give him enough clout to don the lofty title just yet. Even before the film was released, Scott Thill of *Wired.com* wrote that he was impressed with Snyder's devotion to the source material when meeting him for an interview for *Wired Magazine*, but he was somewhat disconcerted by the marketing campaign for the film. He wrote that Snyder "is an ebullient guy and a quick study of source material, and I can report that he was committed to taking panels right from those acclaimed comics and stuffing them into his camera.... And that is no easy feat, to be sure, but it's much easier than dreaming up such imagery and committing it to paper or cinema without anyone else's help." Wary of the implications of calling Snyder a "visionary" months before the film's release, Thill unintentionally pinpointed what some critics found to be a major flaw with the film: Snyder's delicate handling of the graphic novel.

Gordon of *Newsweek* found that Snyder's adaptation reflected the undeniable fact that "he is deeply, sincerely in love with the source material." Yet, this was not necessarily to the film's benefit, as he wrote, "Entire sequences are preserved, frame by frame. But is that a good thing? Speaking as an admirer, but not an apostle, of the graphic novel, I thought the *Watchmen* movie was confusing, maddeningly inconsistent and fighting a long, losing battle to establish an identity of its own." Gordon's main complaint with the film was arguably what Snyder and company prided themselves on the most, their strict adherence to the original work. Not surprisingly, he found the title sequence for the film to be one of its most enjoyable elements. The title sequence portrays "how the history of the 20th Century might have flowed if masked heroes had really existed. Although panels and dialogue from the graphic novel inspired some of the shots in the sequence, many — such as the bomber Miss Jupiter dropping the A-bomb on Hiroshima, or Dr. Manhattan being present at the Apollo moon landing — were entirely new imaginings of events in the *Watchmen* world" (Aperlo, *Art* 43). Gordon noted, "It's a testimony to Snyder's potential that the best part of his *Watchmen*— those marvelous credits— is the only place where he was forced to fend for himself, with no blueprint to guide him. Or paralyze him." Gordon was not alone in his admiration of the title sequence; many critics, even those who did not like the film,[6] enjoyed Snyder's vision for these few moments, scored to Bob Dylan's "The Times They Are a' Changin.'"

Yet, for many critics, the title sequence did not offer enough redemption for what they perceived as the rest of the film's muddled narrative structure. Hoberman of *The Village Voice* wrote that Snyder's *Watchmen*'s "failure is one of imagination — although faithfully approximating Dave Gibbons' original drawings, the filmmakers are unable to teleport themselves to the level of the original concept.... Snyder's movie is too literal and too linear." The graphic novel was an "original concept" within its medium, and in order for the film to approximate the graphic novel, it could not recreate the graphic novel for the screen; it would have to have been unique. Like many other critics, Hoberman's assessment of the film was justified by imprecise quantification and based on his perception of *Watchmen* the graphic novel. Similarly, Orr of *The New Republic* acknowledged, "In the 1980s, *Watchmen* was the definition of envelope-pushing, a bleak violent subversion of a relatively innocent genre." But with Snyder's *Watchmen*, Orr found "there are problems both with the tale, which was an awful lot more subversive 20 years ago than it is today, and the telling, which in contrast to Moore's radical experimentation is disappointingly staid and straightforward, imprisoned by its own legend." Notice how Hoberman and Orr used similar ways to describe their reactions to Snyder's film, finding it to be "literal," "linear," "staid and straightforward." Their assessments, although negative, suggested that Snyder provided a faithful adaptation of the original work, yet still these critics and many others found the film lacking. What these reviewers wanted to see was something that was virtually impossible to achieve: an original film, but one that "faithfully approximated" an existing source.

Snyder has said in various interviews that his *Watchmen* was meant to be viewed as a deconstruction of superhero-film conventions in the same way that he interpreted *Watchmen* the graphic novel as having deconstructed superhero-comic conventions: "In the sense of the deconstruction of the movie, it's sort of a tearing down of superhero movies. Sort of reunderstanding it and understand how it flows in pop culture right now, and how the superhero movie is the movie.... What does it mean? Why do we love the characters?" (Romanelli, "Zack"). However, some reviewers did not perceive Snyder's treatment of the film as such. Instead, many found the narrative so close to the original that, as David Edelstein of *New York Magazine* described, Snyder's treatment of Moore and Gibbons' text was so "reverent" that it "kills what it seeks to preserve," resulting in a film that was "embalmed." He further explained, "Moore and Gibbons used every tool they could invent to push their medium to its limit — and their work is in the hands of people who've decided to cast off many of their own medium's tools in a misguided attempt at fidelity." By remaining faithful to what was printed on the page, the film was seen to lose some of its potential at being original and self-referential; for some reviewers, the film was unable to comment on the film industry and film conventions while recreating ones found in graphic novels.

Mondello of *National Public Radio* believed that "really rabid *Watchmen* fans" would find Snyder's adherence to the graphic novel a "good thing;" however, "it's going to leave everyone else wondering if the director knows much about movie pacing or movie narratives. Or movie audiences." Likewise, Berardinelli of *Reelviews Movie Reviews* saw Snyder's adherence to the graphic novel as a "structural flaw." He wrote, "The nuances are gone. The film is too busy, too narratively dense, and too awkwardly structured for it to achieve the level of absorption that one can get from reading the books.... It replicates material from the comics but keeps the viewer wondering if the narrative is ever going to attain momentum." Like so many other reviewers, Berardinelli's assessment of the film's narrative quality was based on his perception of the one in the graphic novel.

Perhaps even the director himself underestimated the graphic novel's narrative complexity when adapting it for the film, especially for those viewers who were unfamiliar with the source material. Snyder was quoted in Aperlo's *Watchmen: The Art of the Film* as ironically saying, "The thing people would always say about *Watchmen* is it's the unfilmable graphic novel because it's so dense. When you look at it, it looks like a phone book. But the story itself is pretty simple" (28). The main narrative strand (Rorschach's investigation of the Comedian's murder and the formation of his mask-killer theory) is arguably "simple" or straightforward, but this only accounts for a fraction of *Watchmen* the graphic novel as a whole, which includes so much more than the story of the present day. Aperlo continued, "The way that Snyder and his crew went about achieving that density on the screen without overcomplicating the narrative, was to maintain the same high degree of visual detail as the graphic novel" (28). However, one must question if this was enough to guide audience members who were unfamiliar with *Watchmen*'s premise. *Watchmen* the film may have been overwhelming or confusing for newcomers to the narrative, but for others, who were familiar with *Watchmen* the graphic novel, the film could have potentially provided an *under*whelming experience, leaving out the expository materials and other parts of the story that were unadaptable for film.

Paul Gravett explains in an interview for *The Mindscape of Alan Moore* that the "danger with adapting comics very directly into film is that you start to wonder 'what is the point of it?' because when someone makes the effort perhaps through the film to get back to the comic, he'll realize how much better the experience is reading the comic than it is just seeing it on the screen." That "someone" could perhaps describe Lev Grossman of *Time* magazine. Grossman, the *Watchmen* admirer (along with Richard Lacayo) responsible for historically placing the novel among *Time* magazine's top 100 English-language novels since 1923, had a mixed response to the narrative's recreation on film. In an "Entertainment Podcast" for *Time.com*, Grossman noted that *Watchmen* the graphic novel "consists of a large number of overlapping strands and fugal motifs that are really meant to be sat with and absorbed over many different readings. They're not really meant to be administered in a single dose forcibly in one sitting. It's almost too much to comprehend." Snyder faced a losing battle in whatever way he treated the text, as Gordon of *Newsweek* aptly suggested: "That's the trouble with loyalty. Too little, and you alienate your core fans. Too much, and you lose everyone — and everything — else." Based on a work that inspired strong feelings among so many readers (both positive and negative), Snyder was bound to disappoint some.

Squidgate

Among all of the reports that Snyder was staying faithful to the graphic novel, news surfaced in late 2008 that Snyder did, in fact, change a major part of the *Watchmen* narrative — the ending. "Squidgate," an appropriate term for Snyder's controversial decision to alter the ending of *Watchmen*, appeared on *Ain't It Cool News'* message boards in November of 2008.[7] *Watchmen* fans were thoroughly divided over reported changes as they waited for the March 6 release of the film to judge for themselves how the new ending measured up to expectations. In an interview with Garth Franklin of *DarkHorizins.com*, Snyder reacted to the negative outcry by *Watchmen* fandom over rumors that he had decided to nix the psychic squid: "The fans, god love 'em, they're all up in arms about the squid. What they should be up in arms about are things like shooting the pregnant woman, 'God is real and he's American,' whether THAT's in the movie." Romanelli wrote of this interview that "what seemed to irritate fans about this quote the most was not that Snyder came off as being condescending toward them, but that it amped up their fears that even though Snyder was painstakingly including lots of the little details of *Watchmen* into his film, he was perhaps missing the big picture and creating a movie whose ending will fall flat and ultimately makes little to no sense" ("The Squid"). Unfortunately, this was exactly the reaction that some reviewers had when they were finally able to see the alternate ending; yet their disappointment was not over inclusion or exclusion of the psychic squid, but rather the emotional impact of the graphic novel's ending as compared to the film's.[8]

Vinson of *G4TV.com* wrote that the film's "ending doesn't carry the same kind of emotional weight or message as the book. It also seems forced. It's less character-centric and more centered on creating big action." Noah Berlatsky of the *Chicago Reader* elaborated on similar concerns:

> Moore was careful to include a number of civilians in the comic, most prominently a cranky white news vendor and a young black comics reader. In the movie, these two characters die in each other's arms as they did on the page, but that's the first and the last you see of them. They're cannon fodder for the special effects, not characters you care about. As a result *Watchmen* focuses on the choices and sacrifices of the superpowered — the superman's burden, if you will — rather than what those choices mean for everybody else.

Grossman even noted, "By the end of the movie I was feeling just a little bit disconnected from the action and struggling to care about all the people that die." Each of these reviewers were disappointed with the new ending not because of the missing squid, but rather the missing elements from the graphic novel that highlighted the stories of some "civilian" characters, including the two Bernies at the newspaper stand, Detective Fine and his partner Joe Bourquin, Joey, the Promethean Cab Company driver, and her girlfriend, Aline, Dr. Malcolm Long and his wife, and even the watch-seller. The first six pages of the final chapter of the graphic novel portray a panoramic view of the street corner that is depicted throughout, and readers become familiar with the lives of these characters. These six pages, however, depict the destruction *after* the attack. The characters that readers come to know over the previous eleven chapters now lie dead in the street. The emotional impact of the scene resonates through the recognizable faces. Vinson, Berlatsky, and Grossman all reacted to the change in the narrative in similar ways, as all three read and found the ending of the graphic novel to be *more* powerful than the film's adaptation.

Yet, not all *Watchmen* fans and aficionados were entirely dismissive or disliked the altered ending. In fact, some critics, like David Chen of */Film* (*SlashFilm.com*), found Snyder's *Watchmen* to be a success overall:

> I thought that while the film preserved the spirit of the book's ending, it changed its emotional weight for the worse. Still, I understand why the change was made,

as the final chapter of Moore's *Watchmen* does deliver one of the biggest "WTFs" I've ever experienced while reading a book. But overall, Snyder's visual style seemed particularly suited to translating the panels of a graphic novel to the big screen, and despite my disagreement with some of them, you can feel that his personal touches were made with love, and weren't considered lightly.

Similarly, Romanelli viewed Snyder's ending as more cinematically viable than if he used Moore and Gibbons' original creation that was intended for the printed page: "The new ending worked very well. It managed to get across all the ambiguous themes of morality that the climax of the graphic novel had, with the added depth of wrapping one of the main character's story arc into it that was very satisfying to see on screen.... In some ways, [this ending] might resonate better, especially with the uninitiated" ("Review"). Not only would the ending perhaps "resonate better" with those "uninitiated," meaning those who were unfamiliar with *Watchmen*, but it was also perhaps one of the *only* viable solutions to bringing a massively complex narrative to a close within a commercially viable running-time length. To include all or even some of the civilian characters' stories would take a significant amount of time, and with a theatrical running time of two hours and thirty-six minutes already, it was unlikely that many audience members would be willing to sit through an even longer film in the theater. A longer running time also meant theaters would have had to show the film fewer times per day than they would if it were shorter, resulting in less potential revenue. Additionally, the film's presentation in IMAX would not have been possible, as IMAX has a limit for the length of films that it can accommodate, and these screenings were enormously successful during the opening weekend of the film, selling out all 124 midnight shows for opening day, which accounted for 5.5 million dollars of revenue (Pierson). Artistic direction and decisions were bound to clash with big business' bottom line. Snyder's director's cut of the film was over three hours long, which needed to be pared down to the lengthy film that actually made it to theaters. Snyder may have insisted that his film was not concerned with pleasing mainstream audiences, and it was more important for the film to stay true to the original source material, but the film industry was still just that — an industry that intended to make a profit.

Nothing Will Ever Measure Up

Viewing the film as an entity separate from the graphic novel was as challenging for those who admired the graphic novel as it was for those who disliked the original text. Some had preconceived notions about the film because of their dislike for the graphic novel; others found problems with its applicability to a modern-day audience or how it compared to other superhero films, and still other reviewers sided with Moore, deciding that *any* film adaptation of *Watchmen* was a second-rate *Watchmen*. That is, the film never should have been made. Owen Gleiberman of *Entertainment Weekly* was one such critic:

> The fun of graphic novels, or a crucial part of the fun, is that they're like movies that have been frozen onto the page. They're kinetic stories that you can *almost* see move. That fun, of course, is more or less eliminated the moment that you transform a graphic novel *into* a movie.... On the page, *Watchmen* was a paranoid, mind-tripping pastiche of everything from *The Incredible Hulk* to *Naked Lunch*. But when characters who are knowing throwbacks are literally brought to life on screen, they can seem more like half-hearted ripoffs.

If the "fun" of graphic novels is the fact that they are like motion pictures without the motion, then any adaptation of a graphic novel to film is immediately a failure, as it deprives the viewer of the enjoyment of imagining the motion and sound. It is the difference between an intellectual or conceptual exercise and a sensory experience. It was the former that Gleiberman found so gratifying when reading the graphic novel, rendering the film a disappointment because it only provided the latter.

Likewise, Orr of *The New Republic* found the film lacking in that Snyder "does not undertake the more literary ventures that gave the original such unexpected texture: the *Tales of the Black Freighter* mirror narrative, the 'found' book excerpts, etc. As a result, *Watchmen* [the film], which ought to highlight the strengths of its source material, too often reveals the weaknesses instead." Ironically, Orr used the word "literary" to describe what was lacking from the film; that is, the problem with the film was most simply that it was a film. Stephen Whitty of *The [Newark] Star-Ledger* had a similar reaction, yet qualified it by noting that perhaps the film medium simply could not provide an experience that matched what *Watchmen* offered on the page:

> The comic pushed things past the breaking point, with a meta-fictional structure that included interpolated diaries, psychological reports, even other comic books. Which has helped bedevil Hollywood for years: How do you turn that into a movie?... The problem is that, as similar as they appear to be, a comic is not a storyboard for a movie; it's its own form, and perfect in its own way. And the original *Watchmen* went well beyond storyboards, and perhaps beyond what a movie can do.

The discussion over *Watchmen* the film versus *Watchmen* the graphic novel's narrative structure continued in the comments section at the bottom of Whitty's article that was posted to the Web. In a response to a comment on his review, Whitty wrote:

> What made *Watchmen* wonderful — and I am someone who read the novel, and liked it, and saw the movie, and was lukewarm — was ... a real metafictional depth. The movie cut all of that out to focus on the story and the action. And to assume that the best thing about *Watchmen* was its fight scenes is like assuming that the best thing about *Moby Dick* was its whaling scenes. I understand why the filmmakers did that. I'm fully aware of the fact that it may have been impossible to do this any other way (except, perhaps, as some sort of interactive game). But what

made *Watchmen* stand out from other stories wasn't the plot, but the way in which it was told. And that's missing here. Alan Moore said it first, and correctly — *Watchmen* was already in the form it was made for.

Orr and Whitty found the metatextual structure of *Watchmen* the graphic novel to be the most enjoyable aspect of the reading experience. For these two critics, the expository materials and the stories-within-the-story comprised a great deal of what the *Watchmen* experience *should* have been. Even for Gleiberman, whose reading experience was explained in terms of film, the physical act of turning the pages was what made the graphic novel so gratifying.

After viewing Snyder's *Watchmen*, Amy Biancolli of the *Houston Chronicle* also saw little value in adapting the narrative from graphic novel to film. She noted some of the arguments for why *Watchmen* was thought to be "unfilmable" for so long:

> It's too nonlinear, some argued. Too violent. Too sexy. Too long. Too mature. Too cynical. Too complicated. Too dark. In truth, it's all of those things. But the tale of outcast vigilantes in a rotting alternate America was never "unfilmable." The question isn't whether *Watchmen* could be turned into a movie. The question is, should it? And judging from Zack Snyder's garish, uneven and excessively cruel interpretation, I'd say no. It shouldn't.

Biancolli ironically distinguished herself from those who believe the film to be unfilmable; yet, the argument that *Watchmen* was unfilmable was virtually the same argument as to whether or not the film should have been made. Note the way in which she described what appeared to be two separate arguments; the narrative was "too" (insert adjective) to be made into a motion picture, and Biancolli's assessment of the finished project was that it was "*excessively cruel*" and "garish" (too brash or gaudy). Her explanation through imprecise quantification merely showed the reader her personal preference for what she would like to have seen in the film. She described the movie as an "uneven" adaptation; the film in some ways did and in others did not measure up to her reading of the graphic novel. Biancolli concluded her review of Snyder's *Watchmen* with this analysis: "The biggest problem, top to bottom, is overkill. It *is* too long; it *is* too violent.... Alan Moore pulled his name from the credits, just as he pulled it from 2005's far-better *V for Vendetta*. Good move — but not because *Watchmen*'s 'unfilmable.' Because it is, at times, unwatchable." Ironically, *Watchmen* the film was "unwatchable" for Biancolli precisely because it could not consistently measure up to the power of the narrative in its graphic novel form. She, like so many other critics, could not separate her expectations for the film from the final product.

On the March 9, 2009, edition of National Public Radio's *Talk of the Nation* entitled "Are Critics or Crowds Right About *Watchmen*?" Neal Conan asked John Ridley, someone familiar with both the comic-book and film industries, for his take on the *Watchmen* film. Ridley found that the overwhelming majority of critical reactions were a result of critics' inabilities to come to the film without a certain level of fixed expectations: "If you come into it [the film] and you have all these presuppositions about what it should be and don't just sit down and say, 'Look, I'm going to look at this movie for what the film is,' then you are going to be disappointed.... You've got to go into it and say, 'Forget about what I've read before; this is what it is.'" The problem was that few critics and even viewers were able to "forget." Some felt disappointment in their efforts to measure up the film against its graphic novel counterpart, while others felt gratified or even *validated* in seeing the film fail to live up to so many viewers' expectations. Professor Milton Glass ends his "Introduction" to *Dr. Manhattan: Super-powers and the Superpowers* with the conviction that "we are all of us living in the shadow of Manhattan" (4.32); so too was Snyder's movie: the filmmakers and audience alike were all "living in the shadow" of the cultural phenomenon that was *Watchmen*.

Closing Remarks

As I neared the completion of writing *Watchmen as Literature*, I sat down to discuss the project with my professor and mentor, Dr. Stanley Blair, at Monmouth University. I explained to him that I knew my time with *Watchmen* had not finished, even though my manuscript was almost complete. With a smile, he replied, "When you find the right project, it writes you." He was right. This book has written me, completely changing me as both a writer and reader. As Dr. Manhattan says to Veidt before his final exit from Earth, "Nothing ever ends," and my time spent with this text surely has not ended with the final page of this book. Likewise, the work within these preceding chapters is by no means intended to be exhaustive or meant to examine the graphic novel through every facet of contemporary literary criticism. There is still much to be said about *Watchmen* and its lasting effect on both American popular culture and scholarship. I encourage you to take what is here and think about, expand upon, and critically consider one writer's attempt to guide readers through reading *Watchmen*. I would like to extend to you what Hector Godfrey says on *Watchmen*'s final page: "I leave it entirely in your hands."

Chapter Notes

Chapter 1

1. Although literary criticism is normally written in present tense, this chapter (like chapter 9) is written in past tense in recognition that it intends to cover a discrete time period in *Watchmen*'s history.

2. Arnold noted that even though many consider Eisner's work as the first graphic novel, "It was not actually the first long-form graphic story nor [even] the first to use the phrase."

3. See Hajdu for a detailed history.

4. *Watchmen*'s characters are original, but based on a group of defunct Charlton Comics' characters. See Moore's character development notes in *Absolute Watchmen*.

5. In 2009, it is expected that WSFS will introduce a new category for the Hugo Awards specifically for graphic narratives. See "Nominations."

6. To enhance the readability of this and subsequent chapters, "Moore and Gibbons" will be eliminated from the remaining parenthetical references pertaining to *Watchmen*. Only chapter and/or page numbers will be included in parenthetical references, and it is implied that any material quoted or cited from *Watchmen* is attributed to the collaborative effort of Alan Moore and Dave Gibbons.

7. See Levine 46.

8. For other examples of *Watchmen* scholarship from the 1990s, see Fishbaugh and Spinrad.

9. It should be noted that Harris-Fain did acknowledge both artist Dave Gibbons and colorist John Higgins in his 1989 review; however, much more emphasis was placed on Moore's work than the contributions of the other two. Neither Gibbons nor Higgins are mentioned in his letter from 1998, perhaps for no more reason than to be concise.

10. In 1987, *Dark Knight* won four Jack Kirby Awards for Best Single Issue, Best Finite Series (completed in 1986), Best Graphic Album, and Best Art Team. It was additionally nominated for Best New Series, Best Writer, Best Artist/Writer (single or team), and Best Artist. See Hahn.

Chapter 2

1. At least, *most* graphic narratives use both images and words. Some use few (if any) words. Eisner broadly defines the graphic narrative as "a generic description of any story that employs images to transmit an idea. Film and comics both engage in graphic narrative" (*Graphic* xvii). Also see pages 140–48 in *Graphic* for some examples of graphic narratives that use very few words.

2. See chapter 2 of Eisner's *Comics and Sequential Art* and chapter 6 of McCloud's *Understanding Comics* for more information.

3. See page 28 of chapter 5 when Rorschach's mask is ripped from his face by the police. Also see page 9 of chapter 10. Before Rorschach pulls his mask over his face and says, "All I need," his word balloons match those of Dreiberg's, but once the mask is on, his word balloons return to their characteristically disheveled appearance.

4. Here and throughout, all ellipses

in quotes from the word balloons in Alan Moore and Dave Gibbons' *Watchmen* are original unless otherwise noted.

5. See chapter 5, "Parallel Histories," for more information on how "silent location" panel-to-panel juxtapositions are used throughout the novel.

6. For more information, see Strizver.

7. On page 29 of chapter 6, see the word "one" (first word in the fifth row from the bottom) for an example of an unevenly printed word. See the word "possibly" (first word in the second row from the bottom) for an example of a misprinted or improperly inked word on the same page. The documents also include typos, adding to their realism: there is a space missing from between the words "exists" and "that" on page 31, and "education" is misspelled on page 30.

8. A group of Knot Tops attempt to mug Dreiberg and Juspeczyk later in chapter 3, and another group of Knot Tops are responsible for Mason's death in chapter 8 (3.11–15, 8.27–28).

9. Background and foreground detail is not limited to the actions of characters. Inanimate objects from the setting can function in roles similar to the characters themselves. In chapter 7, Dreiberg's costume looms in the foreground of many of the panels, looking on as he and Juspeczyk discuss their past crime-fighting days. For more information, see chapter 8, "Faceless Heroes," for further analysis of this scene.

10. Also compare the location of the sun and shadows in relation to the newsstand in the second panel on page 8 (morning), the third panel on page 12 (midday), and the fourth panel on page 17.

11. In fact, the entire chapter's structure is symmetrical. See Gibbons 140–51 and 204–5. Also see Whitson.

12. See also chapter 5, pages 1–3 and 23–28.

13. All descriptions of colors in this section and throughout pertain to the digitally recolored version unless otherwise noted.

14. See Gibbons 265–67 for some side-by-side comparisons of the originals and the digitally recolored versions, including this example of Dr. Manhattan in Vietnam.

15. It is not my intention here to categorize the virtually unlimited facial expressions and body language cues that graphic-narrative artists use to convey information about characters. For a detailed discussion of this, please see McCloud, *Making Comics* 58–127.

Chapter 3

1. McCloud labels this category as "additive." See page 154 in *Understanding Comics*.

2. Other examples include when Rorschach eats from a can of beans in Dreiberg's kitchen ("Chlop. Thlup."), when Dr. Manhattan's reassembled circulatory system frightens two men in the lavatory at Gila Flats (Eeeeiiiighh!), and when a young Juspeczyk strains to lift barbells during a routine workout at her mother's home ("Haahhh") (1.10, 4.9, 9.11).

3. McCloud defines his duo-specific interaction as one where words and images seem to depict "roughly the same message" (*Making* 130).

4. Please see chapter 5, "Parallel Histories," for a discussion of how page construction affects the reader's perception of time and space.

Chapter 4

1. McCloud labels this image/word interaction as a "parallel combination." See *Understanding* 154 or *Making* 130.

2. In its original form as a series of twelve comic books, each chapter's title page served as the cover of each issue.

3. Moore and Gibbons 12.32.

4. In chapter 5, Rorschach sits in the Gunga Diner. His journal retrospectively narrates: "Entering diner, bought coffee then sat watching my maildrop, immediately across the street" (11). In the last panel on the next page, Rorschach (disguised as Walter Kovacs) is seen digging through the maildrop in the background (12).

5. When Seymour participates in the narrative during the panels, one could argue

that this serves as part of the extradiegetic frame rather than part of the diegesis, derived from the journal entries. Seymour can be found in chapter 7 on page 12 (in the background on the television screen), chapter 8 on page 10, chapter 11 on page 24, and in chapter 12 on page 31 and 32.

6. Moore and Gibbons 7.28.

7. The note attached to this document reads, "The following text is reprinted from the *Journal of The American Ornithological Society*, Fall 1983" (7.29). One may ask why this document does not include "with permission of the author." As far as anyone knows, Dreiberg and Juspeczyk are no longer living at the end of the novel. Therefore, permission could not be obtained from the author, even if the author himself is reprinting it. This complicates the inclusion of the words "with permission of the author" on the three documents from Mason's book. There are two plausible reasons for this: the first being that if the note read "with permission from the estate of Hollis Mason," readers would know that Mason does not survive to the end of the novel. The other possible reason could be that Dreiberg serves as an executor to Mason's estate, and would have had Mason's permission if he were still alive.

Chapter 5

1. Term compliments of Dr. Stanley S. Blair, Monmouth University.

2. Another way that time can be manipulated is through the use of polyptychs, a series of panels that has one continuous background or image, but represents distinct moments in time. There are a few examples of polyptychs throughout the novel, which is one way that time can be slowed down or dissected into moment by moment intervals. However, polyptychs still rely on panel size and the amount of dialogue within each panel to determine how the reader will perceive the time qualitatively. For some examples, see 2.10 and 16, 7.27 and 28, and 8.4 and 5.

3. What Peeters refers to as a page layout reinforcing "regular reading," Cohn believes "is really describing the decisions and strategies of the reading subject" (par. 7). The panels do not disappear once the reader moves to the next panel; he or she may return to them at any time, and nothing stops a reader from reading the panels out of order. Additionally, a reader can make connections across two pages, the recto and verso pages of an open book. The use of a conventional nine-panel page strengthens the linear, mathematical progression of time. Concurrently, however, every page layout has the potential to convey different sequences of time based on each individual reader's perception of the presentation.

4. For an example of how pacing and panel arrangement was tested or enhanced in the planning stages of the novel, see Dave Gibbons' thumbnail sketches throughout *Watching the Watchmen*. There is a particularly good example of this on page 221 where Gibbons notes above one thumbnail detailing Ozymandias' story that it was later discarded because it was "too-spacious."

5. In chapter 1, this panel is viewed from the opposite direction. The reader sees Rorschach in the foreground, facing the front of the panel. Dreiberg is in the background, holding the Comedian's button.

6. During the police investigation of Edward Blake's murder in chapter 1, there is a flashback to the evening before when Blake is killed. In chapter 12 the narrative jumps forward a month at the end, but both of these examples still occur in 1985.

7. In this example and the example to follow, the panel-to-panel transition occurs on a single page. This strategy is used frequently to transition between different elsewheres from the bottom of a verso page to the top of the next recto page, or even as one turns the page (recto to verso). However, this panel-to-panel pattern is much less frequently used on a single page. Transitions that utilize the turning of a page for emphasis will be discussed later in this chapter. See "The Open Door Motif" section in this chapter.

8. Chapter 5, entitled "Fearful Symmetry," is one large, symmetrical structure. See Whitson. Gibbons also discusses the symmetry of chapter 5 in *Watching the Watchmen*. See pages 140–51 and 204–05. This

may account for so many similar panel compositions utilized throughout this chapter.

9. See 1.1 and 4, 2.19. Bernard even has two conversations with Rorschach; see 3.2–3 and 22.

10. For some examples of similar panel compositions used to create simultaneity between different times and places (elsewheres and whens), see 3.9, 11, 18, and 23.

11. For examples of the former, see 1.6–8, 19–20 and 5.17–18. For examples of the latter, see the last panel on 10.13 and the first on 10.14.

12. The eight locations in chapter 8 include (1) Sally Jupiter's home in California, (2) Hollis Mason's apartment, (3) the newspaper stand, (4) a portion of *Tales of the Black Freighter*, which Bernie is presently reading, (5) Dreiberg's apartment, (6) Rorschach's jail cell, (7) the *New Frontiersman*'s office, and (8) the secret island where Max Shea, the missing writer, and others are creating Veidt's creature.

13. In his interview for *The Mindscape of Alan Moore*, Gibbons refers to chapter 4 in *Watchmen* as a "quantum gestalt" and a "meditation on time."

Chapter 6

1. 4.13, 1.4, 10.30, 4.11, 4.32, 1.17, 7.7, 7.8

2. Nelson Gardner (Captain Metropolis), Laurie Juspeczyk (the second Silk Spectre), and Edward Blake (the Comedian) were also members of the failed organization. To illustrate the distinction between natural and conventional heroes, as well as the dynamic nature of the characters, we will focus on Drieberg, Rorschach, Veidt, and Dr. Manhattan.

3. For more information, please see chapter 8, "Faceless Heroes."

Chapter 7

1. Veidt saved three Vietnamese men from persecution and even death by bringing them to Antarctica to work for him (11.30). He also performs a gymnastics routine dressed as Ozymandias for a Southern Indian Famine Relief benefit. The television broadcast appears in the background of panels in Dreiberg's home, and the poster advertisement is pictured on Veidt's wall in his high-rise office (7.14–15, 1.17).

2. Notice how when Veidt returns to the privacy of his Antarctic retreat, he changes from civilian clothes into his Ozymandias attire (10.7). Also, he dresses as Ozymandias for the image that accompanies his interview with Doug Roth in the expository materials after chapter 11, and while performing a gymnastics routine for charity (11.29, 7.14–15).

3. There are numerous references to Veidt's perfected appearance. For example, Doug Roth's July 12, 1975, article for *Nova Express* describes Veidt as having a "perfect Swiss-watch of a body," and states, "Every girlfriend I've had in the past four years has wanted to lay this guy, more than Jagger, more than Springsteen or D'Eath or any of those also-rans…" (11.30).

4. After all, he is a wanted criminal according to the police (1.20).

5. By the end of the chapter, Dr. Long's writing even changes. His notes resemble Rorschach's minimalist speaking style, evident in his depiction of buying a newspaper at Bernard's newsstand the evening before and the evening after Rorschach tells him of his transformative experience while investigating Blaire Roche's disappearance. First Dr. Long writes, "Bought a gazette on my way home, including a small piece about Kovacs which the newsvendor pointed out excitedly" (6.16), but the evening after hearing Rorschach's startling story, he simply writes, "Bought paper" (6.27).

6. See Nuttall for a detailed discussion of Rorschach's adherence to the truth.

Chapter 8

1. For one example, see Campbell's discussion of Psyche starting on page 97.

2. Well, unexpected for all except perhaps Dr. Manhattan.

3. See the discussion of Dreiberg's body language in the last panel on 1.13 in *Watchmen* in chapter 6, "Hooded Honor."

4. After showing Juspeczyk to the spare room at his home, Jupeczyk thanks Drei-

berg, saying, "Thanks for looking out for me, Dan. You're like a big brother, you know that?" (5.19).

5. Later, Fine says, "I made a mistake. Thought a warning would be enough. Hell, I didn't know he was planning on his pal's escape…" (8.24).

6. Campbell bases this analysis (and much of the monomyth stages) on Sigmund Freud's three constructs of the personality: the id, ego, and superego. In the most basic terms, the "id" represents the desire for one to satisfy his or her carnal needs (hunger, thirst, sex, etc.) without regard to whether or not it is socially appropriate and acceptable. The "superego" represents one's moral compass, and functions as a conscience. The "ego" balances between the "id" and the "superego," and operates on the reality principle, working to satisfy the "id" while still respecting social norms and personal moral standards.

7. The underworld is a more traditional representation of the other world in the hero's journey. See Campbell's multiple examples in the section entitled "The Road of Trials," pages 97–109.

8. In addition to the "River Styx" in Greek mythology, the symbol of a body of water separating life from death or death from rebirth is one that is used in a variety of cultures and contexts. See page 251 in Campbell for an interpretation of the Christian rite of baptism.

9. In fact, there is evidence that the Comedian thinks Rorschach is crazy. In a flashback in chapter 2, he says, "Rorschach's nuts. He's been nuts ever since that kidnapping he handled three years back" (18).

10. See chapter 4, "The Watchmen," for a more detailed discussion.

Chapter 9

1. Corliss, Richard. "*Watchmen* Review: (A Few) Moments of Greatness." Rev. of *Watchmen*, dir. Zack Snyder. *Time.com, Time* magazine, 4 March, 2009. Web. 23 March, 2009.

2. This chapter focuses on the theatrical release version of the film from March of 2009. Although literary criticism is nor-mally written in present tense, this chapter (like chapter 1) is written in past tense in recognition that it intends to cover a discrete moment in *Watchmen*'s history.

3. Please see chapter 1, "Invading the Ivory Tower," for more information on *Watchmen* the graphic novel's history and reception.

4. Before the film's teaser trailer was released to theaters, a website was established for eager fans to follow the production's progress. The production diary (with entries as far back as July 2007) is available at <http://rss.warnerbros.com/watchmen/>.

5. The website tie-ins are just one of many marketing strategies that Warner Bros. and Paramount used to promote the film. See Romanelli's "*Watchmen* Ads Abound," "*Watchmen*'s March Madness," and "Manhattan-on-Thames."

6. A. O. Scott of *The New York Times* writes that the opening credits display a "witty pop sensibility," but the "breeziness" of the tone "undermine[s] the ambient gloom of the source material." Christopher Orr thought it was "nice" but "hamfistedly" set to the music. Anthony Lane of *The New Yorker* writes that the title sequence is the *only* worthwhile part of the film, and J. Hoberman of *The Village Voice* says it represents "far wittier filmmaking" in comparison to the rest. Owen Gleiberman of *Entertainment Weekly* gives the film a "B-," but notes that the title sequence has a "marvelous audacity."

7. This is a very long discussion thread of more than 3000 posts entitled "Watchmen (Spoilers for Realies!): Now w/ Poll." Reactions to the altered ending (Squidgate) begin on page 50 of the thread with a post on November 17, 2008, by Ribbons, who cites an article posted on *AintItCool.com*'s homepage from the same day entitled "No Squid for You!! 30 Minutes of *Watchmen* Screens in UK & Snyder Talked 5th-dimensional Squidish Thingies!!" [sic]

8. Reviews were not unanimous in their disappointment with the ending of the film. In fact, some reviewers found the ending to be an *improvement* on the graphic novel's ending. See Orr.

Works Cited

"Adventurer." def. 2, 5. *Oxford English Dictionary Online*. 2nd ed. Oxford University Press, 1989. Web. 18 May, 2009.

Aperlo, Peter. *The Art of the Film: Watchmen*. London: Titan, 2009.

_____. *Watchmen: The Film Companion*. London: Titan, 2009.

"Are Critics or Crowds Right About *Watchmen*?" Narr. Neal Conan. *Talk of the Nation*. National Public Radio, 9 March, 2009. Transcript. *ProQuest Direct*. Web. 23 March, 2009.

Arnold, Andrew D. "The Graphic Novel Silver Anniversary." *Time.com. Time Magazine*, 14 November, 2003. Web. 19 January, 2009.

Beahm, George. "Graphic Novels: Comics, Magazines, or Books?" *Publishers Weekly* 6, November 1987: 22.

Berardinelli, James. Rev. of *Watchmen*, dir. Zack Snyder. *Reelviews.net*. Reelviews Movie Reviews, 4 March, 2009. Web. 23 March, 2009.

Berlatsky, Noah. "Superficial." Rev. of *Watchmen*, dir. Zack Snyder. *Chicago Reader*. Creative Loafing Media, 12 March, 2009. Web. 23 March, 2009.

Bernard, Mark, and James Bucky Carter. "Alan Moore and the Graphic Novel: Confronting the Fourth Dimension." *ImageTexT: Interdisciplinary Comics Studies* 1.2 (2004): n. pag. Web. 2 September, 2008.

Berry, Michael. "Time Warp Nude and the End of the World." Rev. of *Last Fall* by Bruce Stolbov, *The Forge of God* by Greg Bear, *Time Pressure* by Spider Robinson, *On Stranger Tides* by Tim Powers, *Watchmen* by Alan Moore and Dave Gibbons, and *Robot Raiders* by Ellen W. Leroe. *San Francisco Chronicle* 6, December 1987, sec. Rev.: 5.

Biancolli, Amy. "Watch Out — Superhero Flick Is Over the Top." Rev. of *Watchmen*, dir. Zack Snyder. *Chron.com. The Houston Chronicle*, 4 March, 2009. Web. 23 March, 2009.

Boucher, Geoff. "Serious About Comics: A Guide for Those Who Are Ready to Embrace, or Return, to Graphic Novels." *Los Angeles Times*, 17 November, 2005, home ed.: E28. *ProQuest Direct*. Web. 6 February, 2009.

Bush, George W. "President Discusses Global War on Terror." *George W. Bush Administration White House Web Site*. George W. Bush Presidential Library, 5 September, 2006. Web. 18 March, 2009.

Cadden, Mary, Anthony DeBarros, Carol Memmott, Jocelyn McClurg, Bob Minzesheimer, and Craig Wilson. "New Stars Made, Old Ones Rediscovered in 2008." *USA Today*, 15 January, 2009: D5. *ProQuest Direct*. Web. 6 February, 2009.

Campbell, Joseph. *The Hero with a Thousand Faces*. Princeton, NJ: Princeton University Press, 1949.

Carney, Sean. "The Tides of History: Alan Moore's Historiographic Vision." *ImageTexT: Interdisciplinary Comics Studies*, 2.2 (2006): n. pag. Web. 4 August, 2008.

Chen, David. "Movie Review: *Watchmen* — A Cinematic Achievement in Adaptation." Rev. of *Watchmen*, dir. Zack Snyder. *SlashFilm.com*. /Film, 6 March, 2009. Web. 23 March, 2009.

Clinton, William J. "Address to the Nation by the President." *Clinton Presidential*

Materials Project. William J. Clinton Presidential Library and Museum, 20 August, 1998. Web. 18 September, 2008.

Cohn, Jesse. "Translator's Comments on Benoît Peeters, 'Four Conceptions of the Page.'" *ImageTexT: Interdisciplinary Comics Studies*, 3.3 (2007): n. pag. Web. 8 August, 2008.

"Context." Entry 1, def. 4a. *Oxford English Dictionary Online*, 2nd ed. Oxford University Press, 1989. Web. 18 May, 2009.

Corliss, Richard. "*Watchmen* Review: (A Few) Moments of Greatness." Rev. of *Watchmen*, dir. Zack Snyder. *Time.com. Time Magazine*, 4 March, 2009. Web. 23 March, 2009.

Dardess, George. "Review: Bringing Comic Books to Class." Rev. of *History of the Comic Strip* by David Kunzle, *Adult Comics: An Introduction* by Roger Sabin, *Comics and Sequential Art* by Will Eisner, and *Understanding Comics* by Scott McCloud. *College English*, 57.2 (1995): 213–22. *ProQuest Direct*. Web. 21 January, 2009.

"Diegesis." def. 1b. *Oxford English Dictionary Online*, 2nd ed. Oxford University Press, 1989. Web. 18 May, 2009.

Diliberto, Joseph J. "Comics Are Good for More Than a Laugh." *Star Tribune*, 23 June, 1989, Minneapolis ed.: 19A.

Du Mars, Roger Dean. "The Comic Book Grows Up. Graphic Novels: Not Just Kid Stuff." *CSMonitor.com. The Christian Science Monitor*, 28 December, 1988. Web. 15 January, 2009.

Dyer, Jeff. "Great Graphic Novel Enjoys a Comeback." *Telegraph-Herald*. 24 August, 2008: E4. *ProQuest Direct*. Web. 6 February, 2009.

Edelstein, David. "Hopelessly Devoted." Rev. of *Watchmen*, dir. Zack Snyder. *NYMag.com. New York Magazine*, 27 February, 2009. Web. 23 March, 2009.

Eisner, Will. *Comics and Sequential Art*. New York: Norton, 2008.

_____. *Graphic Storytelling and Visual Narrative*. New York: Norton, 2008.

Eklund, Christopher. "Comics Studies." *Modern North American Criticism and Theory: A Critical Guide*. Ed. Julian Wolfreys. Edinburgh: Edinburgh University

Press, 2006, pp. 207–13. *Questia*. Web. 15 January, 2009.

Ellis, Allen, and Doug Highsmith. "About Face: Comic Books in Library Literature." *Serials Review* 26.2 (2000): 21–43. *Science Direct*. Web. 13 January, 2009.

Elwood, Robert. *The Politics of Myth: A Study of C.G. Jung, Mircea Eliade, and Joseph Campbell*. Albany, NY: SUNY Press, 1999.

Felluga, Dino. "Modules on Greimas: On the Semiotic Square." *Introductory Guide to Critical Theory*. Purdue University, 28 November 2003. Web. 13 June, 2007.

_____. "Terms Used by Narratology and Film Theory." *Introductory Guide to Critical Theory*. Purdue University, 28 November, 2003. Web. 1 January, 2009.

Fishbaugh, Brent. "Moore and Gibbons' *Watchmen*: Exact Personifications of Science." *Extrapolation* 39.3 (1998): 189–98. *Literature Online*. Web. 5 July, 2008.

Franklin, Garth. "Special Feature: Zack Snyder on *Watchmen*." *DarkHorizons.com*. Dark Horizons Multimedia, 7 November, 2008. Web. 23 March, 2009.

Genette, Gérard. *Narrative Discourse: An Essay in Method*. Trans. Jane E. Lewin. Ithaca: Cornell University Press, 1980.

Gibbons, Dave, Chip Kidd, and Mike Essl. *Watching the Watchmen*. Photographs by Dan Scudamore. London: Titan Books, 2008.

Gleiberman, Owen. Rev. of *Watchmen*, dir. Zack Snyder. *EW.com. Entertainment Weekly*, 2 March, 2009. Web. 23 March, 2009.

Gordon, Devin. "Till Death Do Us Part." Rev. of *Watchmen*, dir. Zack Snyder. *Newsweek*, 1 March, 2009. Web. 23 March, 2009.

Gravett, Paul. *Graphic Novels: Everything You Need to Know*. New York: HarperCollins, 2005.

Grossman, Lev. "A Fan's Take on *Watchmen*." Rev. of *Watchmen*, dir. Zack Snyder. *Time.com. Time Magazine*, 5 March, 2009, MP3 file.

Hahn, Joel. *Comic Book Awards Almanac*. 2006. Web. 10 January, 2009.

Hajdu, David. *The Ten-Cent Plague: The Great Comic-Book Scare and How It*

Changed America. New York: Farrar, Straus and Giroux, 2008.

Harris-Fain, Darren. Letter. *Extrapolation* 39.1 (1998): 85–89. *ProQuest Direct*. Web. 21 January, 2009.

_____. Rev. of *Watchmen*, by Alan Moore and Dave Gibbons. New York: DC Comics, 1987. *Extrapolation* 30.4 (1989): 410–12.

"Hector." Entry 1, def. 1. *Oxford English Dictionary Online*, 2nd ed. Oxford University Press, 1989. Web. 12 January, 2009.

Held, Jacob M. "Can We Steer This Rudderless World? Kant, Rorschach, Retributivism, and Honor." *Watchmen and Philosophy*. Ed. Mark D. White. Hoboken, NJ: Wiley, 2009, pp. 19–32.

Hick, Darren. "A Glimpse Behind the Curtain: Nominations for the Journal's Top 100." *TCJ.com*. The Comics Journal, 2002. Web. 25 January, 2009.

Hoberman, J. "Zack Snyder Didn't Ruin *Watchmen*: He Just Sapped It of Its Superpower." Rev. of *Watchmen*, dir. Zack Snyder. *The Village Voice*, 3 March, 2009. Web. 23 March, 2009.

Honeycutt, Kirk. "Film Review: *Watchmen*." Rev. of *Watchmen*, dir. Zack Snyder. *The Hollywood Reporter*. Neilson Business Media. 26 February, 2009. Web. 23 March, 2009.

Hooker, Richard. "Greek Philosophy: Pre–Socratic Philosophy." *World Civilizations: An Internet Classroom and Anthology*. Washington State University, 6 June, 1999. Web. 18 June, 2007.

Hughes, David. "Who Watches the Watchmen?" *The Greatest Sci-Fi Movies Never Made*. London: Titan, 2008, pp. 147–59.

Hughes, Jamie A. "'Who Watches the Watchmen?': Ideology and 'Real World' Superheroes." *Journal of Popular Culture* 39.4 (2006): 546–57. *ProQuest*. Web. 5 September, 2006.

Itzkoff, Dave. "Behind the Mask." Rev. of *Absolute Watchmen*, by Alan Moore and Dave Gibbons. *The New York Times Book Review*. 20 November, 2005: 17. *ProQuest Direct*. Web. 6 February, 2009.

Jameson, Fredric. *Archaeologies of the Future: The Desire Called Utopia and Other Science Fictions*. New York: Verso, 2005.

Jensen, Jeff. "Watchmen: An Oral History."

EW.com. Entertainment Weekly, 847 (2005): n. pag. Web. 4 September, 2008.

Kart, Larry. "A Comic Book as Gripping as Dickens." Rev. of *Watchmen*, by Alan Moore and Dave Gibbons. *Chicago Tribune*, 2 December, 1987, c ed.: 3. *ProQuest Direct*. Web. 14 January, 2009.

Keeping, J. "Superheroes and Supermen: Finding Nietzsche's Übermensch in *Watchmen*." *Watchmen and Philosophy*. Ed. Mark D. White. Hoboken, NJ: Wiley, 2009, pp. 47–60.

Kendricks, Neil. "Zap! Cartoonists with an Attitude Draw Cynicism into the Mix." *The San Diego Union-Tribune*, 19 August, 1993, 1–10 ed.: n. pag. *ProQuest Direct*. Web. 21 January, 2009.

Kennedy, Pagan. "P.C. Comics." *The Nation*, 19 March, 1990: 386+. *Questia*. Web. 21 January, 2009.

Kennicott, Philip. "Blight *Watchmen*: Graphic Novel's Edge Is Dulled in Adaptation." Rev. of *Watchmen*, dir. Zack Snyder. *The Washington Post*, 5 March, 2009. Web. 26 March, 2009.

Klapp, Orrin E. "Heroes, Villains and Fools, as Agents of Social Control." *American Sociological Review*, 19.1 (1954): 56–62. *JSTOR*. Web. 20 June, 2007.

Klock, Geoff. *How to Read Superhero Comics and Why*. New York: Continuum, 2006, pp. 25–76.

Knapp, Bettina L. *A Jungian Approach to Literature*. Carbondale: Southern Illinois University Press, 1984. *Questia*. Web. 10 December, 2006.

Lane, Anthony. "Dark Visions." Rev. of *Watchmen*, dir. Zack Snyder, and *Leave Her to Heaven*, dir. John M. Stahl. *The New Yorker*, 9 March, 2009. Web. 23 March, 2009.

Layman, John. "Beyond Outstanding *Watchmen*: Watch This Man." *The San Diego Union-Tribune*, 7 Sept. 1997, 1–2 ed.: Books7. *ProQuest Direct*. Web. 21 January, 2009.

"Legend." Entry 1, def. 8. *Oxford English Dictionary Online*, 2nd ed. Oxford University Press, 1989. Web. 18 May, 2009.

Levine, Beth. "Graphic Novels: The Latest Word in Illustrated Books." *Publishers Weekly*, 22 May, 1987: 45–7.

Llyr, Jonathan. "An Open Letter from *Watchmen* Screenwriter David Hayter — Updated." *Hardcore Nerdity*. Ning, 11 March, 2009. Web. 23 March, 2009.

Loftis, J. Robert. "Means, Ends, and the Critique of Pure Superheroes." *Watchmen and Philosophy*. Ed. Mark D. White. Hoboken, NJ: Wiley, 2009, pp. 63–78.

Long, Tom. "Comic-Book Adaptation *Watchmen* Is a Messy Superhero Film for Grown-Ups." Rev. of *Watchmen*, dir. Zack Snyder. *DetNews.com*. The Detroit News, 5 March, 2009. Web. 23 March, 2009.

Lovejoy, Arthur. *The Great Chain of Being*. Cambridge: Harvard University Press, 1982.

Maurstad, Tom. Rev. of *Watchmen*, dir. Zack Snyder. *GuideLive.com*. The Dallas Morning News, 6 March, 2009. Web. 23 March, 2009.

McCloud, Scott. *Making Comics: Storytelling Secrets of Comics, Manga and Graphic Novels*. New York: Harper, 2006.

_____. *Understanding Comics: The Invisible Art*. New York: Kitchen Sink Publications, 1993.

McConnaughey, Janet. "Comic Books Getting Serious." *Chicago Sun–Times*, 28 March, 1993, late sports final ed., sec. Sunday News: 40. *LexisNexis Academic*. Web. 25 January, 2009.

McConnell, Frank. "Comic Relief: From 'Gilgamesh' to 'Spiderman.'" *Commonweal*, 28 February, 1992: 21–22. *ProQuest Direct*. Web. 21 January, 2009.

Mescallado, Ray. "The Twenty Best Mainstream Comics." *The Comics Journal* 210 (1999): 123–4.

Miller, Dean A. "The Hero from on High." *The Epic Hero*. Baltimore: Johns Hopkins University Press, 2000, pp. 1–69.

The Mindscape of Alan Moore. Dir. DeZ Vylenz. Shadowsnake, 2008. DVD.

Mondello, Bob. "In *Watchmen*, a Long Look at Life in Spandex." Rev. of *Watchmen*, dir. Zack Snyder. *NPR.org*. National Public Radio, 5 March, 2009. Web. 23 March, 2009.

Moore, Alan. "Nite Owl." *Absolute Watchmen*. New York: DC Comics, 2005.

_____. "Ozymandias." *Absolute Watchmen*. New York: DC Comics, 2005.

_____. "Rorschach." *Absoulte Watchmen*. New York: DC Comics, 2005.

_____. "The World." *Absolute Watchmen*. New York: DC Comics, 2005.

Moor, Alan, and Dave Gibbons. *Watchmen*. New York: DC Comics, 1986.

Motion Picture Association of America, "What Do the Ratings Mean?" *MPAA.org*. MPAA, 2005. Web. 23 March, 2009.

"Natural Law." *The Columbia Encyclopedia*, 6th ed. Columbia University Press, 2004. *Questia*. Web. 12 June, 2007.

Navasky, Victor S., et al. "Our Holiday Lists." *The Nation*, 26 December, 1987: 793+. *Questia*. Web. 30 January, 2009.

"Nominations Begin for 1st Graphic Novel Hugo Award (Updated)" *Anime News Network*, 7 January, 2009. Web. 20 January, 2009.

Nuttall, Alex. "Rorschach: When Telling the Truth Is Wrong." *Watchmen and Philosophy*. Ed. Mark D. White. Hoboken, NJ: Wiley, 2009, pp. 91–99.

Orr, Christopher. "The Movie Review: Watchmen." Rev. of *Watchmen*, dir. Zack Snyder. *TNR.com*. The New Republic, 6 March, 2009. Web. 23 March, 2009.

"Pantomime." Entry 1, def. 1. *Oxford English Dictionary Online*, 2nd ed. Oxford University Press, 1989. Web. 18 May, 2009.

Peeters, Benoît. "Four Conceptions of the Page." *Case, planche, récit: lire la bande dessinée*. Trans. Jesse Cohn. Paris: Casterman, 1998, pp. 41–60. Rpt. in *ImageTexT: Interdisciplinary Comics Studies* 3.3 (2007): n. pag. Web. 8 August, 2008.

"Persona." def. 2b. *Oxford English Dictionary Online*, 2nd ed. Oxford University Press, 1989. Web. 18 May, 2009.

Phillips, Michael. "Who Watches Who Walks Out of *Watchmen*?" *Chicago Tribune.com*. Tribune Interactive, 9 March, 2009. Web. 23 March, 2009.

Pierson, David. "*Watchmen* Dominates Movie Box Office." *LATimes.com*. Los Angeles Times, 9 March, 2009. Web. 23 March, 2009.

Puig, Claudia. "*Watchmen* Forgettable After Opening Blast." Rev. of *Watchmen*, dir. Zack Snyder. *USAToday.com*. USA Today, 6 March, 2009. Web. 23 March, 2009.

Queenan, Joe. "Drawing on the Dark Side." *The New York Times*, 30 April, 1989, late ed.: A32. *ProQuest Direct*. Web. 14 January, 2009.

Radford, Bill. "Magazine Shows Scope of Comics with Diverse Top 100 List." *The Gazette*, 18 April, 1999: LIFE4. *ProQuest Direct*. Web. 25 January, 2009.

_____. "Millennium Editions Feature Classics." *The Gazette*, 14 November, 1999: LIFE2. *ProQuest Direct*. Web. 25 January, 2009.

Reagan, Ronald. "Message on the Observance of Afghanistan Day." *The Public Papers of President Ronald W. Reagan.* Ronald Reagan Presidential Library, 21 March, 1983. Web. 18 September, 2008.

Reynolds, Richard. *Superheroes: A Modern Mythology.* Jackson: University of Mississippi Press, 1994.

Ricoeur, Paul. "Narrative Time." *Critical Inquiry* 7.1 (1980): 169–190. *JSTOR*. Web. 27 June, 2008.

Romanelli, Glenn. "Manhattan-on-Thames." *WatchmenComicMovie.com*, 4 March, 2009. Web. 23 March, 2009.

_____. "Review: *Watchmen* Works." *WatchmenComicMovie.com*, 6 March, 2009. Web. 23 March, 2009.

_____. "The 'Squid' Is Out." *WatchmenComicMovie.com*, 10 November, 2008. Web. 23 March, 2009.

_____. "*Watchmen* Ads Abound." *WatchmenComicMovie.com*, 1 March, 2009. Web. 23 March, 2009.

_____. "The *Watchmen* Effect." *WatchmenComicMovie.com*, 14 August, 2008. Web. 15 August, 2008.

_____. "*Watchmen* Producers Speak." *WatchmenComicMovie.com*, 20 February, 2009. Web. 23 March, 2009.

_____. "*Watchmen*'s March Madness." *WatchmenComicMovie.com*, 1 March, 2009. Web. 23 March, 2009.

_____. "Zack Snyder Breaks It Down." *WatchmenComicMovie.com*, 6 March, 2009. Web. 23 March, 2009.

Rowe, Peter. "The Big Battle: It's Edge vs. Respectability as Graphic Novels Move into the Mainstream, but Make No Mistake: The Art Form Retains Its Grit and Its Power." *The San Diego Union-Tribune*, 22 July, 2007: E1. *ProQuest Direct*. Web. 6 February 2009.

Salm, Arthur. "*Time*'s Top 100 Did Not Make His Top 10 List of Best-Book Lists." *The San Diego Union-Tribune*, 6 November, 2005, 1–3 ed.: Books2. *ProQuest Direct*. Web. 6 February, 2009.

Saraceni, Mario. *The Language of Comics.* New York: Routledge, 2003. *Questia*. Web. 3 July, 2007.

Saussure, Ferdinand de. *Course in General Linguistics.* Trans. Roy Harris. Ed. Charles Bally, Albert Sechehaye, and Albert Riedlinger. Chicago: Open Court, 2002.

Scott, A. O. "For a Cold War, a Blue Superhero (and Friends)." Rev. of *Watchmen*, dir. Zack Snyder. *The New York Times*, 6 March, 2009. Web. 23 March, 2009.

Smoler, Fredric Paul. Rev. of *Watchmen*, by Alan Moore and Dave Gibbons. New York: DC Comics, 1987. *The Nation*, 10 October, 1987: 386–7. *ProQuest Direct*. Web. 14 January, 2009.

Solomon, Charles. "The Comic Book Grows Up: Graphic Novels—'Comics for Adults'—Are Enjoying Immense Popularity ... but Why?" *Los Angeles Times*, 16 April, 1989, home ed.: 6. *ProQuest Direct*. Web. 14 January, 2009.

Spanakos, Tony. "Super-Vigilantes and the Keene Act." *Watchmen and Philosophy.* Ed. Mark D. White. Hoboken, NJ: Wiley, 2009, pp. 33–46.

Spinrad, Norman. "The Graphic Novel." *Science Fiction in the Real World.* Carbondale: Southern Illinois University Press, 1990, pp. 59–76. *Questia*. Web. 18 July, 2008.

Strizver, Ilene. "Initial Letters." *For Your (Typographic) Information* 1.3 (2003): n.p. PDF file.

"Text." Entry 1, def. 2b. *Oxford English Dictionary Online*, 2nd ed. Oxford University Press, 1989. Web. 18 May, 2009.

Thill, Scott. "Is *Watchmen* Director Zack Snyder Really 'Visionary'?" *Wired.com*. CondéNet, 22 December, 2008. Web. 25 March, 2009.

Thomas, David. "Awards Honor Best in Comics World." *Denver Post*, 19 July, 1996, Rockies ed.: F14. *ProQuest Direct*. Web. 21 January, 2009.

Thompson, Ann. "Filmmakers Intent on Producing New Comic-Book Movies." *Sun–Sentinel*, 26 August, 1986: E7. *ProQuest Direct*. Web. 25 March, 2009.

Thomson, Iain. "Deconstructing the Hero." *Comics as Philosophy*. Ed. Jeff McLaughlin. Jackson: University of Mississippi Press, 2005, pp. 100–29. *Questia*. Web. 2 September, 2008.

"The Top 100 Comics." *ReadYourselfRAW. com*, n.d. Web. 25 January, 2009.

Varnum, Robin, and Christina T. Gibbons, eds. Introduction. *The Language of Comics: Word and Image*. Jackson: University Press of Mississippi, 2001, pp. ix-xix.

Versaci, Rocco. *This Book Contains Graphic Language: Comics as Literature*. London: Continuum, 2007.

Vinson, Dana. "*Watchmen* Movie Review." Rev. of *Watchmen*, dir. Zack Snyder. *G4TV.com*. G4 Media, 6 March, 2009. Web. 23 March, 2009.

Voger, Mark. "Super History: Montclair Exhibit Covers Evolution of Comic-Book Heroes." *Asbury Park Press*, 8 July, 2007: E1+.

Wells, Dominic. "Tights and Teleology." Rev. of *Watching the Watchmen* by Dave Gibbons. *The Independent on Sunday*, 9 Nov. 2008: 49. *ProQuest Direct*. Web. 6 February, 2009.

White, Hayden. *The Content of the Form*. Baltimore: Johns Hopkins University Press, 1990.

Whitson, Roger. "Panelling Parallax: The Fearful Symmetry of Alan Moore and William Blake." *ImageTexT: Interdisciplinary Comics Studies*. 3.2 (2007): n. pag. Web. 1 September, 2008.

Whitty, Stephen. "*Watchmen* Review: Fails to Live Up to Compelling Original." Rev. of *Watchmen*, dir. Zack Snyder. *NJ.com*. *The Star-Ledger*, 4 March, 2009. Web. 23 March, 2009.

Wolf-Meyer, Matthew. "The World Ozymandias Made: Utopias in the Superhero Comic, Subculture, and the Conservation of Difference." *Journal of Popular Culture*, 36.3 (2003): 497–517. *EbscoHost*. Web. 4 September, 2008.

Selected Annotated Bibliography of *Watchmen* Scholarship and Related Resources

Aperlo, Peter. *The Art of the Film: Watchmen*. London: Titan, 2009. Focuses on the production of the film. Includes interviews with director Zack Snyder, production designer Alex McDowell, costume designer Michael Wilkinson, and others. Also explained are the processes by which decisions were made for costumes, sets, and CGI cinematography. Pages 62 and 63 feature Dave Gibbons and John Higgins' reimagining of *Watchmen*'s ending for the film, and a section of the book explains the making of the film's Owl Ship.

_____. *Watchmen: The Film Companion*. London: Titan, 2009. Provides character descriptions and plot details with interviews from the cast and crew. Also includes some information on production and post–production work.

Atkinson, Doug. *The Annotated Watchmen: Your Complete Guide to the Classic Series*. n.p. 1995. Web. 1 September, 2008. This website features a page for each chapter of the novel. Explanation of the chapter titles, motifs, and allusions, as well as cross-references to different chapters, are provided on a panel-by-panel basis. Other features include short descriptions of all characters and links to the chapters in which they appear, an explanation of

Watchmen's world, and a chronological timeline of events.

Bernard, Mark, and James Bucky Carter. "Alan Moore and the Graphic Novel: Confronting the Fourth Dimension." *ImageTexT: Interdisciplinary Comics Studies* 1.2 (2004): n.p. Web. 2 September, 2008. Sequential art is perhaps the best art form for representing the fourth dimension (simultaneity of all spaces and times), even when compared to newer and more modern media. *From Hell* and *Watchmen* best exemplify how Moore uses the graphic-novel form to represent the fourth dimension and to make it a primary narrative theme. Dr. Manhattan experiences the fourth dimension on a continuous basis, and as the reader reads *Watchmen*, he/she is experiencing time in this same way.

Carey, Edward. "Analyzing *Watchmen* with Peter Sanderson." *ComicBookResources.com*. Comic Book Resources, 31 January, 2007. Web. 2 September, 2008. Overviews the second part of a series of lectures on *Watchmen*, which were presented at the Museum of Comic and Cartoon Art (MoCCA) in New York. The superhero genre's foundation lies in Nietzsche's idea of the Übermensch. Fans do not often view Veidt as a hero, but have many reasons why Rorschach is one. Various characters' masks and superpowers are also discussed, and parallels are drawn with other notable graphic works.

_____. "MOCCA Presents: '1986: The Year That Changed Comics.'" *ComicBookResources.com*. Comic Book Resources, 15 November, 2006. Web. 2 September, 2008. Overviews the first part of a series of lectures on *Watchmen* and focuses on the novel's reinvention of the superhero genre, integration of multiple sources that are considered high art, and allusions to the history of the comic-book form.

Carney, Sean. "The Tides of History: Alan Moore's Historiographic Vision." *ImageTexT: Interdisciplinary Comics Studies*. 2.2 (2006): n.p. Web. 4 August, 2008. Moore's work not only explores how time and the progression of history are completely out of man's control even if he believes otherwise, but also portrays characters who search for meaning in life (*Marvelman*), experience simultaneity of space and time (*Watchmen* and *From Hell*), and discover the merging of the sacred and the profane (*Promethea*).

Fishbaugh, Brent. "Moore and Gibbons' *Watchmen*: Exact Personifications of Science." *Extrapolation* 39.3 (1998): 189–98. *Literature Online*. Web. 5 July, 2008. Rorschach, Ozymandias, Dr. Manhattan, Nite Owl, and Silk Spectre each symbolize how science and technology affect humans: Rorschach symbolizes "soft sciences" and psychology, Dr. Manhattan represents the chemical and "hard sciences," Ozymandias is a mixture of both, and Nite Owl and Silk Spectre embody how man interacts with and uses science. Heroism, the credibility of the characters, and their histories are also discussed.

Gibbons, Dave, Chip Kidd, and Mike Essl. *Watching the Watchmen*. Photographs by Dan Scudamore. London: Titan, 2008. Numerous sketches, layout roughs, page prints, and schematics from *Watchmen*'s creation, some of which were used and others of which were eventually redone, all including commentary from Gibbons.

Also included are narratives detailing how Gibbons and Moore came to work together on the project, their unusual amount of creative flexibility during the project, the overwhelming and somewhat unexpected acclaim for the series, and the flurry of memorabilia and marketing strategies that ensued after the series' release and subsequent binding into a "graphic novel." John Higgins, colorist on the original series, also provides a brief commentary about his involvement.

Gravett, Paul. *Graphic Novels: Everything You Need to Know*. New York: HarperCollins, 2005. Provides some basic graphic-novel reading strategies and then groups a wide range of titles by theme, including stories of war, superheroes, childhood, crime, and many others. Includes a section on *Watchmen*.

Hughes, David. "Who Watches the Watchmen?" *The Greatest Sci-Fi Movies Never Made*. London: Titan, 2008, pp. 147–59. Traces *Watchmen*'s long and seemingly endless road to the big screen starting shortly after Moore and Gibbons finished work on the comics in the mid–1980s. This chapter was published before the film's March 2009 release, but does acknowledge Zack Snyder's intent to make the film.

Hughes, Jamie A. "'Who Watches the Watchmen?': Ideology and 'Real World' Superheroes." *Journal of Popular Culture* 39.4 (2006): 546–57. *ProQuest*. Web. 5 September, 2006. One's chosen ideology and interaction with social constructs, such as government, schools, and religion, are factors in determining one's ability to be defined as a hero. Louis Althusser's idea of "Ideological State Apparatuses" or (ISAs) defines social institutions which promote ideologies. This is then applied to characters in the novel.

Jensen, Jeff. "Watchmen: An Oral History." *EW.com*. Entertainment Weekly, 847 (2005). Web. 4 September, 2008. Interview with Alan Moore, Dave Gibbons, Len Wein, and Barbara Kesel (editors), and John Higgins (colorist) about the development and production of *Watchmen*.

Topics discussed include the team's feelings about a film adaptation; Moore's meticulous attention to detail; and influences on various films, music, and popular culture symbols, from Disney's *The Incredibles* to the popular television series *Lost*.

Klock, Geoff. "The Bat and the Watchmen: Introducing the Revisionary Superhero Narrative." *How to Read Superhero Comics and Why*. New York: Continuum, 2006, pp. 25–76. *Watchmen* and *The Dark Knight Returns* changed the face of the superhero genre by reinventing the superhero's role in society, self–perception, and identity formation. This text draws heavily from Harold Bloom's work, and rejects interpretations based on the works of Jung, Campbell, and Lévi-Strauss.

The Mindscape of Alan Moore. Dir. DeZ Vylenz. Shadowsnake, 2008. DVD. Disc one of this two-disc set provides a lengthy interview with Alan Moore, and begins with a discussion of his childhood in Northampton, his discovery of American comics, and his beginnings as both author and illustrator for various short works. He indicates that 1980s British politics and world events influenced *V for Vendetta* and *Watchmen*. He presents views on a wide range of issues, including fame, erotica or pornography, the relationship of film to comics, monotheism, magic, materialism, conspiracy theories, the time/space relationship, and his notion of "Ideaspace." Particular attention is also paid to *Swamp Thing, Lost Girls*, and *From Hell*. Disc two provides interviews with author Paul Gravett and illustrators Melinda Gebbie (*Lost Girls*), Dave Gibbons (*Watchmen*), David Lloyd (*V for Vendetta*), Kevin O'Neill (*League of Extraordinary Gentlemen*) and Jose Villarubia (*Promethia* and *Mirror of Love*).

Moore, Alan. *Alan Moore's Writing for Comics*. 1985. Rantoul, IL: Avatar, 2008. Moore provides suggestions for aspiring writers by way of explanation of his own creative process: the importance of having an idea, fleshing out round characters, and developing a plausible world in which the narrative can take place. Appended is a 2003 essay in which Moore comments on his earlier essay and provides some new suggestions for the more seasoned writer from his more experienced perspective.

_____. "The Mark of Batman: An Introduction." *Batman: The Dark Knight Returns*. By Frank Miller. New York: DC Comics, 1986. As the world changes, the nature of its heroes also necessarily change. Comic books have had to contend with negative social stigmas and have been labeled as childish, campy, and filled with the "same old muscle-bound oafs"; however, Miller's *Dark Knight* reflects how a superhero narrative can resonate with a sophisticated society and audience. Moore also praises Miller for reinventing a traditional character and his world.

Moore, Alan, and Dave Gibbons. *Absolute Watchmen*. New York: DC Comics, 2005. Includes digitally remastered coloring printed on heavy paper stock in a larger format than the trade paperback. Some corrections have been made to account for a few minor errors in the first printing's artwork. Also included are essays by both Moore and Gibbons, Moore's original notes on the Charlton Comics characters from which the *Watchmen* characters are drawn, selections of Gibbons' preliminary sketches, and reproductions of Moore's notes (with Gibbons' highlighting) that guided the visual layout for the work.

Reynolds, Richard. *Superheroes: A Modern Mythology*. Jackson: University of Mississippi Press, 1994. Analyzes the superhero genre by primarily focusing on *X-Men* nos. 108–143, *The Dark Knight Returns*, and *Watchmen*, in addition to examining Thor, Superman, and Batman. It explores the effect of costumes on identity, how supervillains and superheroes are political foils of one another, and the evolution of what constitutes heroes in comics and graphic novels.

Romanelli, Glenn, ed. *WatchmenComic-Movie.com*. 2009. Web. 8 March, 2009. The most comprehensive website for everything *Watchmen*. This regularly updated site features information on the film, the comics, and other products from the world of *Watchmen*. Sections of the website include links to Alan Moore interviews, analysis and criticism of the graphic novel, numerous news items and interviews related to the film, and much more. The website also includes a discussion forum where users can post their thoughts on the *Watchmen* film and graphic novel.

Spinrad, Norman. "The Graphic Novel." *Science Fiction in the Real World*. Carbondale: Southern Illinois University Press, 1990, pp. 59–76. *Questia*. Web. 18 July, 2008. The science fiction genre includes such graphic novels as *Watchmen*, *Greenberg the Vampire*, and *The Dark Knight Returns*. The graphic novel is not an entirely new art form, but rather a composite of previously established forms, a continuation of an ever evolving form of communication. The use of expository material and the reworking of heroic ideals and conventions are specifically discussed in relation to *Watchmen*.

Thomson, Iain. "Deconstructing the Hero." *Comics as Philosophy*. Ed. Jeff McLaughlin. Jackson: University of Mississippi Press, 2005, pp. 100–29. *Questia*. Web. 2 September, 2008. The existentialist philosophers Heidegger, Nietzsche, and Kierkegaard's understandings of the hero are very different from Moore's. Whereas existentialism stressed moving above and beyond heroes by deconstructing past conceptions, *Watchmen* leaves readers with an indifferent attitude toward the future of heroes. When examined more closely, however, the novel serves as a sort of resurrection or rebirth of perhaps, at the time, an overly-exhausted form.

White, Mark D. ed. *Watchmen and Philosophy: A Rorschach Test*. Hoboken, NJ: Wiley, 2009. Examines *Watchmen* through a philosophical lens. Includes fifteen essays focusing on power, ethics, metaphysics, and the comic-book medium.

Whitson, Roger. "Panelling Parallax: The Fearful Symmetry of Alan Moore and William Blake." *ImageTexT: Interdisciplinary Comics Studies*, 3.2 (2007). Web. 1 September, 2008. Chapter five in *Watchmen* draws heavily in both form and content from Blake's poem "The Tyger." Blake and Moore both experience parallax (virtual isolation due to two seemingly conflicting perspectives) driven primarily by their alternative perspective in what they perceive to be unjust worlds. The chapter's symmetry reflects how Moore derives a sense of his identity from Blake and allows him to write himself into the text, looming over characters who seek their own identities.

Wolf-Meyer, Matthew. "The World Ozymandias Made: Utopias in the Superhero Comic, Subculture, and the Conservation of Difference." *Journal of Popular Culture*, 36.3 (2003): 497–517. *EbscoHost*. Web. 4 September, 2008. Rorschach and Veidt are aligned with extreme conservative and extreme liberal political philosophies, respectively. Conservatism is paired with immaturity, and liberalism is paired with intelligence. Most people identify with Rorschach's character because the readership is immature and adolescent.

Other Recommended Sources on the Graphic-Narrative Form

Eisner, Will. *Comics and Sequential Art*. New York: Norton, 2008. This foundational work in comics-art theory covers the reading process for these works, the image/word interaction and connection, and the importance of frame, timing, and expressive anatomy. Also discussed is sequential art's place and application as it becomes increasingly popular in a digital format.

_____. *Graphic Storytelling and Visual Narrative*. New York: Norton, 2008. Concerned with narrative development, style, and tone, this work explains that the reader is an integral consideration when constructing the narrative. Artists gain the reader's "attention" and maintaining it for the entirety of the story ("retention") by understanding different types of narratives and one's audience. Also crucial to a successful narrative is that the artist understands how to tell these stories through interacting images and words with believable characters and settings.

McCloud, Scott. *Making Comics: Storytelling Secrets of Comics, Manga and Graphic Novels.* New York: Harper, 2006. Explains strategies for how to effectively convey a narrative through sequential art, discussing everything from the image/word relationship to facial expression and body language to developing realistic settings. This book expands upon the sequential-art theory found in *Understanding Comics* and is aimed at readers interested in creating comics, but is accessible and useful to any comics reader. Provided at the end of each chapter is a useful notes section with exercises for aspiring artists. A brief bibliography of recommended sources is also included.

_____. *Understanding Comics: The Invisible Art.* New York: Kitchen Sink Press, 1993. One of the foundation materials for understanding the comics and graphic-novel medium. Begins with the history and evolution of sequential art from cave paintings up to modern interpretations, and includes the connection between words and images, page layout and paneling strategies, the importance of icons, design, and color, as well as explanations of how time and space are created and manipulated.

Index